THE
FILENES

by
George E. Berkley

INTERNATIONAL POCKET LIBRARY
(Division of Branden Publishing Company)
Boston

Library of Congress Cataloging-in-Publication Data

Berkley, George E.
  The Filenes / by George E. Berkley.
    p. cm.
  Includes bibliographical references and index.
  ISBN 0-8283-2035-7 (alk. paper)
    1. Filene family.
    2. Businesspeople--Boston-Biography.
    3. Filene's (Department Store: Boston, Mass.)--History.
    4. Department stores--Massachusetts--Boston--History.
    I. Title.
HC102.5.F5B47 1998
381'.141'0974461--dc21   98-16772
                             CIP

INTERNATIONAL POCKET LIBRARY
(Division of Branden Publishing Company)
17 Station Street
Brookline Village Box 843
Boston, MA 02447

PRINTED IN CANADA

ACKNOWLEDGEMENTS

As it so happens, most of the research for this book was done many years ago and so my recall of all those whose assisted me has become a bit blurred. Certainly, the person who aided me the most was Jerry Burns, who was then the librarian of the Credit Union National Association. During the several days I spent at the Association's headquarters in Madison, Wisconsin, he provided me with access to all sorts of informative material including letters, manuscripts and reports. Many of the latter he had himself solicited and, in some cases, commissioned from various family members, friends, associates and aides. I left Madison most grateful not only to him but to the Credit Union National Association itself for having given him the resources to assemble such a voluminous and, in my view, important archive.

It was Jerry who told me about the collection of Lillian Schoedler papers at the library of Radcliff College, and since Schoedler was the person closest to Edward Filene during the last seven years of his life, these papers proved most useful. I wish to thank Radcliff College for allowing me full access to them.

Others I wish to thank include Justin Kaplan, for arranging an interview with his remarkable father-in-law, Edward L. Bernays; Nan Bailey, for directing me to Austin Benton; Gabriel W. Kirkpatrick, who, as Jerry Burns' capable successor at CUNA, helped me in various ways; Erin Marino of Filene's, Christy Hicks of the Twentieth Century Fund and Mary Beth Dunhouse of the Boston Public Library for help with various last minute matters; and my favorite private library, the Boston Athenaeum, which provided me with various hard-to-find books relating to my subject.

Finally, there are my many interviewees, most of whom are named at the back of the book. All of them were well along in years when I interviewed them, yet nearly all of them retained vivid memories of Edward and Lincoln Filene. I deeply regret that none of them are now with us to see their recollections in print.

This is the greatest gift: to choose a life
one can admire oneself for living.

--Mary Gordon, in *The Company of Women*

For
Robert Safer
and in memory of Shirley and June Ellen

Contents

PROLOGUE

At first glance it may not strike the casual observer as especially impressive. Its solid, somewhat massive walls and its ground floor display windows make it look like merely another department store on Boston's busy Washington Street. It usually requires a second and more searching look to discern the ornate columns, cornices and other features which caused connoisseurs and critics to hail it at the time of its construction as the most outstanding example of store architecture in the United States.

Yes, the Filene building was and is a structure of some beauty or at least distinction. But its claim on our attention does not rest on its architecture alone. The activities it housed were far more important and far more interesting as well. For within its walls a series of bold, imaginative innovations emerged which not only changed the course of American retailing but opened up wholly new approaches to human organization. Today many supposedly advanced companies are earning plaudits for cautiously experimenting with principles and practices that were successfully at work within this eight-story edifice nearly a century ago.

Yet even this does not reveal the building's entire story. There is still more to tell. Out of its top-floor executive offices came not just some bold new ideas for retailing and managing but also a broad range of economic, social and political initiatives which have affected the lives of us all.

Behind this array of activity and accomplishment stood two brilliant brothers who became millionaires while earnestly seeking to contribute to the society which made their financial success possible. In their extraordinary journey through life, they at first cooperated, then separated, and finally clashed.

They were two unusual, remarkable men. And this is their story.

Chapter 1
THE FIRST FILENES

The city of Posen lies in eastern Germany near the country's historically unstable Polish border. Early in the 19th Century Posen was, for a while, actually part of Poland but by 1830 it had reverted once again to Prussia. It was in this year that the first Filene was born. His name was Wilhelm Katz.

Wilhelm was the second son of a ribbon merchant, and since ribbons were then an important part of women's apparel, it was possible for those who sold them to become quite well off. This had apparently happened to Wilhelm's father for in 1847 the elder Katz, taking advantage of recent legislation opening up new opportunities to Jews, sent Wilhelm and his older brother Rudolph to Berlin to study law. But the ribbon merchant's efforts to establish his sons in a learned profession went sadly awry. Soon after they boys arrived in the German capital, Rudolph fell ill and, after a brief struggle, died. The tragic event caused Wilhelm, who was greatly attached to his older brother, and who was the only family member present at his death, to abandon his studies and return home.

Like most critical events in a young person's life, his brother's death had both long term and short term effects on Wilhelm. In the long term it deepened his sensibilities and extended his range of human sympathy. More immediately it left him disconsolate and without direction.

It was now 1848, a year when the spark of freedom suddenly ignited the continent of Europe, spawning numerous uprisings, all of which were soon quashed. Moping aimlessly about the house, Wilhelm Katz easily fell prey to the revolutionary ferment and to the "American Fever" which followed in its frustration-filled wake. He decided to immigrate to the United States.

His announcement understandably alarmed his parents. They had already lost their first son to illness; they did not want to lose their second one to the New World. They persuaded Wilhelm to go to England instead and stay with some relations they had in Manchester.

The youth did so but the American Fever which had seized him did not abate. Soon after arriving in England, he boarded a ship bound for New York. He had turned his back on the Old World for good.

Starting out in a strange country with little money and no connections, Wilhelm worked at various odd jobs before finally learning a tailor's trade. He apparently experienced little difficulty learning English for he was a youth of some education who had already spent time in England. And since he had come to America not just to make his fortune but to realize his ideals, he soon began following his new country's politics with considerable interest. He became an abolitionist, a free-soiler and an admirer of that craggy Midwestern lawyer, Abraham Lincoln.

But although such issues would always interest him, he still faced the need to make his way in his new homeland. One step he took to facilitate this was to change his name. Wilhelm Katz became William Filene.

What prompted him to choose such a name remains something of a mystery. So far as can be determined, the name does not exist in German or, for that matter, in any other language. One possible clue lies in the similarity between Filene and feline, the French word for cat. (Katz, of course, is the German word for cat.) Wilhelm may have had a penchant for Frenchified names for he would call one of his later retail businesses Guillaume's Glove Store. Guillaume is the French equivalent for William.

After changing his name, William Filene decided to change his address. He set out for Boston where in 1851, at the age of 21, he opened W. Filene & Co., Tailors and Drapers, in the city's downtown shopping district.

For the next eight years his firm is listed under that name in the Boston Directory. But in 1860 W. Filene & Co. appears under a new listing, that of Millinery Goods, Wholesale. This new listing, however, only tells part of the story. For by this time William's business activities had branched out beyond Boston, while his personal life had also taken on a new dimension.

The Year 1856 looms especially large in the life of William Filene. It was the year he opened his first strictly mercantile operation. It was also the year he met Clara Ballin.

Since arriving in America, William had established and maintained contact with the country's emerging German-Jewish community. Most of its members had also arrived in 1848, and once in this country they tended to protect their sense of identity, keeping somewhat apart not only from other Americans but also from other Jews. They welcomed a young man like William who not only shared their ethnic background but who appeared to be ambitious and somewhat educated as well as pleasant and personable.

Sometime after settling in Boston, William came to know a German-Jewish family in Salem called Conrad. With their assistance and possibly their participation, he opened up in Salem a "Fancy Goods" store featuring trimmings, ribbons, buttons and skirts. It was also through them that he met his future wife.

Clara Ballin was a cousin of the Conrads from the old country. Born in 1833 in a picturesque village on the Main called Seignitz, she had, as a youngster, attended a local private academy, a school she would later refer to as "an exclusive and advanced institution." There is apparently some justification for her boast since the school was co-educational, which made it advanced, and since it had only 12 pupils, which made it at least seem selective. After attending the academy from age seven to twelve, she studied under a private tutor until she became seventeen.

Clara was therefore a woman of some education, especially for her time. She was also apparently a young woman of some means. One branch of the family owned a factory in New York, and in 1855 Clara's mother and father decided to send her to this country to learn English. Clara herself welcomed the decision. Indeed, she had probably persuaded her parents to make it.

Clara arrived accompanied by an uncle. She met many members of the German-Jewish community, learned English, and took an immediate liking to a country which, like herself, was young and vibrant with life. When her uncle went back to Germany after a year, she decided to stay on, putting off, with one excuse after another, her parents' persistent pleas to come home. During this period she met William Filene at the home of some friends in Hartford, Connecticut. William was immediately attracted; so was Clara.

The two differed in appearance for she was short while he was quite tall. They also differed in temperament for Clara was forceful and determined while William, despite his earnest striving for success, still retained a soft, indecisive streak. Thus while William proved assiduous in his attentions, he became hesitant and timorous when it came to asking the crucial question, let alone setting an actual date. Clara soon began to tire of her swain's shilly-shallying, and since her family was still begging her to come back, she wrote him from New York saying farewell. The note jolted William into action. He boarded the next train for Manhattan and proposed marriage as soon as he saw her. In fact, he now wanted to marry right away.

Clara accepted his proposal but not his wish for an immediate wedding. She had already made her arrangements to depart, so her now impatient lover would have to wait. She went back to Seignitz, spent three months with her family and then returned to America bringing with her a trousseau that filled thirteen trunks.

William was there to meet her when she landed in New York and once more, pressed her to marry him immediately. But one of Clara's thirteen trunks had been delayed and, as it so happened, it was the one containing her wedding dress. A month later when the trunk showed up, the couple were wed and set out for Salem to begin their new life.

Married in 1858, William and Clara Filene became the parents of five children during the next seven years. The first, a boy whom William named Rudolph after his deceased brother, was born in 1859. The second, born on September 3, 1860, was named Edward Albert after the Prince of Wales who was touring the United States at that time. Emma, the only girl, and Bertram would come during the next four years while the youngest, Abraham Lincoln entered the world on April 5, 1865, just nine days before the assassination of the president for whom he was named.

The marriage also proved fruitful in other ways. The Salem store, while scarcely a smashing success, survived and slowly grew. Since Salem itself was a far from flourishing city--it had lost its once famed and lucrative seafaring trade and was trying to re-establish itself as an industrial community--William's success, limited though it may have been, was nonetheless encouraging. It enabled him to close out his tailor shop in Boston and open up a wholesale house instead. This represented a rather shrewd business move, for the wholesale house, small though it undoubtedly was, permitted him to stock his Salem store at lower cost and therefore sell at lower prices. This is evident from his first advertisement which appeared in a Salem newspaper in June, 1860.

William Filene, says the ad in somewhat awkward English, "would respectfully call the attention of the public of Salem and vicinity to the fact that purchasers can save a large percentage in calling at our place of business for articles in our line...thanks to direct purchases from manufacturers for our wholesale store in Boston." The term "our line" was then explained as including "Dress Trimmings, Embroideries and Laces, Chenille Head Dresses, Bonnets and Dress Rucks, India Rubber" and the ubiquitous and all-inclusive "Fancy Goods."

***

The advent of the Civil War rattled the nation's economic structure, opening up numerous opportunities for those with the will and means to take advantage of them. In 1863, during one of the dips which the economy experienced in the course of the war, William went to New York and bought a wholesale business at a bargain price. He subsequently invested in an iron works as well, though he knew nothing about such operations. Where he got the money for these ventures is unknown but very likely it came from Clara's dowry.

For a while he commuted to New York every week or so while continuing to operate his businesses in Salem and Boston. But sometime after the war's end he closed out his Boston area activities and moved his family to New York. His businesses there were prospering, enabling him to install the household into a luxurious home at 92nd Street and Fifth Avenue. The site at that time lay between a park and a pasture, making the move to the big, bustling city actually seem more like a move to the country.

But the Filene family's new prosperity proved short-lived. In the Fall of 1869 the Federal government thwarted a move by speculator Jay Gould to corner the gold market, thereby causing the financier's extensive operations to collapse. Gould's financial failure triggered a series of others which sent the economy into a tailspin. Businesses by the hundreds went bankrupt. Among them were the firms of William Filene. As Clara later acerbically put it in a brief memoir of the family's early days, "We stayed in New York just long enough for Mr. Filene to lose every dollar he had."

***

William now found himself at almost forty years of age forced to start again from the beginning. It would be no easy task, and the fact that he now had seven mouths to feed scarcely lightened it. But after disposing of all his assets, except the family's furniture and clothes, to pay his business debts, he set out once again for the Boston area where he had achieved his first bit of business success.

This time he went to Lynn, a grubby but growing city which had become the nation's shoe-making center. After much searching he found a store or rather half a store he could rent. He could not, however, find anything resembling decent housing. When he reported this back to his wife, she wrote him to take anything he could find until she could join him. So William rented the lower rooms of a one family house situated some distance from his new business.

Clara sold part of their furniture to pay for their train tickets, and shipping the rest, she gathered up her brood and departed for their new home. As she wrote in her memoirs forty years later, "We joined Mr. Filene, and together began our fortunes all over, in the face of aspects that appeared most discouraging."

These discouraging aspects confronted them as soon as they stepped off the train. It was a chilly, early Spring evening and a light rain was falling. William met them at the station, and since he could not afford the rental of a carriage, they had to tramp through the town en route to their new quarters. It was a march they would long remember. It took them down muddy streets lined with grimy, windowless factory buildings and tanneries. The latter gave off an acrid stench which the falling rain only sharpened. It was quitting time and so the streets were filled with weary and shabby workers treading home. The one festive note, provided by the numerous saloons with their garish gas lights, raucous shouts and staggering customers only made them shudder. And so the family, with William carrying the two babies and with the three older children trudging fearfully at their parents' side, walked on, silent and depressed at this first glimpse of their new community and their new life.

***

The chilling prospect that encountered them on the evening of their arrival did not, fortunately, prove predictive of the family's future. Once ensconced in their new compressed living quarters and established in their equally compressed store, the Filene's fortunes began to revive. In four weeks William asked his business landlord to tear down the partition and rent him the whole store. He was selling women's wear and with so many young women flocking to work in the city's thriving shoe factories, the Filenes did not lack customers. On Saturday nights they stayed open until eleven, sometimes having to lock the doors to keep new customers from jamming their still small shop.

Clara had now become William's business associate and she was contributing greatly to the store's success. With a good head for figures, she kept such books as were kept. She also served as cashier, and, in so doing, maintained a close eye on which goods were moving and which were not. She even handled most of their business correspondence, ordering new goods, sending back unwanted ones and seeing to it their orders were filled on time.

Two developments that occurred shortly after their arrival in Lynn helped her play such a role. One was the discovery of a modest but decent cottage for rent only one street away from the store. This enabled her to move from one place to the other much more easily and quickly.

The second development proved much more significant, especially to the children involved. The small co-ed school which Clara had attended as a girl had since blossomed into an all-male academy with an enrollment of three hundred boys. Clara persuaded one of her sisters who was visiting the United States to take her three oldest youngsters back to Germany and, presumably with the financial aid of their grandparents, enroll them in her alma mater. Her main motive for doing so was probably the belief that they would secure a much better education than they would in joining the working class children of Lynn in that city's none-too-impressive public schools. However, the decision also gave her more time to help her husband get back on his feet.

Within a year of their move to Lynn, their business had grown enough to warrant renting a larger store in a new and better location. The following year Clara went to Germany and brought the boys home. They now began attending the Lynn schools while helping their parents behind the counter in their spare time. Their assistance allowed William to open up a second store for men and boy's clothing some twelve blocks away. Soon this enterprise was also flourishing.

The next year, 1873, saw disaster threaten again. The stock market collapsed once more, creating a nation-wide depression. Hundreds of banks and other businesses went under throwing several million people out of work. Oliver Wendell Holmes, Jr., walking up Beacon

Hill to his new law offices that winter, shuddered at the sight of men sleeping in the doorways in the freezing cold.

But the new crash did not catch William unprepared. Though he had expanded, he had done so prudently without contracting heavy debts. Furthermore, he was selling clothes, goods that people always needed. Consequently, his enterprise weathered the new financial storm. In fact he may have profited from it for in 1875, as the depression was ending, he purchased at a bargain price still another store, this one in Bath, Maine.

During this same year, he also rented a new home for his family in a more expensive part of town. This new house came with 200 fruit trees, a stable, and quarters for a few cows. Each child could now have his or her own room. The Filenes had no horses or cows and their furnishings only sufficed to equip a few of the mansion's many chambers. But they luxuriated in their new living quarters. Clara could later refer to it as "a large estate" and she would tell triumphantly, if not too grammatically, what ensued. "Living there one year when we bought and paid, in cash." Fortune was once again smiling on William Filene.

***

Turning 45 in May, 1875, William Filene could feel a sense of satisfaction and even pride. Coming to this country as a penniless and friendless youth of 18, he had become a comfortably situated middle-aged man with, presumably, many more productive and profitable years ahead. He had made a good marriage and could look forward to providing well for his five children. In this respect, at least, he had achieved his American dream.

But the William Filene or Wilhelm Katz, who had crossed the Atlantic over a quarter of a century earlier, had been motivated by more than the mere desire to make money. That he probably could have achieved by staying in Posen and taking over his father's ribbon store. He had also come to the new world to advance and attain his ideals of freedom and brotherhood. Had the prosperous, mature merchant forgotten them in his quest for financial security?

The answer is no. During his long, laborious struggle to put himself on a sound financial footing, he never stopped believing in or supporting those ideals. They continued to animate the prosperous merchant as they had the penniless youth.

We have already seen how William had soon become an abolitionist. During the 1850's when he was trying desperately to make a go of things in Boston, he still found time to take in lectures and go to meetings. He went to churches as well. He was particularly impressed by a Unitarian clergyman named Theodore Parker and frequently attended Parker's church to listen to this fiery minister's liberal sermons.

Once he had established himself in Lynn, he began sampling the churches of that and neighboring cities, and when his sons returned from their stay in the German academy, he would often take them with him. As Edward later recalled, "He started me off at least so I wasn't taught a lot of so many things that weren't so. In reference to religion, we had a store in Lynn and were a pretty busy family and didn't go out hardly at all. Father and I worked pretty close together and Father used to take us to church and say he wanted us to see and hear and ask questions, but not to join any church until we were at least of age."

Did he ever take them to a synagogue? Apparently not, for William had turned his back on his ancestral religion for good. Admittedly, it was convenient for him to do so since anti-Semitism had already become quite pervasive in American society. But other factors probably played a greater role in prompting him to do so. He associated Judaism with the traditional past that he wanted to shuck off. It seemed counter-revolutionary and anti-scientific and therefore unpalatable to William who was very much a child of his times. Many Boston churches, on the other hand, especially those associated with the new "Boston religion" called Unitarianism, were reaching out and embracing the new currents of thought that were coursing through the nineteenth century. They were also becoming involved with the social issues which these new ideals were spawning. William thus found these churches more compatible than synagogues to his intellectual interests and spiritual sympathies.[1]

William did not confine his interest in modern religious ideas and ideals, and his sympathy with basic human values, to occasional visits to various churches. These moral commitments entered into the very texture of his personality and influenced his everyday personal life. Once as a young bachelor, to cite just one illustration, he had dressed up and set out to attend a party when he came across a poor woman struggling to get home while carrying a heavy load of laundry and shepherding a large brood of children. William immediately offered to assist her.

The woman lived some distance away and by the time he had gotten her and her children home, it was past midnight. Yet he willingly, if not happily, gave up his party to perform a *mitzvah* or good deed to someone he did not know. (Except, of course, he would not have called it a mitzvah since he probably did not know this Hebrew word.)

What is of more interest and of far greater importance when it comes to understanding the achievements of his sons Edward and Lincoln, is the way these human and humane concerns governed his business activities. For the William who stood behind the counter was the same man who went to church on Sundays and helped strangers on the street.

As noted earlier, William enlisted his whole family into the service of his store. Even Lincoln by the age of ten was coming in after school to sweep out from behind the counter and run errands. But William looked on his sons as more than unpaid labor. They were also associates whose views he valued. He rarely gave them direct orders and frequently sought their advice. "My father rarely acted alone," Lincoln would recall in later years. "Even when my brother and I were still young men, he would ask us 'What do you think of this? Had we better do it his way?'"

When it came to dealing with his growing number of employees, William Filene adopted a similar approach. He held regular meetings at his home on Friday night and encouraged his workers to drop in, take some refreshment and give their opinions concerning the store's operations. Such conclaves were almost unheard of in those days, indeed they are rare enough today, and they transformed William's workforce into a large and loyal cadre of collaborators. Furthermore, even when he had 200 on his payroll, he still knew nearly all of them by name.

That such practices represented more than just superficial gestures is attested to by one of his employees in an article about William ten years after his death. He "won the hearts of all who knew him," she wrote, "for he was an approachable man, a man to whom everyone felt they could go and talk about whatever troubled them, sure to find a willing ear and sure to receive...sympathy, philosophy, and wisdom."

As the writer of this article also made clear, Clara was William's partner in this respect as in everything else. She not only supported his concern for his employees' welfare but often suggested new ways for him to manifest it. When they moved to their larger store in Lynn, she urged him to set aside a room where the sales girls could rest and to make provisions for them to have proper lunches.

The same consideration which William showed for his workers also guided his approach to his customers. He firmly believed that a merchant's and a customer's best interests were one and the same. Taking advantage of a customer in any way represented in his view not only poor moral principles but unsound business practice. Providing shoppers with what they genuinely wanted at the lowest possible prices was the sole way of assuring their continued patronage and his stores' continued growth.

His ability to empathize and sympathize with others extended even to other business firms. Once when the banks had plenty of money available, one of his supervisors told him that he was paying more than he needed to pay for credit. His bank was charging him six per cent and the supervisor maintained he could get the rate reduced to five per cent.

William agreed to his proposal and, sure enough, the employee did succeed in persuading the bank to chop one per cent off his interest charges. But later on when money became tighter, William found himself cut off from all credit even though he was willing to pay a higher rate. It took a good deal of effort for him to find new funds with which to operate.

William refused to react to the incident by cursing the banks as so many other small businessmen might have done. Instead he felt he had learned a lesson. "Banks have to make money like everyone else. If you help them to make a reasonable profit when business is good, they are apt to remember it and return the favor when things are slack. It's only a simple business principle."

The principle was obviously meant to apply to a much wider area than simply borrowing from banks. For William it meant never trying to squeeze someone to make a bit more in immediate profit. Think of the other party, have some regard for their interests, and also think of the long term. As we shall see, the lessons William learned from his experience with the banks he also passed on to his sons Edward and Lincoln. And they put these lessons along with all the other principles and practices which their father taught them, to remarkable and even revolutionary use.

***

That William Filene succeeded in conducting his businesses with honesty and humanity does not mean he lacked or failed to exercise good business sense. As his former employee, Margaret Murray, wrote, his kindliness and probity did not interfere with his "true financial judgement, a careful supervision of resources and investments in merchandise." When it came to re-supplying his shelves, for example, he always solicited bids from competitors before re-ordering even those items that had sold well.

This cautiousness, acquired at great expense in the crash of 1869, plus his determination to treat his employees, his customers and his business connections with fairness and sympathy, paid off handsomely. To the three stores he had acquired by 1875, he added another within two years. This one was in Salem which was now becoming something of a manufacturing center itself, although it would never rival Lynn in this respect.

As the decade drew to a close, and as William neared his 50th birthday, he began once again to think of bigger things. But this time he set his sights not on New York but on Boston where he had operated a business before and which, though far from being the hub of the universe as it claimed, was at least the hub of New England. He started preparing for a major move but the strain of the years had taken its toll, and in July of 1880, he suffered a stroke. He recovered but his doctor warned him that his days of full-time activity must end. For the Filene enterprises to go forward, or even survive, he would need a capable full-time manager.

William turned to his sons. His oldest, Rudolph, had unfortunately shown little flair for merchandising or, for that matter, anything else. But with his second son, Edward, it was a different story. This bright though somewhat peculiar youth had displayed a distinct knack for retailing. So on Edward's nineteen year old shoulders the family's fortunes would now depend.

Chapter 2
THE UGLY DUCKLING

O n a mid-April morning in 1865, Edward Filene, then four years old, was lying on the living-room couch of his Salem, Massachusetts home when he heard his father come into the kitchen. His father's entrance greatly surprised Edward for the older man almost never came home at this hour. The boy's uneasiness further increased when he heard his father and mother conversing in low, somber tones.

Soon his father came into the living room and, ignoring his young son for the moment, began pacing up and down, glancing occasionally out the window and tugging at his dark, full beard as if he were in great pain. He then went out through the front door.

Edward, suspecting, fearing that something was seriously amiss, started to follow him. The boy moved slowly, hesitantly, first steadying himself on the furniture, then the door post, then the porch railing. On reaching the railing he paused to take in the dilapidated dwellings huddled together along the street, nearly all of them fronted by weedy yards and scraggly trees. At the corner loomed the grey, shapeless bulk of the Catholic Church. Down the hill in the distance sprawled the empty warehouses, left-over ruins from Salem's days of glory as a world center of shipping and trade.

Edward knew the scene well. Since becoming lame a year before, he had spent hour after hour lying on the couch looking at the street. But today it all seemed much more ominous and oppressive. This feeling was greatly heightened by the sudden pealing of a church bell in the distance. Then the bell of another church joined in and then another and another. Why were they doing this since it was a weekday, he wondered. He had no way of knowing that a president, beloved by most of the people of Salem but especially by his father, had fallen to an assassin's bullet.

As the sounds of the bells increased in intensity, he limped down the porch steps, holding on to the guard rail as he did so. Hearing a noise behind him, he turned and saw his father on the steep roof of the porch. His father was holding a banner curled up under one arm while steadying himself against a window casement with the other.

The older man then released his grip on the casement and let himself slide down the roof until he found support at the gutter. But his banner, caught by a gust of wind, slipped open, revealing a bare expanse of black cloth unrelieved by any design or emblem.

The sight of his father sliding down the roof with the black banner unfurling startled the boy and he began to scream in terror. His father hastily descended from the roof and his mother came rushing out of the house. They picked him up, tried to quiet him, attempted to find out what was wrong. He could not say. But nothing ever erased the memory of the mysterious dark horror he felt when he saw his father with the black banner sliding down the roof and heard the tolling of the church bells in the air. Seventy years later, Edward A. Filene recalled the scene as the most vivid and most frightening incident of his child hood.

***

Edward was three and a half when he suffered a bad fall. The mishap rammed a stone against his side, leaving him unable to walk, at least not without great pain. For a year he lay in bed or on a couch waiting desperately for the injury to heal. Gradually he improved and slowly learned to walk all over again. But it was not easy. His mother, seeing him totter on his unsteady legs, would grow pale and hurry to his side to catch him. He fell often but eventually managed to move about, dragging his lame leg after him.

Eventually he succeeded in getting to the front gate by himself and, when Rudolph accompanied him, could make it to the deserted warehouses by the now decrepit docks. These forlorn buildings served as a recreation center for the boys of Salem who liked to throw rocks through their already broken windows.

But since some degree of lameness persisted, Edward's attempts to join other boys in play rarely turned out well. When his mother sent him and Rudolph out to play she carefully instructed Rudolph to watch out for his younger brother. But no sooner were they out of sight when Rudolph would run ahead. At first, he would stop from time to time to allow the limping Edward to catch up, but eventually he would meet up with other boys and go off with them. Edward would struggle for a while striving to keep up, then abandon the futile effort and limp back to the house.

When Rudolph returned home, flushed and conscience-stricken, their mother would merely look at him with pain and disappointment. It made the older boy so miserable that he would voluntarily avow never to do it again. But afterwards, when no one else was around, he would come up to Edward and whisper fiercely, threateningly, "Why didn't you wait? I came right back!" And the next time the same thing would happen all over again.

Sometimes Edward did join the other boys at play but these occasions provided little joy or real recreation. He still limped and he was awkward in other ways. "I got the idea," he later recalled, "that playing was something you were forced to do, like going to bed early, because adults expected you to." And, he added, "I never hated any part of my work so much as I hated being made to play."

Although he was still too young for work, he was spending much of his time at the family business. With Rudolph in school, Clara customarily took Edward and the three younger children with her to the store. There she installed the youngsters behind a little desk that served as the office, and there, restlessly but quietly, they played in whispers. This was play that Edward could perhaps enjoy for as the oldest brother present, he need not suffer any indignities. Also he found the store fascinating with its well-oiled floors, its shelves bulging with bolts of cloth and its interesting parade of customers, some of them foreign seamen.

Here too he frequently experienced unpleasantness and occasionally even terror. Sometimes rough male customers used crude language that visibly distressed his mother. Once a customer insulted his mother and Edward always remembered the terrible agitation he felt until his father unexpectedly came in and threw the man out.

When business slacked off, Clara bundled up the children and, carrying Lincoln and Emma while letting Edward and Bertram toddle along beside her, took them home. When Rudolph returned from school, he and Bertram often went off to play. Emma and Lincoln were put to bed. And Edward was left sitting by himself, waiting impatiently for his father to come home.

His father's only distraction was working with tools and Edward loved watching him do so. At one time, the older man tried to invent a new type of cooking pot, one that would sink into the stove and not just rest upon it. In this way, so he reasoned, the food would cook uniformly all around the pot and not just on the bottom. Such a pot would also prevent heat from escaping from the stove. Edward followed with fascination his father's futile efforts to translate the idea into a patentable cooking utensil.

Edward had ideas of his own but they did not concern pots or even inventions. He did once dream of owning a store but this was the usual childish vision of a candy store and a few stomach aches from over-indulgence cured him of this ambition. He also felt a yen to become a railroad engineer, again hardly remarkable for a boy in those adventurous days of railroading. His biggest fantasy, however, was of being a conqueror, of riding off to battle on a black horse, of slashing off enemy heads four at a time and then of returning home to ride down the streets in triumph, while crowds of onlookers admired and applauded him. This last fantasy, while not entirely unique to the world of masculine childhood, is still distinctive enough to help us understand the troubled youngster he was and the troubled man he became.

***

We do not know the exact year William moved the family to New York City. It was probably 1868 or early 1869 since we do know that the Filenes did not stay there long. The uprooting appears to have made little impact on Edward for his memory of it always remained dim. But the same cannot be said for the second major move in his life, namely the one to Germany and the private academy in Seignitz. This move markedly increased the sufferings of the child while leaving deep scars on the later adult.

The Handels Institute as it was now called, operated in a heavy-handed, semi-military manner. Its atmosphere was harsh, its discipline was brutal. The boys were strictly separated into age groups so that the three brothers saw little of each other. Moreover, as non-Germans they undoubtedly had to suffer a good deal of verbal and even physical abuse from their Teutonic classmates. For Edward, small in stature and still lame, it was an on-going nightmare.

At one point during his stay a rebellion broke out. Some of the students had become aroused over the fierce beatings which the instructors so freely administered. The rebels took over one of the buildings and refused to come out. Finally, the kindly, grey-haired wife of the headmaster entered the building and persuaded them to surrender. She assured them they would not be penalized for their action. But as soon as the boys yielded, the school's instructors seized them and beat them severely, with the worst blows falling not on the rowdiest rebels but on those from the least well-off families. The whole experience made a deep impression on Edward's young mentality. It left him with a horror of, and an aversion to, the cruelties of discrimination and betrayal. These feelings greatly influenced his later policies and practices.

Edward, however, took no part in the student insurrection. In fact he took part in little that went on at the school. He responded to the stresses of his situation by succumbing to frequent, and largely psychosomatic, illnesses. He thereby ended up spending much of his time lying alone in his small room. He was not, however, idle. The school's regimen required the boys to read numerous German classics and other serious works as well as texts on various subjects. In his sickbed he sought to keep up but found the relentless cramming of information it required not only unpleasant but also unrewarding. He came away from the experience convinced that how to think was far more important that what to think. He soon thereafter developed a passion for the thinking process that would last his entire life.

"You can hold a pint-sized pot under Niagara," he would later say in reference to his German school days, "but even with the whole of Niagara pouring down upon it, you can't possibly take away more than a pint. In fact, you're apt to take away less, since the very force of the water is more apt to empty than to fill the pot." Trying to persuade American educators to focus more attention on rigorous thinking and objective analysis and less on the mere acquisition of information would become one of his many adult pursuits.

While lying in bed he also found time to read other books. Many of these were also ponderous for light reading was hardly a staple of German schools at the time. However, he did manage to find a copy of Grimm's fairy tales and he read it through avidly. The one that particularly impressed itself on his 11 or 12-year-old consciousness was, rather predictably, "The Ugly Duckling." Indeed, of all the stories he read as a child, this was the one he most remembered.

Although the tale is at least vaguely familiar to most literate adults, it might be useful in view of its significance to Edward to review it briefly. The ungainly and unsightly duckling in the story is mercilessly teased and hounded before finally being ostracized by his family as well as by the other members of the flock. In vain, the young fowl exclaims, "You don't understand me." Eventually, the duckling, alone and bereft of friends or family, finds salvation through becoming a swan. The story ends with these words:

> He thought how he had been persecuted and despised, and now he heard them saying that he was the most beautiful of all the birds. Even the elder-tree bent its branches straight down into the water before him, and the sun shone warm and mild.

Edward would never, not even in the most figurative, farfetched sense of the term, become a swan, that is, acquire any of the swan-like features of grace and beauty. But, in certain respects, and to some degree, he would succeed in making the elder trees bow down.

***

One can easily imagine Edward's ecstatic joy when his mother finally came to bring the boys back. What a sense of relief he must have felt as he boarded the train that would take them to their homeward-bound ship. And how appealing the still drab and grimy city of Lynn must now have looked when he arrived.

But although his life in unattractive Lynn undoubtedly represented a major improvement over his life in picturesque Seignitz, the return home brought fresh humiliations. The initial cause was a trivial one as are so many of the things which cause great anguish to youngsters. The academy had outfitted all its students with heavy green coats as part of the school uniform. The coats, a product of German crafts-manship at its best, proved exceptionally sturdy and Clara insisted that they continue wearing them. Unfortunately they also proved to be conspicuous and conspicuously foreign-looking. They stood out with great visibility in the streets and school houses of Lynn, making Edward and his two brothers objects of mockery and scorn. "Here come the green coats," the other boys would shout when the three Filene brothers came into the school yard.

Edward suffered the longest from the ordeal for he was smaller than Rudolph and Bertram, and since the coats seemed almost impervious to wear, he had to wear their coats when they outgrew them. In his green coat the ugly duckling had, in his own eyes at least, become still uglier.

Before he finally shucked off the last of the green coats, Edward found himself beset with still a new humiliation, one that proved to be neither trivial nor tractable. Most youths develop some acne as they head into adolescence but Edward, with what at times seems to have been almost a knack for faring worse than his fellows, contracted an eczema. It was something of an on-again, off-again malady that proved nearly impossible to control. Emotional tension, among other things, tended to make it flare up.

The eczema, added to the slight limp which continued to plague him, plus his short stature, greatly affected his relations with those around him. He always felt people were staring at him whether they were doing so or not. The image of himself as the ugly duckling burned still deeper into his consciousness.

As might be expected, all these afflictions greatly affected Edward's relations with his peers. While he did manage to maintain some rather remote contacts with a few other youths, and even to join them occasionally in hunting, fishing and horseback riding, he apparently went through childhood and youth without making one close friend. When it came to girls, his problems intensified for here his skin disorder did him, in effect, double damage. It made him fearful about approaching girls to begin with, and when he did think of doing so, the fear and tension which the eczema had already aroused in him would make the eczema itself worse. Edward Filene grew to manhood without anything resembling a romantic experience.

William now expected his boys to help out in the store and Edward, cut off as he was from normal relationships with youngsters his own age, welcomed the work as an outlet for his energies. But the stores provided more than an escape from loneliness. He genuinely loved retailing and took to it with eagerness and skill. As a result, the aging William began leaning on his second son more and more.

But while Edward showed a distinct flair for merchandizing he also showed an increasing impatience with the way it was carried on in his father's stores. These were still small operations catering to a working class clientele. For Edward, this meant standing behind the counter hour after hour waiting endlessly, or so it seemed, while impoverished working women and housewives tried to make up their minds as to whether to buy a yard or two of material or a small article of little value. He knew well the reason for their hesitation. He knew that with their scanty funds such a purchase would represent a major expenditure, and that a wrong choice could have near disastrous effects on their family finances. Yet the teen-aged merchandiser could not help but find their procrastination nerve-racking. At times, standing behind the counter and waiting while a woman customer fingered a piece of goods, the exasperated youth could barely suppress the urge to cry out, "Do you want it or not?"

Edward thus fully shared his father wish for a store that would carry higher-priced goods and cater to a higher-income clientele. He even became impatient with his father's cautiousness in moving towards this goal. But both father and son desperately desired a bigger and better store, and both toiled together to achieve it.

***

While Edward acquired few if any real friends from among his peers during this period, he did form a friendship with an older man. This was Thomas Woodley, a tenant in one of the houses that William, as his fortunes improved, had acquired.

Woodley was an English shoemaker, a craftsman not a factory hand, who had read and studied widely on his own. Through his studies he had become an atheist, or at least an agnostic, with a consuming interest in natural science. He had come to the firm belief that all nature was governed by logical principles. The fish swam in season, the leaves dropped from trees, all in accordance with natural laws. In short there were no miracles.

This simple deduction he passed on to his young disciple who embraced it devoutly. It guided Edward's thinking throughout his life. In his seventies he was still uttering and acting on Woodley's basic maxim: There are no miracles.

Edward learned something else from Woodley, something that was already playing a role in his life and would play a bigger role later on. This was the notion that one did not need formal schooling to acquire an education. Indeed, one could learn as much if not more on one's own as one could in a school house. So while continuing to attend the local schools and while continuing to work for his father, Edward embarked on an ambitious if somewhat erratic program of self-education.

He stashed away books in the desks of each of his father's stores, and whenever business slacked off he picked one up and read it for a few minutes before the next customer showed up. Even when traveling the twelve blocks between the two stores, Edward found time for his self-taught education. Boarding the street car while carrying change from one store to another, he would go through two or three pages of Darwin while simultaneously guarding the money, nodding to acquaintances and watching out that he did not pass his station.

In addition to Darwin he also read, or read away at, Bancroft's American history, the essays of Oliver Wendell Holmes and other currently popular, educational works. He even found time to include a bit of fiction such as the novels of George Eliot. All this hurried, on-the-run reading proved a mixed blessing. While it gave him a taste for, and an acquaintance with, issues and ideas far beyond the narrow range of simple shop-keeping, it also tended to blur them in his mind. In later life he often confused works of science, works of social problems and works of literature, skipping from one to another without distinction and attributing to one writer ideas which properly belonged to another.

He also at about this time began writing his thoughts down in a notebook, a practice he pursued until his death. Many of his jottings reflect the concerns common to a serious-minded adolescent of any era. For example, he pondered, and pondered deeply, the question "Is there a god?" His answer indicates the influence of Woodley and, to some extent, his father. Since there were natural laws, so Edward reasoned, and since they seemed to fit the human condition, they probably came from an omnipotent force. This force, he concluded, could be called God.

But Edward did not stop there. If the laws which appear to govern man are natural, that is God-made or at least God-sanctioned, then to act in conformity with them was to act in accordance with God. And since these laws enabled and even encouraged personal success, the attainment of such success was not only acceptable but admirable.

Edward, however, was not willing to let himself and other strivers for success off too easily. Everything in nature has its price, so he reasoned, and the price of success required those who obtained it to pay something back to the society which had made the success possible.

As Edward later put it, he came to realize "that it was an evolutionary and not a miraculous world and that all I was enjoying was made up of the sacrifices and martyrdom of those who preceded me, and...just as I wouldn't let a man give me a cigar without 'treating back,' so I began to think of 'treating back' for all that had been given me...of paying back the benefits that I was receiving from civilization which was the result of what untold generations had constructed through bitter experience, self-denial and martyrdom."

And so this serious and intense adolescent began to view the success he so desperately wanted, the success that would affect his figurative transformation into a swan, as something he could achieve through serious and intense effort. However, it required conformance to the laws of civilization which in themselves were an outgrowth of the laws of nature. It also required a pay-back to civilization itself for making such success possible.

These ideas, germinating in the mind of the youth, would take root and flourish in the mind of the mature man. They would shape and influence Edward Filene's actions for the rest of his life.

***

As with so many bright youths, high school appears to have played no significant role in the real education of Edward Filene. Nevertheless, Lynn had a high school and he attended it, finishing in 1879. His grades were apparently quite satisfactory but not especially outstanding. He received no particular honors at his graduation.

But burning with a thirst for knowledge as well as with a desire for success, Edward began to think of going further. He finally decided to aim as high as he could: Harvard College.

Harvard then, even more than today, stood out as the country's premier institution of higher learning. Socially as well as intellectually it towered over a still sparse academic landscape. For the son of a Jewish emigrant shopkeeper to think of going there struck many as not just the height of ambition but also of audacity, if not absurdity. Nearly everyone Edward knew, including members of his family, tried to persuade him to abandon such a vain pursuit. But the young man refused to listen. He would never pay much heed to the fears and doubts of pessimists, and once he had decided that Harvard could provide him with a passageway to wisdom and wealth, he exerted an all-out effort to take advantage of it.

Edward studied at every spare moment he could find. Happily, German was to be one of the examination subjects and in this language he was already quite proficient. In May of 1880 he sat for the exams. They consisted largely of translating from and into Greek, Latin and German plus solving some problems in mathematics. The next month the letter from Cambridge arrived bearing the results. Edward A. Filene had passed the exams and could join the freshman class entering in the fall. The ugly duckling had taken his first step, and a formidable one, to becoming a swan.

But the ecstatic joy which Edward experienced at the news was soon shattered. Only a few weeks after the crucial envelope from Cambridge arrived, his father suffered his stroke and turned to him for help. Edward Filene would not be among the freshman trooping into Harvard Yard in September.

"I had to give up my dream of a university training," Edward subsequently wrote in speaking of that traumatic summer of 1880. "How well I remember my disappointment. I thought I should never become a really useful man without this Harvard education."

He always claimed that he quickly recovered from the blow, that he soon found in retailing all the knowledge he was looking forward to acquiring at Harvard, that operating his father's stores taught him more about sociology, psychology, economics, labor relations, design, etc., than he could have learned attending college classes. But his journals of the time showed that his first notion was to work hard for ten years, acquire $100,000, set aside half of the sum to take care of his parents and then use the other half to realize his dream of a Harvard degree. The fact that he would then be a man of 30 entering school with a class of 18-year-olds apparently did not worry him.

This new Harvard dream was also destined to remain unfulfilled. But the yearning which inspired it never expired. In going over Edward's papers after his death, his executors found certificate number 276, issued by the acting Dean of Harvard, stating that Edward A. Filene, having passed his exams, was herewith admitted to the college. From young manhood through middle age and into old age, this faded scrap of paper had remained one of Edward Filene's most cherished possessions.

***

Edward would suffer many defeats throughout his ambitious, active life but would rarely spend much time grieving over them. Instead he would pick himself up and plunge into something else. This pattern of behavior was already at work in the summer of 1880. Though terribly hurt by the turn of events which saw a Harvard education placed in his hands and then, within a month, snatched away, he was far from crushed. With his quickly fabricated and quite flimsy plan for attending college in the future to spur him on, he threw himself into his new life as his father's full-time manager.

He did not lack aid and assistance. Though only 15, Lincoln had already demonstrated a marked talent for retailing. Less studious and much more gregarious than his older brother, he was nonetheless bright and willing. So Lincoln quit high school--he only finished his sophomore year--to help out. Meanwhile William remained in overall control, supervising the stores and dictating their major policies.

Working closely and constantly with his father, Edward inevitably found things to criticize. For example, the older man never took inventory of the stock of his stores. His only way of determining his profits was to buy and sell real estate. If he owned more property at the end of a year then at the beginning, he had made money; if he owned less, he had lost. When his son sought to persuade him to make a more systematic check of his operations by taking inventory, William merely shrugged his shoulders and said, "Why bother? My stock is just as good at the end of the year as at the beginning."

But despite these and other occasional differences they worked well together, and with Lincoln as well as Clara helping out, they forged ahead.

In 1881 William felt ready to realize his long-standing dream of owning a store in Boston, a store that would cater at least to the middle class if not to the "carriage trade." Cautious as he had now become, he started out modestly. His new Boston enterprise was situated on Winter Street, a side street in Boston's shopping district, and was only 24 feet square. Yet it boasted an attractive facade plus marble floors. William believed that a store was judged first and foremost by its entrance and he took care that his new Boston outlet met such a test.

The Filenes advertised in the Boston papers to announce their arrival. They touted the small store as "one of the most modern of the day with its genuine white marble floors and most artistic windows." Purchasers, it said, "can save a large percentage on emeralds and embroidered sleeves from 25 cents to $3 a pair...dress trimmings in the latest patterns...lisle thread and silk gloves and mitts...and cotton stockings."

The store apparently did well almost from the start and the next year they opened the Guillaume Glove Store a few doors away. Lincoln, now 16 and showing great promise as a merchandiser, was placed in charge.

Edward, however, supplied the driving force that kept all of William's now numerous operations going. He would journey to Boston early in the morning, go over the stock and discuss problems with the clerks. At noon he would give his report to his father. The Boston stores closed earlier than the Lynn ones and so after checking the day's receipts, he and Lincoln would take the ferry to Lynn and usually remain in one or another of those two stores until they shut up shop for the night.

But riding the ferry from Lynn to Boston and back was not the only traveling Edward was doing. It bothered him greatly that his father's operations were still too small to send buyers to Europe or even New York as their larger competitors did. They had to depend on the salesmen from the major suppliers who made no special effort to bring the latest fashions promptly to their attention or even to show them the full range of merchandise available. The situation, to be sure, had improved as their enterprises grew but they still had to take a back seat to the larger stores when it came to acquiring the newest and most promising items, and since they were operating in the rapidly shifting world or women's apparel, these limitations were greatly hampering their growth.

To overcome the problem Edward began to make short one-day trips to New York on his own. He would board the night train from Boston, arriving at Grand Central early the following morning. After eating breakfast at the station restaurant, he would then start out on a walking tour of Fifth Avenue. He would first carefully inspect the display windows of the larger and more prestigious stores of mid-Manhattan to see what they were selling. He would next proceed down the avenue until he reached 14th Street where with equal care he would scrutinize the shop windows of the cut rate stores. These shops he knew served as dumping grounds for the lines and models that had failed to catch on in the more fashionable shops uptown. He wanted to know just what these lines and models were.

By the end of his walking tour he knew what goods he wanted, as well as those he didn't want, and he would set out for the manufacturers to give his orders. That same evening he would take the midnight special to Boston where the following morning he would leave the train, eat a quick breakfast and head directly to Winter Street, arriving in time to help with the customary pre-opening preparations.

Edward still found time to read and study. These were, at this period of his life, just about his only distractions. He poured through every book on business he could get his hands on--there were not too many available in those days--and then branched out to broader and deeper works. He also continued to keep notebooks, jotting down thoughts, observations and stray bits of information.

These journals show that Edward the young man was as deeply concerned as was Edward the adolescent with such issues as death and the meaning of life. Only he seems somewhat more preoccupied with living life to the full, not in the sense of enjoying all its pleasures, but in the sense of realizing his potential and achieving something worthwhile. "I do not think," he wrote, "that I should fear at all to die--that is, fear the hereafter--but the thought that I am compelled to leave this life with all its possibilities unfinished would be unbearable." Elsewhere he cites Matthew Arnold's poem "The Youth of Man" and quotes lines reflecting Arnold's regrets of old age. "If Arnold feels that," observes Edward, "how much more wretched old age will make a man who distinguishes himself in nothing." Edward was already determined that such a life of non-distinction would not be his.

At times, he exhibits a poetic sensibility of his own. He remembers how Woodley had told him of insects whose entire life lasted but a single day. The idea fascinated Edward and he wondered about those insects born on a sunny day and who therefore died without knowing that it ever rained. As one can see, an unusual merchant was in the making here. But merchant he was becoming despite all his far-ranging interests and perceptions. He was still toiling in his father's stores every week day until 9 p.m. The only exception was Saturday, when he worked until 1 a.m.

Thanks in large part to his intelligent and intense efforts, things were going well. By the fall of 1883, the two Boston stores, one three years old, the other only two, were selling $100,000 worth of goods a year--a sum that would reckon out into the millions in today's inflated values. But Edward was not able to savor the full fruits of his achievement, for by the fall of 1883 he was desperately confronting the most agonizing personal crisis of his young and continually woe-racked life.

***

It struck quite literally like a thief in the night, the night being that of October 12, 1883, for when Edward awoke the next morning he found his face red and inflamed. Moreover the inflammation was spreading up his arms, between his legs and under his arm pits. The eczema that had plagued his youth, and which had never completely disappeared, had now returned with a terrifying virulence. Almost as he watched, it spread over more and more areas of his body.

His father had already left home to go to the stores. His mother and Emma were in Iowa visiting relatives. Edward let Lincoln and Rudolph go to work while he remained in bed, waiting and hoping for the affliction to abate.

It failed to do so. Instead as the days went by it became worse. What especially frightened him was its effect on his eyesight. He could not write and when he sought to read, the words seemed to blur and dissolve after a few sentences. A doctor from Boston was summoned. He diagnosed the case as eczema and gave him zinc lotions and salves, but these nostrums failed to halt the increasing deterioration of his skin. His father, unable to care for him himself, suggested sending him to the Conrads, their cousins in Salem, until Clara and Emma returned. Edward at first balked at the idea but when his brothers pointed out that he had no right to increase his father's worry, he consented. His father also hired a male nurse to take care of him.

The attendant turned out to be a congenial but ineffectual fellow who spent more time relating his adventures in the Civil War than looking after his patient. Fortunately, the Conrads themselves proved sympathetic and supportive. The mother cooked special foods for him while the girls read to him and cleaned his room. But Edward's prickly pride and defensiveness, exacerbated by his humiliating illness, often made their efforts to ease his discomfort difficult. When one of the cousins would offer to read to him he would immediately protest that it wasn't necessary even though reading was the only thing that could take his mind off his illness. She had to insist on doing so before he would say yes.

His mother and sister returned from Iowa, and his mother, alarmed over his condition, took him home immediately. More doctors were summoned. Without exception they all prescribed zinc ointments supplemented by generous doses of potash taken internally. But by the end of the year, his overall condition had worsened. While his eyes had improved so that he could read and even, in a very shaky hand, write, the eczema now covered his entire body. Furthermore, he had lost all his hair.

One doctor told him that his hair would almost certainly never grow back, and this information bothered him more than the eczema itself. "I feel that way because of what strangers might think of me," said the self-conscious Edward in the detailed notes he had started to make on his baffling illness. He then went on to speculate on illnesses such as his, illnesses which did not take one's life but which could cause so much distress.

"I wonder if Socrates ever had a toothache, and how he bore it if he did," Edward ruminated. "I would rather know that than know how fearlessly he took the poison that was to kill him. I can easily imagine," he continued, "a state of feeling made so exalted by innocence and the presence of weeping and sympathetic friends as to take from death all its terror. But a common toothache, or some disease disgusting but not dangerous--how did he meet that?"

Edward's own illness, however, soon became dangerous as well as disgusting. His body had turned a grey, muddy color. His alarmed parents transferred him to a hospital but the move failed to help. Hitherto his hands and feet had been covered only with a fine rash. Now great patches of skin began coming off, leaving the raw flesh swollen and burning. His pain increased until he could hardly sleep at all.

Understandably, his nervousness had mounted to the point where he could not read or write despite his improved eyesight. In helpless horror he lay in bed and watched the outer skin of his body disappear, come off as a smudge of dust "is wiped off a mirror," so he later expressed it. He saw all the ambitions of his childhood and youth disappear along with the scabs of flesh.

The presence of the other patients did little to alleviate his agony. One was a laborer dying of "Galloping Consumption;" another was a stone cutter dying of a diseased heart and liver; a third was a young Italian who was apparently dying of dropsy. It was the latter patient who most aroused Edward's attentions, and to the extent he could think of anything outside of his own predicament, he followed this fellow-sufferer's case with fascination and fear.

The Italian, whose name was Dosia, was only a little older than Edward himself. He seemed to know he was dying but to have determined not to do so. Sometimes in agony he would scream out in defiance "I'm better! I'm a good deal better!" Then at night, seized with delirium, he would ramble endlessly on in Italian, now arguing, now laughing. But Dosia's will to survive never deserted him. Once a doctor, feeling his pulse and finding it almost imperceptible, announced that he would be dead in a few hours. Yet a few hours later Dosia was sitting up reading a newspaper.

Dosia's determination ignited a spark in Edward. He decided to take his own illness in hand. As a first step, he stopped taking the daily potash solutions. Almost immediately he felt better.

This successful initiative led to another and more decisive one. As he put it in an interview a half century later, "I finally came to the conclusion that I would die if I did not get out of that depressing atmosphere. I wanted to live and I intended to live. The doctors told me I would die if I got up, but I made up my mind that if I could get away, I would get well. So I went to Europe."

Once on the continent he headed for Vienna which then enjoyed a world-wide reputation as a center of advanced medicine. The first specialist he consulted shook his head and told him he had only six months to live. He urged the young American to return home so that he could die among his own people. But Edward had heard that prognosis before and had not journeyed to Europe to hear it again. So he sought out a second specialist and then a third. He told both of them that he felt "organically sound" and both agreed with him.

Just what happened next is not completely clear from the scattered and incomplete records he left behind, but it appears that Edward, buoyed up by the pronouncement of the last two specialists, cured himself by a sheer act of will. He simply decided that he would get well and so he got well. What's more, by using the same determined effort he apparently rid himself of what remained of his childhood limp. So he returned from Europe with a comparatively clear complexion and a brisk gait, ready to resume his role as a young man on his way to the top.

***

During the two years that Edward had been battling his mysterious malady, the Filene enterprises had continued to prosper. Lincoln, though only 17, had stepped into Edward's place, and under his father's tutelage, had continued to show the makings of a most successful merchant. When Edward returned, however, the younger brother cheerfully accepted a subordinate role and the three of them, William, Edward and Lincoln, all worked strenuously to advance the family's enterprises.

William decided to dispose of his Lynn, Salem, and Bath, Maine shops and concentrate the family's efforts and resources on their Boston operations. In 1878 he sold the Bath store. Bertram was managing it and unfortunately had not demonstrated the merchandising capability of his two brothers. The store had never done well.

The Lynn and Salem stores were operating in the black but they were draining too much of the family's time and energies. William had always wanted to escape from the toil and trouble of worrying about small sales, of wrapping countless small parcels. He now felt he was ready to do so. A year or two later, these stores were sold as well.

Once the Lynn and Salem stores had been disposed of, William and his sons began looking for a site for an expanded Boston enterprise. They eventually found a suitable structure at 445-447 Washington Street. The building not only offered an excellent location but also plenty of room. It contained five stories, which, with a basement, would give them six floors of selling space. It would make William Filene's the largest women's wear and accessory shop in Boston.

The move to their new address in the fall of 1890 marked a major triumph for the father and his two sons. It also marked a major change in the ethnic makeup of Boston retailing. Up to then, old-time Yankees had owned and operated every major store in Boston. No outsider had ever succeeded in breaking into their select circle. Now William Filene had done so. There was certainly no indication that his Yankee colleagues and competitors welcomed this German-Jewish emigrant to their ranks. But they had no choice. William Filene had arrived.

But having arrived, William Filene decided that it was time to go. He was now sixty and despite the wonderful way his sons had eased much of the burden since his stroke, he was feeling the strain of age and ill health. So he calmly informed Edward and Lincoln that he was turning the business over to them.

The father, so the boys learned, truly meant what he said. Not only was he placing them in charge, he was making them sole owners of the firm he had founded. The new store would be incorporated as

William Filene and Sons but all the shares would be held by the sons. William, for his part, asked only for an annuity of $7,500 a year for himself and Clara. To be sure, this was quite a respectable stipend in those days. An elderly couple could live well on it. But it hardly represented munificence.

Edward and Lincoln thought it was too little for such a large and thriving business. But William knew the contributions his sons had made to his success and the difficulties they would still experience in making the new, and enlarged operation succeed. He also felt that the sum he stipulated would suffice for the needs of his wife and himself. So he stuck to his generous offer and his sons gratefully acquiesced. Henceforth Edward, who had just turned 30, and Lincoln, who was now 25, would own and operate New England's largest clothing store specializing in "Fancy Goods and Women's Ready-to-Wear Apparel."

Chapter 3
ON THEIR OWN

Despite his ever deepening immersion into retailing, Edward Filene remained alert to the many other attractions and alternatives which life presented. He was, in fact, all too aware of what he might be missing. Walking through the Boston Common on a bright Sunday in the Spring of 1888, the twenty-seven year old merchant mused to himself, "On a day like today I feel I could conquer the world. And yet I know that tomorrow I will sell pins."

***

We know what Edward was thinking on that May morning of 1888 for he was still assiduously keeping his journals. The journals themselves have since disappeared, but that quotation has survived. Another surviving quotation of that year sheds still further light on the sentiments churning inside him at this stage of his life. "I ought to be happy, very happy, for there is no real cause for worry," he wrote, "but my ambition is so restless, so unsatisfied that it takes all my philosophy not to 'kick over the traces.'"

Two years later when he became president and half-owner of William Filene and Sons, these feelings had not faded. If anything, they had intensified, for a journal entry of 1890 has him saying, "I cannot think fast enough or logically enough to satisfy myself and allow myself to rest." The restless and ambitious youth had grown into an even more ambitious and restless young man.

But if Edward was approaching his thirtieth birthday still ablaze with all the aching yearnings of his adolescence, this only made him a creature of his times. For the decade that saw him branch outward and upward saw his country do the same. It saw the near doubling of America's industrial production, the spread of the telephone and the electric light, and the installation of the first electric street cars. It saw the arrival of millions of new immigrants on the East coast and the crushing of the last Indian uprising in the West. And in Boston, it saw the erection of H.H. Richardson's spectacular new buildings in the newly filled-in Back Bay, the beginnings of Frederick Olmstead's "emerald necklace"--a linked system of parks stretching through the heart of the city--and the launching of the Boston Symphony.

By the 1890's, however, a reaction was setting in. Americans, or at least some Americans, were starting to question what Theodore Roosevelt later called "a riot of individualistic materialism." In 1892 a new People's party surged out of the West calling for government ownership of the railroads and government-owned banks for farmers. While the Populists, as they were called, failed to dislodge the two major parties, they combined with the Democrats in some jurisdictions to elect four U.S. senators and four congressmen.

The revolt of the western farmers was matched by similar signs of unrest among industrial workers in the East. The same year that witnessed the birth of the People's party also brought the Holmstead strike which took ten lives. Two years later the equally violent Pullman strike gave further evidence that industrial discontent was on the march.

The government itself was starting to pay attention. In 1890, Congress, reacting to the public's rising rancor against business combines, passed the Sherman Act. It outlawed all commercial combinations that tended to restrain trade. For a while this legislation simply lay on the books, unenforced and largely unnoticed. But in 1897 the Supreme Court shocked the business world by using the Sherman Act to dissolve a transportation trust in Missouri. In Massachusetts, meanwhile, Oliver Wendell Holmes, Jr., now a member of his state's Supreme Court, was shocking his fellow Brahmins by handing down daring dissents which upheld the right of a laborer to be paid even for shoddy work, and which called the strike "a lawful instrument in the universal struggle for life."

Holmes on another occasion would say that a man must share the actions and passions of his time lest he suffer the penalty of not having lived. There was never any danger of Edward Filene suffering such a penalty. His striving for success had not walled him off from the broader and deeper concerns that had begun to besiege the American consciousness. For his ambitions centered not just on commercial achievement but on intellectual growth and social involvement. And as he shared in the upward surge of the 1880's, so now he shared the more questioning, reflective mood of the 1890's.

He joined many clubs during this period. Most of them were organizations of progressively-oriented businessmen such as the Twentieth Century Club, the Economic Club, and even the Paint and Clay Club, which was composed of theatrical managers and newspapermen along with young business executives. However, the one that seems to have involved and influenced him the most during the 1890's was the Liberal Club. It included Bostonians from all backgrounds and walks of life--else how could it call itself the Liberal Club?--who with open minds and warm hearts wanted to learn about and think about the pressing problems of their times. Most of their meetings featured a guest lecturer who would answer questions and lead a discussion after his, or occasionally her, remarks.

Edward attended these meetings faithfully and on returning home would stay up to write down those points that had most impressed him, along with any further ideas they might have germinated in his still youthfully fecund mind. His notebooks from this period bulged with such notations interspersed with comments on the price of lace and reminders to speak to a section head about a glove display. Edward also began attending, and contributing to, an annual summer conference sponsored by some advanced Bostonians at Greenacres, New Hampshire. There he heard speakers hold forth on the deep, dark mysteries of the human soul. And again he came home to scribble away in his journals.

Other factors and forces were also expanding the consciousness of Edward Filene. The store was now large enough to import stock from abroad, thus providing Edward with an excuse for making annual trips to Europe. During these missions he not only bought merchandise but shopped around for ideas and imported some of these along with the latest in hats and hosiery. He also continued to read any book of interest that might come his way and even toyed with the idea of writing one. An indication of the far-ranging nature of his interests can be found in the fact that the book he had in mind was to be a novel depicting the evils of nationalism.

Much of what he was reading and hearing, however, dealt with the evils of capitalism, at least as it was then being practiced. Edward, budding young capitalist though he was, shared many of these misgivings. The depression of 1893, which was to be the worst such downturn until the debacle of 1929, only strengthened his suspicions over the direction which economic forces seemed to be taking. During that year he wrote to a reform magazine editor, Edward O. Mean, expressing his desire to help "control the threatening dangers of combinations and trusts" by preparing citizens to manage cooperative distribution agencies. Thus the basic concept of cooperative management which he would do so much during his lifetime to further and foster had already taken root.

In viewing the rising tide of industrial strife which the burgeoning young economy had spawned, Edward's sympathies lay strictly, and strongly, with the workers. Lynn had been a center of labor militancy during Edward's formative years and he had seen at first hand the bitter and bloody battles which the blind arrogance of the factory owners had needlessly precipitated and prolonged. He was convinced that he was now seeing the same thing all over again, only on a larger scale.

The eight-hour-day movement was gaining momentum and Edward supported it, at least in principle. He even thought it too conservative. A three-hour day should be labor's long-term goal, he observed.

But Edward Filene was no utopian dreamer. He was a practical and prosperous businessman. As such he realized that while the nation's economy could make a few people very rich, it could not yet support a substantially shortened work week for the masses. He lamented, as businessmen have lamented ever since, the inability of working people, and most especially the inability of those who claim to speak for working people, to appreciate and accept the built-in limitations of the economy. For more to be distributed, more must be produced. Plundering the rich, or, as Karl Marx had earlier put it, expropriating the expropriator, would not enrich the average man. What were needed were more efficient methods for producing and distributing goods and services. With this realization, another of Edward's lifelong obsessions was born: to help create a more efficient economy.

His concern with and commitment to economic efficiency flowed naturally from his long-time concern with rational explanations plus his belief in the pay-back principle, i.e., the necessity of compensating civilization for the many benefits and bounties it bestows. By the early 1890's, these aspects of his thought had blossomed virtually into a complete philosophy.

His devotion to the process, and powers, of rational thought coupled with his disbelief in divine intervention and magic panaceas--he even placed little stock in those caprices of circumstance that we call luck--caused him to place facts before feelings. Fact-finding and logical analysis, he felt, offered the best, indeed the only, correct approach to action. Every situation should be subjected to systematic study and any subsequent move concerning it should be made only in accordance with the information and insights which such a process provided. There were no miracles; there were only hard work and, more importantly, hard thinking.

Such a scientific approach to problem solving has become nearly routine in business enterprise today, but in the 1890's it represented a bold advance. Edward thus became the first to apply scientific methods to merchandizing and one of the first to introduce them into American business generally. He believed, for example, that through compiling and analyzing appropriate statistics one could make the accurate forecasts so desperately needed in the slippery world of women's fashion. "Forecasting is arithmetical," became one of his lifelong and oft-repeated axioms. When he later developed an interest in politics, he would go to *The Boston Globe* on election nights and marvel at the way the newspapermen could predict the results when only a small fraction of the returns had come in.

His belief in the pay-back principle was strengthened and amplified when he came across a book entitled, *The Law of Equivalence*. Written by a sociologist named Edward Payson, it sought, in effect, to apply the law of the conservation of energy to life. Everything has its price, argued Payson, so that if we choose one course, we must sacrifice all that we could obtain from choosing another. Furthermore, any accomplishment we achieve or benefit we realize will come with a price tag and the price will have to be paid. (Economists today refer to this as the there-is-no-such-thing-as-a-free-lunch principle and some of them consider it the most basic principle of their discipline.)

Edward read through *The Law of Equivalence* with near rapture. At last he had found someone who could express, and express well, what was for him not just a theoretical speculation but a fundamental fact of life. From then on he always kept a stack of Payson's books on hand and gave one to nearly every person he met.

But although he accepted totally all that Payson said, Edward failed to apply it fully to his own life. He never realized that the scientific approach to life which he had so ardently adopted also imposed a price, and a severe one at that. As one commentator would observe after Edward's death, "Early in life he learned the logical approach to human problems and he never learned any other." He did not understand until too late that logic alone could furnish only a frail and often faulty guide when it came to dealing with human beings. So while his analytical approach to life would bring him much success, it would bring him a good deal of sorrow as well.

***

If the early 1890's were critical in Edward's development, they were no less so for his youngest brother and business partner. For while Edward was framing a philosophy, Lincoln was falling in love.

Her name was Therese Weil, and she was the attractive daughter of a German-Jewish stockbroker and his wife. She was also a talented amateur musician who could not only play difficult classical music on the piano at sight but could also play popular tunes by ear.

Although the piano had become Therese Weil's main instrument, it was not the one she had first chosen. And therein lies an important clue to her makeup. Her first love had been the violin and she had worked tirelessly at mastering it until once, when playing, she caught a glimpse of herself in a mirror. The sight of herself standing with her cheek cocked over the instrument, one arm cradling it and the other drawing the bow, made her so self-conscious that she soon thereafter gave up the violin for the piano. Sitting at the keyboard, so she found, gave her less of a feeling of exposure.

As this incident indicates, Therese suffered from extreme shyness. This may account for her responsiveness to her suitor's attentions, since Lincoln, with his short stature--he was actually an inch or two shorter than Edward--and his weak eyesight--he was already wearing rather thick eyeglasses--could hardly be called physically prepossessing. Moreover, he had little love for, and virtually no knowledge of, music. But he did possess unusual warmth and charm. It was not the charm of the manipulator or seducer. It was the charm of a young man who seemed entirely at peace with himself and the world. His gentle geniality would always draw people to him. Now, it was doing the same to Therese Weil.

Winning Therese's affections proved less difficult than winning the approval of her parents, especially that of her mother to whom the still young girl was extremely attached. The family was considered the second most prominent in Boston's ethnically self-conscious, German-Jewish community. Both husband and wife were trustees of the community's only temple. In addition Charles Weil was a founding member of the newly-organized Federation of Jewish Charities while his wife was Vice President of the Hebrew Women's Sewing Society. The Weils held open house on Sunday afternoons, and it was at one of these gatherings that Lincoln and their daughter had first met.

But having Lincoln Filene as a guest at one of their receptions was not the same as having Lincoln Filene as the husband of their sensitive and much-loved daughter. Mrs. Weil in particular tended to look askance at the scrimpy shopkeeper who had never finished high school and who was, at the time, drawing $25 a week from the family business.

But such obstacles never proved much of a deterrent to Lincoln Filene. Having successfully paid court to the daughter, he now proceeded to do the same to the mother. He did have some favorable factors to draw upon. Although his current salary was small, it could be easily increased for he was half-owner in Boston's fastest growing major store. If he lacked education and culture, he certainly did not lack intelligence and poise. And if his physical appearance was unimpressive, his delightful amiability soon made anyone forget the fact.

So Mrs. Weil eventually succumbed to the young store owner's appeal--few people would ever succeed in withstanding it although, unfortunately, one of the rare exceptions would be Edward--and she agreed to accept him as her son-in-law. In May, 1895, the thirty-year-old Lincoln Filene and the twenty-year-old Therese Weil were wed.

The marriage produced two daughters, Catherine born in 1896 and Helen born in 1899. It also produced at least a fair degree of contentment for the couple, who differed so widely in temperament and taste. For while Lincoln never truly appreciated music or any of the arts, he always supported his wife's efforts in this area. On her part, Therese never fully felt at home in business or bureaucratic circles, but she learned to become a gracious hostess and generous helpmate in the many social activities which her husband's numerous interests increasingly involved.

Therese never, however, completely lost her shyness. As a result, a certain aura of reserve always clung to her, causing some to label her a snob. The fact that she pronounced her name in the French manner, i.e., as if it were written Terez, and the fact that like so many shy people she was very conscious of appearances, seemed to add weight to such a charge. But the accusation was essentially baseless. Therese Weil Filene was no snob, as her later activities will abundantly make clear.

***

As for the other three children of William and Clara Filene, they went their separate and largely unsuccessful ways. Rudolph went to New York City, married, fathered one daughter, but apparently achieved little else in life. The rest of the family heard little from or about him.

Bertram's failure to make the Bath, Maine store profitable proved to be predictive of his later career. His brothers set him up in business three times, but each time he failed. Described by one of the few who can remember him as a "sweet, charming person," he was also apparently something of a zealot. Unfortunately, his zeal was usually centered on one or more issues of the day rather than on his need to make a living. Customers coming into his store would usually hear more about his latest cause than about the goods he had for sale. He did manage to marry and raise three children.

Emma also married and had one daughter. But her husband died soon afterward and she never took another. Instead, she too began espousing various causes, especially vegetarianism. All three siblings of Edward and Lincoln married Anglo-Saxons, thus continuing their father's turn away from Judaism. And two of them also demonstrated their father's concern with public issues. But only Edward and Lincoln would ever turn such an interest to notable account and they would do so without any help from their brothers or sister. In fact, the other three Filenes would play little role in Edward and Lincoln's subsequent activities.

As for William, he continued to live on in retirement. He occasionally came to the store to chat with some of his old employees, most of whom revered him. But he and Clara spent much of their time traveling. Edward at one time induced a bank to offer his father an honorary position but could not persuade his parent to accept it. William told his son that instead of finding honors for his father, he should find a good woman, marry her, and raise a family.

In March, 1901 William died at the at the age of 70. Funeral services were held in Emma's Brookline home. Only the family and a few close friends, most of them former employees, were present, but the numerous floral tributes which poured into the house bore ample witness to the way he had lived. In the words of a local newspaper, the deceased, "although naturally retiring in his disposition," possessed "a distinct personality which influenced for good all those with whom he came in contact."

These sentiments were echoed by a Unitarian clergyman who presided at the funeral service and who pointed out that "the world was better that he had lived." A quartet sang some appropriate selections and the body was laid to rest in a local cemetery.

Clara survived her husband by more than a quarter century. Into her early nineties she maintained her own apartment, paid her own bills, and kept tract of her investments and income. Of course, she had the help of her servants and her sons but she remained in charge of her own life up to the end. Never overly concerned about her appearance, she became even less so as she grew older. When an illness permanently removed some of her hair, she purchased a wig. The wig was not a perfect fit and frequently became disarranged, but Clara continued to wear it anyhow.

She was concerned with good health, and strongly believing that women should exercise more, she faithfully practiced what she preached. When visiting Lincoln and his family in their suburban home, she would take the gramophone along with some marching band records out to the porch every morning. She would then proceed to play the records while striding up and down the porch, her arms swinging rhythmically and resolutely in beat to the martial music.

***

If the 1890's saw Edward forming a philosophy and Lincoln forming a family, it saw them both working closely and cooperatively in creating a bigger and better store. Of course, the term "bigger and better" has become a terrible truism which is now applied indiscriminately to all sorts of endeavors. But it accurately and appropriately sums up what the Filene brothers were attempting to do. Although the store, as we have seen, had already reached a substantial size by the time the founder's sons took it over, they wanted it to grow still more. And they knew they could not achieve this growth without making it a better store as well.

Edward needed increased business success to help promote his many principles and causes as well as to prop up his still brittle ego. Lincoln was probably more motivated by the need to provide for his new and growing family. But beyond such considerations, both brothers genuinely loved retailing. As Edward subsequently put it, "I think shop-keeping is like sin; first you endure it and then you embrace it."

Although both brothers had demonstrated a distinct knack for the retailing vocation, Edward had shown the most ability at merchandising. This is only one aspect of successful retailing and when it came to certain other aspects of running a store, such as administration and personnel practices, Lincoln exhibited a brilliance which Edward, to his regret, would always lack. But since merchandizing is obviously the most salient function in store operation, Edward's superior abilities in the area naturally tended to place him in the forefront.

Lincoln was bright enough to recognize, and emotionally secure enough to accept, and even applaud, his brother's remarkable talent as a merchandiser. Furthermore, Lincoln was still the younger brother and was used to playing a subordinate role. So although both were equal partners, and although they took turns in holding the titles of president and general manager, the dynamic Edward, at least during these initial years, supplied much of the driving force that propelled the Filene store forward.

They faced, on the whole, a favorable terrain on which to move ahead. Boston, to be sure, was not enjoying the growth spurt of such cities as Chicago or Los Angeles. Yet it was still adding to its population of over 300,000 and was still serving as a shopping mecca, especially in women's wear, for most of New England.

More importantly, the Filene brothers did not confront any formidable competition. Most of the city's major stores had existed, so it seemed, since the beginning of time. As a result, a certain lethargy had settled over them. A local guide book issued in the mid-1850's had described the city's merchant princes as "cautious, systematic in their business transactions, ready to advance in their proper time, and distinguished from that recklessness which marks the New Yorker." Thus had their sluggishness been cast as a virtue.

Forty years later the situation had not notably changed. Only a department store named Jordan Marsh was showing any signs of enterprise and vigor. The rest remained content to conform to, rather than create, the conditions shaping their fate.

Of course there were obstacles to overcome. The Filene brothers were upstarts and Jewish ones at that. But the Brahmin barons of Washington Street made no concerted effort to block their upward path. For one thing, Boston's big merchants were too cultured and genteel to engage in any overtly vicious tactics. And then the Filenes were well-groomed, well-spoken German Jews who fortunately lacked the frequently offensive mannerisms of their East European co-religionists. Indeed they were not even co-religionists of those black-coated, black-bearded Ashkenazi Jews who were starting to populate the city's North End and Roxbury sections.

A more important reason, perhaps, for the willingness of their fellow Washington Street merchants to accept the Filenes, albeit grudgingly, into their ranks was that they did not threaten them with head-on competition. The big stores were largely department stores; Filenes was, and to some extent would always remain, a specialty store. With limited capital at their disposal, Edward and Lincoln believed they could only grow through a rapid turnover in merchandise. The best wares for realizing such a high turnover appeared to be ready-to-wear apparel, especially women's apparel. So they decided to stick with the merchandising specialty they already knew. It would prove to be a wise decision.

***

Fashion provided the main reason why the field of women's wear featured such high rates of turnover. And fashion was undergoing some rapid changes in the last decade of the last century. The nearly 100 yards of gown, petticoat, and underclothes which had encased middle- and upper-class women of a few years earlier was finally giving way. Drawers had replaced pantaloons, hats had replaced bonnets, and dresses no longer needed to sweep the pavement. They now stopped a full inch above the ground.

Keeping abreast and, if possible, ahead of these trends offered the brothers plenty of challenge. But their biggest challenge during this initial period of their proprietorship came from another quarter. The invention of the sewing machine had led to creation of "sweatshops," small factories where swarms of workers, many of them women and most of them recent immigrants, were turning out standardized goods on an increasing scale. Should William Filene & Sons stock and sell such wares?

The store had built up a bustling business based on the "carriage trade." How would such a clientele react to the introduction of machine-made garments? Would not such goods destroy the store's carefully cultivated tone and name? But, on the other hand, did not such clothes, now streaming out of the small factories of Boston and New York in such profusion, represent the merchandise of the future? If the Filenes passed them up, might they not end up foregoing their own future?

Here Edward found an opportunity to put his belief in systematic analysis into practice. He and Lincoln proceeded to gather all the information they could on the subject. They conferred with manufacturers in both Boston and New York City, going over their figures, inspecting their operations, and carefully examining their products. Finding nothing intrinsically inferior in these garments, they concluded that only popular prejudice stood in the way of their wholesale acceptance by women of all classes. And such prejudices, in their view, would eventually give way before the low prices and decent quality which these goods afforded. They therefore decided that William Filene & Sons would become the first major Boston store to sell machine-made dresses.

But having made this rather bold decision, they then proceeded in a most cautious and systematic manner to implement it. They selected their manufacturers carefully and worked with them closely to make sure they would get the kinds of dresses they wanted. And when the dresses began arriving, they set up a separate department within their store to handle them. This new department was given its own accounting and buying system as well as its own personnel. By segregating the controversial new merchandise in this way, they reduced any possible contamination it might cause to the carefully nurtured Filene name.

Their decision to handle machine-made clothing and the method they devised to carry it out proved highly successful. The new line of merchandise moved well without tainting Filene's reputation as a quality store. The brothers would make extensive use of the separate department approach from then on, and their store would eventually evolve into what in many ways would be a collection of specialty shops. (To some extent, it remains so today.) It is interesting to note that sometime after World War II many large American firms such as DuPont developed the "profit-center" concept under which their various subunits would gain independence and flexibility while being held individually accountable for their own profits or losses. The profit-center concept owes its origins, at least in part, to an innovation initiated by Edward and Lincoln Filene more than a half-century earlier.

Edward's nearly devout belief in the systematic approach, and his zeal in applying it, affected nearly all aspects of their enterprise. He and Lincoln particularly put it to good use in evaluating call slips. Clerks made out such slips whenever a customer requested something that was not in stock. The brothers regularly and rigorously went through these slips, and in so doing, often detected a new fashion trend before it actually appeared.

For example, in going over the slips they once noticed one or two requests for terra cotta or "crushed strawberry" colored gloves. The next week, the number of requests for such gloves had grown. They quickly got in touch with manufacturers and importers and found that none of them had ever heard of the shade. But as the requests increased, Edward and Lincoln decided that a new style was starting to surface so they began asking manufacturers to make gloves and other items for them in this shade. As a result, when terra cotta goods suddenly became the rage, William Filene & Sons was the only store in Boston to offer them.

***

The systematic approach to merchandising, so the Filenes soon found, blended perfectly with what their father had taught them about the need to treat customers honestly and fairly. In fact, this approach actually encouraged the practice of pleasing the customer at almost all costs.

William had always warned them to avoid high pressure selling and to concentrate on developing a satisfied and therefore loyal clientele. Edward and Lincoln took this lesson to heart. Many stores at the time paid extra commissions to clerks who managed to sell slow-moving merchandise. Filene's offered no such inducements. On the contrary, when a clerk once boasted to Edward how he had "soaked" a customer with such goods, he received a severe and unexpected reprimand. Never try to sell a customer an article that you would not sell your mother if she had the customer's money and taste, so the clerks were told.

Such a policy, Edward believed, produced two basic benefits. The first and most obvious one was the cultivation of the customer's trust. The store's success depended more on the creation of permanent shoppers than on temporary sales. Unloading unwanted goods on a customer would get rid of the goods only at the price of getting rid of the customer.

The second benefit which such a policy provided dovetailed with Edward's systems approach. Allowing slow-moving stock to stay on the shelves until its unsalability became glaringly apparent provided vital information. It brought mistakes to light and therefore helped prevent their repetition. Covering up such purchasing errors by foisting them on unwary purchasers would keep the store's buyers, as well as the two brothers themselves, from learning their lesson. It would only encourage them all, so Edward once remarked, to "reload the store with more ammunition with which to drive customers away."

The two brothers even went a step further and exhorted their sales people to send customers to another store if that store was stocking an item which the customer was seeking but which Filene's did not have. Again, this pleased the customer while bringing to light inadequacies in the store's own line of merchandise. When the clerks hesitated at carrying out such an unheard-of policy, Edward sought to assure them that they ran absolutely no risk in doing so. If it happened repeatedly, he said, then there might well be unpleasant repercussions, but they would be felt only by their superiors who had failed to stock their shelves with the wares that were wanted.

Such practices as these encapsuled the basic belief which the two brothers would always adhere to when it came to retailing or to business generally. They accepted as an article of faith that money-making and morality went hand-in-hand, at least over the long term. Today, especially, many might scoff and sneer at such an assumption. But Edward and Lincoln Filene firmly believed it, and for them it always seemed to work.

***

When it came to handling their employees, the brothers adopted the same approach that worked so well with their customers. They combined the pursuit of high profit with the pursuit of high princi-ples. In fact, treating their sales clerks in the same basic manner they treated their customers was crucial, so they felt, to their store's success. As Lincoln later explained it, "If we were to create contentment in front of the counter we had first to create contentment behind it. Many employees learn their manner of serving the public from the manner in which they are served by their managers."

Such an approach came rather naturally to the Filene brothers. They both had witnessed at first hand all the bitter and often bloody industrial strife which had characterized labor relations in the factories and tanneries of Lynn during the previous few decades. Of course, they had no fears of such strife affecting their own business since they employed mostly young women of middle-class values (though not usually of middle class origins) who were only biding their time until marriage would take them permanently out of the work force. But what they had seen in Lynn had convinced them that most employee discontent results from the mistakes of management. They were determined to make as few such mistakes as possible.

In carrying out this determination, they could draw upon their father's example for William had treated his employees as members of his family and in so doing had inspired an astonishing degree of devotion and dedication. Edward and Lincoln sought to follow the path their father had pointed out to them.

In 1892 the brothers gave a dinner for their buyers and another dinner for their department heads. These are almost routine rituals today but were almost unprecedented in that era. Both get-togethers proved highly successful and became annual events.

When it came to dealing with their rank and file employees, the Filenes established a new position, that of welfare director, and charged its holder with looking after their work force's well being. William Filene & Sons thus became the first store, if not the first business, in the country to create such a post. They also inaugurated many new and, for their time, quite advanced welfare policies. For example, by 1898 store employees, by paying five cents a week, could insure themselves against illness. The benefits were not great by present-day standards. They consisted of either $5 a week in sick pay or $50 worth of medical services. But in the context of the times, this plan made their store a leader in the field.

With the sons now in command, the informal weekly meetings which William had instituted became a formalized and fixed feature of the store's operation. The often vigorous discussions that emerged from them centered largely on the standards of service which the store should adopt and act on.

By the end of the 1890's, it became customary to invite outside speakers to address these assemblies once a month. Among such speakers were Harvard president Charles W. Eliot and Harvard's, as well as America's, most distinguished philosopher, William James. Other speakers at the Friday evening sessions would eventually include Louis Brandeis and Lincoln Steffens. At around this time the two brothers, along with a few managerial employees, contributed some books for an employee library. The library was kept initially at the desk where employees signed in for the day.[2]

But not all efforts to look after their employees' interests caught on. For instance, when Lincoln first installed a doctor and nurse on the premises to supply free medical care, almost all the work force refused to take advantage of it. The reason, so the brothers found out, was the employees' fear that any medical problems they might have would be reported to management and lead to loss of their jobs. There were grave limitations, so Edward and Lincoln were discovering, as to how much you could successfully do for people. At the same time, some of their policies, such as the regular meetings, the outside speakers, and the library, were only stimulating many employees to think and do more for themselves. This was causing them to reject some of the store's more paternalistic practices. In a sense, the Filene brothers had become victims of their own success.

An incident that occurred around this time illustrates what was happening. The revolving door had not yet appeared on the scene and so the coming and going of customers frequently flooded the store with gusts of damp, chilly air. A superintendent thought of sending out for soup and coffee for the ground floor sales force. Initially, these workers responded with gratitude to such consideration, but before too long a group of younger saleswomen came to the superintendent to protest.

"What's wrong?" he asked them in astonishment.

"We'd rather do it ourselves," replied the young women.

They asked for a room with a gas stove where they could prepare their own lunches. This was quickly given them. Their operation became popular with other employees, eventually leading them to employ on their own a cook for this purpose. Out of this grew an employee-run restaurant which still operates today.

Such incidents as this taught the brothers another lesson or rather brought to their awareness certain aspects of the lesson their father had already taught them. As Edward later noted, "In the beginning we had tried to do the work for our people under well-meant but despotically benevolent principles. But grown wiser and more democratic by our failures, we agreed to do nothing for our people, but to help them with all our minds and strength to do everything for themselves."

As the failings and flaws of their paternalistic policies dawned on them, Edward and Lincoln cast about for other and more effective ways of dealing with their employees. This eventually led them to conceive and create a new institution that would startle the Boston business world and stir up interest not only throughout the United States but in Europe as well. This institution was the Filene Cooperative Association.

The FCA, as it was customarily called, gathered every employee who wanted to join it into one all-inclusive organization with each member having one vote. Management financially contributed to it but did not control it. All managerial personnel, including Edward and Lincoln themselves, belonged to it, but each of them cast only one vote in its deliberations. The organization operated all employee functions such as the restaurant, the library, the insurance fund, and others. it also functioned as a forum for discussing and dealing with store problems and policies.

In setting up the association, the Filene brothers were not trying to establish a company union which they could manipulate and use to head off any threat of a real union. Trade unionism at that time had made little headway among store employees, and although a Retail Clerks Union was in existence, it had only 2,700 members, with few if any of them in Boston. Moreover, for reasons mentioned earlier, a women's clothing store catering to the carriage trade was one of the last places such a union could hope to organize.

No, the FCA represented the Filenes' continuing--it would be lifelong--quest for combining economic with social achievement. Their conviction that these goals were not conflicting but rather convergent led them not only to create the FCA but to equip it with some remarkable powers.

The crucial test as to how far the Filenes were prepared to go came in the winter of 1901 when the head cashier marched into

Edward and Lincoln's joint office with a complaint. The store had docked part of the pay of one of her girls to make up for a shortage in the girl's accounts. This was standard practice in mercantile houses at the time and was done to keep the cashiers alert and honest. But the young lady in this case had protested the dockage to her supervisor. "If I'm short in my accounts, it's supposed that I've stolen the money," she had caustically commented. "If I happen to be over, it's a clerical error and the store pockets the money. It isn't fair."

Her supervisor had seen the logic of her argument and agreed with her. She now presented it to Edward and Lincoln. The brothers responded by pointing out the need for accuracy as well as the need to protect the store against losses.

"But an overage is just as much of an inaccuracy as a shortage," observed the head cashier.

"To be consistent," said Edward, "we should penalize you for both." He also noted that the penalty in any event was scarcely severe. In this case it had amounted to about one dollar.

When the head cashier remained unconvinced, Edward then suggested a radical step: the establishment of a three-member panel to arbitrate the issue. The panel would consist of a representative selected by the docked cashier, a representative chosen by management, and a third representative chosen by the other two. Edward agreed in advance to abide by the panel's decision.

The proposal was accepted and the panel was set up. It ruled in favor of the cashier and Filene's abandoned its policy of docking pay to make up for shortages. Henceforth the cashiers would be credited with overages but not penalized for shortages.

Both sides actually won. The girl got her docked pay back and saw her case bring a change in store procedure. But the Filenes were the biggest winners for they now had an arbitration process which they could continually use to deal with the prickly problems of employee relations. Their revolution in retailing was now well underway.

Chapter 4
AN ODD COUPLE

I n 1906 a well-groomed young man entered the Filene store and asked for the manager's office. He was a recent Harvard graduate named Austin Benton who shortly before had answered a blind ad for a manager's assistant. The ad, so he had since found out, had been placed by Lincoln Filene.

Many of Benton's friends expressed surprise when he told them he was going for an interview. They even tried to dissuade him. Why would a well-reared, Harvard-educated Anglo-Saxon want to work for a Jewish store? But Benton had decided that he would take the position if it were offered.

When he entered the executive office he found the two brothers sitting back to back at their respective desks. The interview went well, the post was offered, and Benton joined the Filene staff. He spent his working lifetime at the store, eventually becoming its comptroller as well as a member of its board of directors. Some seventy years later, when he was in his nineties, he looked back on many memories, most of them pleasant, of his career at Filene's. But the memory that stood out most sharply in his mind was the first time he entered the office and saw Edward and Lincoln sitting back to back. Such a set-up put the two brothers close to one another but facing out in different directions. In a way, this seemed to symbolize their relationship for although they shared many of the same values and goals, their personalities differed so widely that they appeared to approach such values and goals from entirely different directions.

***

In his twenties, Edward Filene sported a full and luxuriant beard. In his thirties, he trimmed it to a van dyke. By his mid-forties, he had reduced it to a close-cropped, bristly moustache. The moustache, combined with his neat, almost dapper, dress, plus the pince-nez he occasionally wore, gave him quite a distinguished appearance. He resembled at times a Prussian aristocrat.

Unfortunately for those who had to work with and, especially, under him, such a resemblance was more than superficial. For despite his deep and earnest commitment to the values of cooperation and compassion, Edward Filene, often displayed the arrogance and abrasiveness associated with Prussianism at its worst.

Stories abound of Edward's appalling insensitivity and rudeness to his employees. When a young executive's wife, in passing him on the back stairs, sought to put in a plug for her spouse by saying, "Hello, Mr. Filene. My husband is working awfully hard for you," Edward gruffly replied, "And he's getting well paid for it, too." He then continued on his way, disdainfully refusing to give the mortified young woman a second look. When, in one of his daily walks through the store, he asked a young salesgirl what she was making and she jokingly responded, "Oh, not half what I'm worth," Edward quickly snarled back, "That's still twice what you deserve" and marched off in a huff.

On still another occasion he came up to a secretary who was separating out call slips and stacking them into various piles. Though she was only following the store's established procedures, the process gave her desk a messy look. "An untidy desk is an indication of an untidy mind," barked Edward as he took his hand and swept all the slips onto the floor. This meant that the young woman would have to work well into the evening to re-assort them. When she tearfully began to remonstrate his action, Edward became furious and dressed her down severely.

His personal staff bore the brunt of his abrupt and frequently abusive ways. As the business grew and as his outside activities proliferated, Edward began employing several assistants along with anywhere from three to five secretaries. They all found working for him an experience they would never forget.

He frequently expressed his wishes like an old-time Army officer giving commands. Be here at 9 a.m., do this by 5 p.m., etc. But this was not the worst part of working for Edward Filene. He would not hesitate to call an aide on a Saturday evening or Sunday or holiday and summon him to his office or home to work on something he wanted done right away. He never apologized for or tried to soften such a demand. It was issued in a matter-of-fact manner as if the employee had nothing better to do. He would even expect married staff members with children to abandon their families and come to his house on Christmas Day to help him with his own Christmas activities.

He rarely gave his aides much personal encouragement. "A subordinate who was not prepared to withstand a barrage of questions," so one ex-staff member later related, "was foolish to submit an idea to him at all...One of his most maddening inquiries, and one that lost him the services of man after man, was to say when a particularly good job was reported, 'Why didn't you do it better?'"

This former aide, whose name was Frederick W. Stuart, would recall a time when a dispute had arisen between Edward and the other management members over a statement the store was going to issue. Negotiating in behalf of Edward, Stuart managed to get all of Edward's ideas accepted with only some minor modifications in wording. Returning in triumph to the office, he proudly showed his boss the final document. Edward read it through, grunted, and then, holding up his original statement, exclaimed, "I can't help thinking that if you had really tried hard, we could have gotten this."

The irony of Edward's behavior, as contrasted with his beliefs, is woefully apparent. Here was a man who advocated high wages but who rarely and only reluctantly raised any of his own staff's salaries. Here was a man who steadfastly supported shorter hours for workers but who went to the State House to get his own female secretaries listed as managerial executives for the sole purpose of exempting them from the laws limiting the hours of labor for women. Here was a man who ardently preached the virtues and benefits of cooperation but who could scarcely get along with anyone. As another staff member once said of him, "In his work for humanity, apparently, he cannot stop to consider people."

Edward thus suffered from the curse which has afflicted so many reformers and radicals throughout history: an inability to love man in the flesh as much as in the abstract. Those who have seen Socialist parties split continually into warring factions while professing belief in the brotherhood of man know this phenomenon well. Edward could never become a Socialist, but the discrepancy between his idiosyncracies and his ideas could plague him all his life.

***

The callous disregard Edward often displayed for other people's individual feelings and interests was not his only distasteful characteristic. He had at least two others. One of them was stinginess.

Here again stories abound. After wearing a tuxedo for thirty years, he took it back to the tailor who had made it and asked him to rebuild the suit so that he would not have to buy a new one. On another occasion, he was giving a dinner-theater party when the broker called with the tickets. When the "scalper" sought to charge him a 75-cent fee for each ticket instead of the usual 50 cents, Edward became infuriated. He called off the event and sent his guests home rather than pay the additional dollar and fifty cents this would have entailed.

As might be expected, such parsimonious practices often ended up costing him dearly. In 1920 Edward purchased a dignified but not ostentatious house at 12 Otis Place, a small square at the foot of Beacon Hill. Thanks to a vacant lot in front of it, the house offered a panoramic view of the Charles River, which flows between Boston and Cambridge. Edward loved to look at the river and always meant to buy the lot in order to protect his view.

One day the lot's owners came to him saying that an apartment house developer had expressed an interest in the land. Would he like to buy it instead? Edward said yes but when they named their price he deemed it outrageous and insisted on a substantially lower one. He thought they had made up the story of the developer in order to shake him down for an exorbitant profit. Unhappily for him, he was wrong and when he kept refusing to pay their price, the owners sold it to the interested builder. Soon thereafter, Edward found his cherished view partially obstructed by an apartment house.

His endless efforts to economize carried over to his work at the store. Although Filene's always paid more than competitive wages and stood ready to pay well for good merchandise, Edward was constantly looking for ways to reduce costs. He eventually had a stamp prepared bearing the message, "How can we make or save a dollar on this?" Henceforth every piece of paper that came to his desk was returned to its sender emblazoned with this question.

A third obnoxious trait which was just starting to show itself in the early nineteen hundreds but which would become a predominant part of his personality, was an intense and inordinate thirst for public attention and acclaim. Edward Filene loved to be seen in public with prominent personalities, to be recognized by head waiters in prestigious restaurants, and to be invited to sit at head tables at important dinners. If he could be one of the speakers, so much the better. If he could be the featured speaker, his bliss was complete.

His craving for personal publicity was almost boundless. Miserly though he might be in some respects, he rarely stinted when it came to paying for good ghost writers and publicity consultants. As his prominence increased he subscribed to news clipping services and avidly pored through the packets they sent him. Edward Bernays, who served for a while as his public relations consultant, would remember him as a man who "seemed entirely uninterested in anything that was not directly concerned with himself and his ideas." According to Bernays, Edward Filene "lived a life surrounded by his own ego."

* * *

The above catalogue of Edward Filene's flaws are enough to make anyone turn away in dismay and disgust. But they would be unwise to do so. There was much more to Edward Filene than the long litany of his weaknesses suggests. And even the weaknesses themselves, when seen in the context of his unhappy past, take on a less horrendous hue.

Edward Filene was not just a brilliant man but a bold one. He never fled from a fight. Indeed, he almost relished battling for his ideas, and if he failed to incorporate them into his own life, he never faltered in trying to implant them into the world in which he lived. In so doing he would willingly defy any establishment.

On a long stay in India, he became outraged at the social caste system that the British had imposed on the natives' own religious one. He therefore decided to ignore it despite the fact that his action cost him many congenial contacts among the country's high-placed British overseers. On the ship which took him on the round-the-world cruise, of which his stay in India was a part, he frequently deserted his fellow first-class passengers to talk with those in the steerage sections. That some of his fellow travelers raised their eyebrows over this did not faze him one bit.

At home he could be just as disdainful of social and economic barriers. He could also be just as defiant of those whose favor he would otherwise seek. While he did like to be seen with prominent people, he did not hesitate to risk their disfavor by speaking out if he felt they were doing wrong. And while he courted the press, he freely told a magazine interviewer on one occasion that he felt the Boston newspapers treated Filene's and other big advertisers too deferential ly. He said this, knowing full well that it would be published and that the local papers would hardly react kindly to this implication of cravenness on their part.

His boldness often translated into a certain amount of physical courage. As a young man he purchased a half-interest in a sailboat. He did so not because he loved the sea but because he feared it and thought it best to meet his fear head-on or, as he put it, "a little dangerously." (He apparently had never learned to swim.) As a middle-aged man he took a 1200-mile, week-long automobile trip through the heart of India in 1907. Cars were, of course, not only rudimentary but rare in those days, and he and the Scotsman who accompanied him lumbered along roads where no auto had ever traveled and passed through villages where no one had ever seen such a machine. As an elderly man in the 1930's, he became one of the first to take advantage of passenger plane service even though the safety record of such service was far below what it is today.

An incident recounted by Lincoln's eldest daughter Catherine sheds some further light on this part of Edward's personality. When Catherine secured her driver's license sometime around 1915, she and her uncle Edward would frequently go off on weekends together. Once they were having dinner at a hotel in New Hampshire when a huge and loud lumberjack began making crude overtures to the girl. The management quickly intervened and steered the fellow away. But that night as Catherine lay in her bed she heard the man, now apparently quite drunk, pound on her door. Suddenly she heard a thud followed by silence. When she opened the door, she saw the lumberjack sprawled unconscious at the feet of her short, fiftyish uncle. It seems that Edward had studies ju-jitsu while stopping off in Japan on his world cruise and had just put to use what he had learned.

Another weekend trip the uncle and niece took together illuminates still another, more appealing aspect of Edward's complex nature. This was a trip to Provincetown where they stayed with an artist. Nearly seventy years later Catherine vividly recalled her uncle's intense interest in the man and his work, how perceptively Edward probed in order to learn the artist's attitude toward his art, how he went about it, etc. Edward never developed much genuine appreciation for any of the arts except literature, but he always sought to learn more about any serious aspect of life and esteemed every sincere effort at mastering it.

Edward was constantly on the alert for broadening and educational experiences. On a canoe trip down a North Carolina river in 1918, he met a Methodist minister and attended services in his church. In his stay in Japan he engaged a scholar to explain to him the various sites and shrines and to fill him in generally on Japanese culture. On what would become his annual trips to Europe, he talked with bankers and barbers, commercial magnates and coachmen, labor leaders and homeless men on park benches.

Reading too offered an educational experience that he did not neglect. Although he liked to say that he read little, the existing evidence indicates that for a busy businessman he read a great deal. He was fairly familiar with most of the more talked-about works on economic and social issues of his time. And although his taste for fiction was limited, he was acquainted with, and seems to have appreciated, the novels of H.G. Wells. He did not always read profoundly. "I skim through a book to get the general idea," he once remarked. But his journals show that at least some books received more rigorous perusal. In his world cruise journal, for example, he notes in one entry how he spent the morning finishing Lowell's *Soul of the East* and records his intention of reading it through a second time. One gets the impression that this intention was carried out.

As he traveled and observed, listened and read, so he wrote, furiously filling page after page of his notebooks with facts and figures, with impressions and ideas. Almost nothing escaped his keen, catholic curiosity. One can find in one of his journals a complete description of the training a brakeman receives on the Pennsylvania Railroad written down in detail as described to him by a brakeman he interviewed.

Jammed as they are with the hurried scribbles of a man, and a mind, continually on the move, these notebooks nonetheless do not lack literary merit. Later, a left-wing novelist who disapproved of Edward Filene politically and detested him personally, conceded that Edward's journals showed a compelling conciseness and clarity.

In the many books, articles, and speeches which later poured forth under his name, Edward made extensive use of ghost writers. But he went over their copy painstakingly (and, for them, often painfully) to make sure that each sentence expressed exactly what he wanted it to say. Some years after his death, his principal ghost writer, Charles Wood, told an interviewer that in all of the hundreds of pages he turned out for Edward to put his name to, there was not a single idea that was not Edward's and Edward's alone.

For Edward Filene never lacked ideas. Many, as he freely acknowledged, he picked up from his travels and his reading. Some of them were quite silly, such as the cigar shaped like a pipe which he came across in Switzerland and tried to have manufactured in the U.S. Others would eventually catch on, such as the water skiing he noticed in Germany and thought would become popular here. Many of his more original ideas, such as the one for motorized roller skates, were also silly but others, such as the one for motorized lawn mowers, became staples of American life.

These, of course, are only some of the more minor notions that on occasion engaged his fancy. More major ones will be described in the chapters that follow. And, as we shall see, he would score some surprising successes in putting many of them into operation. Furthermore, many of those that failed did so not because they were faulty but because they were premature. Even today, nearly a half-century after his death, the world may still not be quite ready for all that the fertile mind of Edward Filene had to offer.

***

If Edward's more notable assets fail to offset and override his many personal liabilities, then many of these liabilities take on a softer hue when we examine them more closely. It is perhaps not possible to love Edward Filene, and this is why few outside his family, and not many within his family, ever managed to do so. But a greater awareness of this troubled and, in many ways, tragic figure should dampen our distaste and even arouse our sympathies.

For one thing, Edward's manner was not always disagreeable. When he was traveling or when he was relaxing at his home, he could be quite pleasant and accommodating. He was at his worst when he was in his store. As one commentator put it, "the moment he stepped into his office, he began to bristle."

Yet even here his conduct toward his collaborators and aides, harsh though it often was, usually carried no personal ill will. Furthermore, if he could give criticism, he could also to some degree take it as well, providing the argument being advanced against him was couched in a rational and impersonal manner. "He never takes offense at opposition," Frederick Stuart said of him, "if he believes it is sincere and without animosity, and cannot conceive that other people should feel differently." And Stuart added, "His criticisms are always sincere, by the way, and without animosity."

He did drive his aides mercilessly, goading them on so much that one secretary once accused him of practicing the "goadin" rule. But after leaving his employ, most of them seem to have felt that the experience, while it was not one they would want to repeat right away, was also one they would not want to have missed.

One explanation for Edward's behavior in this respect can be found in his bookplate. It bears the words "When work is for the common weal, then work is worship, work is prayer." Edward always believed that virtually everything he was doing served mankind and therefore anyone who was assisting him had joined in a holy crusade. He therefore expected them to demonstrate the same zest and zeal for his ideas that he did. He simply couldn't understand it when they failed to do so.

He always paid his staff well, and if he rarely raised them or, for that matter, praised them, then he felt he had good reasons for not doing so. Giving such "rewards" in his view would be tantamount to bribery. People should not expect rewards for the privilege of utilizing their talents to accomplish great and worthy projects such as those he was continually undertaking. Needless to say, few of his aides fully shared this view. Consequently, he always seemed to have a vacancy on his staff and was always looking for a new assistant to fill it.

If his parsimony in giving pay raises can be explained, then so can the apparent miserliness which affected so many other of his activities. While he rarely gave money to charity, especially organized charity, he did give away much of the sizable fortune he accumulated in the course of his life to various public causes. For the most part, they were causes which he had originated and which were designed, among other things, to help do away with poverty. He explained his refusal to give money to philanthropic agencies as part of his general refusal to subsidize poverty. He believed in poverty's elimination, so he repeatedly maintained, not its endowment.

As a businessman he was certainly cost conscious, probably one of the most cost conscious of his time. Yet here again this should be seen in a broader context. His ghost writer Charles Wood summed up the situation well when he wrote, "There are only two things that one can do with money--keep it or get rid of it and Mr. Filene never seemed to enjoy doing either. Money, both the getting of it and the getting rid of it, was just a responsibility to him. He was never in business for profit, but to be in business without making a profit seemed to him a crime. 'Show me how we can make or save a dollar on this' was not inspired by acquisitiveness," said Wood. "It was a moral precept. If one did not make a dollar out of a business transaction, it was an unsound transaction--a transaction which, if generally imitated, must result in universal ruin."

Edward's never-ending desire to reduce costs reflected an almost desperate determination to drive down the expense of distribution. At the end of his life he considered himself a failure for not having succeeded in doing so. But developments after his death, developments that owed a great deal to his early efforts in this direction, would show that he succeeded more than he knew.

There are still further aspects of his penny-pinching that need to be explored. On a personal level, much of his apparent tight-fistedness came from a very genuine and deep-rooted horror of waste. This aversion partly grew out of the constrained circumstances of his boyhood. But to a much greater extent it resulted from ideas his father had instilled in him. "The first thing my father taught me," Edward once said, "was that a man who wastes things like gas and electric light, because he does not have to pay for them, is a fool because finally he has to pay a share of the total waste, and, more than that, he is not a good citizen."

As his father's son, Edward Filene always turned out the lights no matter who was paying the bill. "If I go out of a hotel room and leave an electric light burning, and I think of it before I get on an elevator, I know if I go down in that elevator I will come back and turn that light out," he told one of his would-be biographers. (He would have several.) To another he explained it in these words, "I am afraid that if I get in the habit of not doing what I ought to do I shall lose whatever power I have, and I know that it is not that one or two cents, but the total of the waste."

But there is yet another side to Edward's frequent over fastidiousness when it came to money matters, and this side relates more directly to his basic problem. For although Edward Filene was a complicated man and no biographer can hope to psychoanalyze him, nevertheless it would appear that at the heart of most of his problems lay what can be called his "ugly duckling complex." Enmeshed in a web of insecurities at an early age, he grew up into an insecure and highly defensive man.

His defensiveness seems to have colored and, to a greater or lesser degree, contaminated nearly all his personal relationships. When he refused to pay the ticket scalper the extra 25 cents and when he rejected the frequent appeals for money that others so often pressed upon him, he was probably more motivated by the fear of being taken advantage of than by anything else. This man, who could and did give away millions, would resist to the utmost any attempt, real or imagined, to play him for a fool for a few cents.

But money matters were perhaps the least of the areas that his deep-seated feelings of inferiority caused him distress. The walls such feeling had erected around him essentially cut him off from achieving any real closeness to most people.

There were some exceptions, one being his mother, whom he genuinely adored. She seems to have had a special place for him in her heart, possibly because of the childhood lameness which caused her so much concern. She called frequently at the store, striding into the executive offices to ask in a resolute voice, "Where's my Eddy?" Edward always made himself available to see her and frequently they had lunch at his desk. In addition, he usually visited her at her home on Sundays. While he never owned a car himself, he provided his mother with a fashionable Pierce Arrow complete with chauffeur. (However, Edward frequently borrowed both car and chauffeur for his own purposes. He never learned to drive.)

Another exception was children, especially pretty little girls. He kept a stock of dolls in his office and whenever he spotted a cute little girl in the store he would take her and her mother or whoever the child was with up to his office and give the youngster one of the dolls. The little girl's pleasure would make him glow with genuine, if rare, warmth.

Wherever he went he noticed children and would often stop to talk with them. He even had a children's playroom constructed in his home. On Thanksgiving and Christmas he held parties for the youngsters of his aides and friends--he did have a few of the latter--and joyfully played games with them on the floor. Afterwards, they would send him little thank-you notes which he treasured.

Edward could relax with and enjoy the company of children in a way that he could never do with adults, for children posed no threat to him. Unfortunately, it is probably for the same reason that no child of his own ever romped in his playroom or shared his holiday activities. For Edward Filene never married.

When asked why he had never taken that critical step, Edward offered various replies. On one occasion he said he had asked "her" twelve times to marry him and was too superstitious to ask again. On another occasion he said that when he was in his mid-thirties he reached an "understanding" with a young woman but business pressures forced him to continually postpone the wedding date. Then, when he and his fiancee were once returning from the theater in a street car, he noticed a man he had been trying to see for some time on a business matter. He went over to him, sat down, and began discussing what he had in mind. After some minutes, Edward had consummated a business deal but had lost a prospective bride. When he looked around, his intended had vanished--for good.

There is a third story that claims Edward was out walking with a girl he was interested in when a man he knew came along in an automobile. The driver offered to demonstrate his new car to Edward and Edward quickly climbed aboard. After cruising about for a half-hour, they returned to the spot where they had met and Edward was amazed at not finding his escort patiently waiting for him.

Although this last story may have no more validity than any other, it does express a tragic truth about Edward Filene. He was often so heedless, so unaware of the feelings of others, that he could very well have abandoned a young lady on the sidewalk, expecting her to remain rooted to the spot until he returned.

Did romance ever play any real role in his life? There is no indication that it ever did. His journals and other writings make not the slightest reference to such feelings and no one remembers him consistently courting any member of the opposite sex.

Did he have any sex life at all? Was he, perhaps, homosexual? If he were homosexual, no one ever seems to have discerned the least indication of it. But there is also no evidence to show that he ever went to bed with a woman. In fact, only one instance has come to light of Edward even trying to.

It occurred in 1924 when he met a young widow named Dorothy Turner Warner on a trip to Europe. Edward was quite taken with her and when she came to Boston in the fall to visit her sister, he invited her to his home for dinner. She came, thinking they were going to discuss the many exciting projects he had going at the time to promote world peace. Instead, she found herself, so she later told her sister, being chased around the dinner table by her 64-year-old host.

Actually, those who knew him during this phase of his life say he often seemed to respond to attractive young women but no one can recall any relationship that seemed to have the slightest sexual coloration. In his seventieth year, he did, however, engage a secretary-assistant with whom he got along extraordinarily well. From her he elicited some of the warm affection which he craved and in her arms he would eventually die.

But this relationship, though it did soften him somewhat in his later years, arrived too late and provided too little to effect a fundamental change. He continued to crave the public approval and acclaim that served as a substitute for the normal, intimate human contact that he had lacked for so long. This missing element in his life can be summed up in the revealing if seemingly insignificant fact that almost no one outside his immediate family ever called him Edward. To most of his associates he was always addressed, as well as referred to, as E.A.

It is no wonder then that those who recall him agree that Edward Filene lived an essentially lonely life. It is also no wonder that even when they talk about his more obnoxious traits, they do so not with rancor or scorn but with bemusement tinged with a hint of sadness. It is as if they somehow sensed the frightened child that lay within the often fearful man.

***

When we turn to Lincoln Filene we find a sharp and startling, if certainly welcome, contrast. Spared Edward's lameness and eczema, spared also the horrors of the German academy along with the parental separation it entailed, and benefiting, perhaps, from being the baby of the family, Lincoln developed an almost totally different personality than that of his older brother. Like Edward, Lincoln would achieve substantial success as a private businessman and public benefactor. Unlike Edward, he would also succeed as a husband, father, and friend.

Indeed, when it comes to these latter categories of achievement, his success was nothing short of spectacular. Though hardly impressive physically, with his short, stumpy legs, balding head, and thickly bespectacled eyes, he nevertheless exuded an aura of geniality and good will which virtually cast a spell over those who came in contact with him. He would live many years longer than his brother so that a biographer in the 1980's would have little trouble locating people who knew him well. All of them, associates, employees, and offspring, agreed wholeheartedly on this one point: to know Lincoln Filene was to love him.

He was quite skilled and proficient in most areas of retailing, but in the store he gravitated to the administrative side. Dealing with people came naturally to Lincoln; it was where his greatest genius lay. And his ability in this area apparently reached near-genius dimensions. He could enter a room where several hard-headed men were bitterly disputing and in a few minutes would have them all smiling and talking amicably to one another. Harshness and hostility seemed to dissolve when exposed to his good-humored warmth.

His walks through the store differed greatly from those of his brother. Edward was always looking at merchandise, prices, displays, etc., and his overactive mind was always thinking of new things to do or new ways of doing them. Lincoln, while by no means oblivious to such concerns, always seemed to be focusing more on people, his employees and his customers, but especially the former. If anyone looked troubled, he would immediately ask what was wrong and what he could do to help. Often he would station himself at the door after closing time so that he could say good night to his departing work force.

He frequently found himself trying to repair some of the human problems which his brother's insensitive behavior could create. A young employee named William Reardon remembered how Edward once came up to him in the store and chastised him severely for something he was doing or failing to do. "After he was through with me I felt like nothing," said Reardon. "But hardly had Edward left when Lincoln came up beside me, put his arm around my shoulder, and told me what a good fellow I was."

Lincoln's own personal staff adored him. "Anyone would do anything for Mr. Filene," says Mrs. Tracey Brown, who served as his financial secretary for thirty-five years. This does not mean he was lax as a boss. A methodical man, he expected his staff, for example, to have gone through the newspapers and clipped any stories he might be interested in, such as items relating to economic conditions, stores and people he knew, and to have the clippings on his desk when he arrived. He expected them to be reasonably punctual. And he took great care to see that his personal staff received no benefits that other store employees did not receive.

But his demands on his staff never interfered with his concern for their well-being. When one woman staff member failed to show up or report in for two days, Lincoln did not become annoyed, but alarmed. He sent a store nurse to her home and the nurse found the woman, who lived alone, dead from a heart attack. The funeral was held in Manchester, one of the more distant suburbs, but Lincoln closed his office for the better part of the day so that he and the other members of his staff could attend the ceremony.

While Edward would often keep his aides working at night, Lincoln, at least on occasion, would take his out to dinner. On those rare occasions when he would require some of them to work in the evening, he saw to it they received compensatory time off. He also never kept things from his assistants. "If you can't trust your employees, then you shouldn't be employing them" was a maxim he both preached and practiced.

But what seems to have endeared him most to his employees, as well as to others who knew him, was not so much what he did but how he did it. If nearly everyone knew they could go to him for help, they also knew that he would downplay the help he would almost certainly give them. Although he appreciated a modicum of gratitude, he abhorred profuse thanks and often carried out his many acts of kindness indirectly. He would, for instance, have a third party actually render the sought-for assistance and then inform the recipient of it. When the recipient would come to him to express his or her thankfulness, he would seek to make light of the whole thing, often dismissing it with a joke.

Lincoln, as a matter of fact, loved jokes. He loved both hearing them and telling them. He also loved to tease, but his teasing was always good-natured or good-humored. No one ever smarted or suffered from one of his well-meaning jests. Those who describe Lincoln frequently use an adjective that one seldom hears applied to successful businessmen. The adjective is "twinkly." And with his sparking blue eyes glistening through his thick glasses, his warm comforting manner, and his lively and lovable sense of humor, the unusual term seems to fit.

Lincoln Filene did not, of course, lack limitations and liabilities. For example, he was not at his best in hard-nosed negotiations. He tended to dislike such dealings and often turned them over to others. He also, say many, allowed people to take advantage of him. He never became as familiar or as fast with figures as Edward was. Finally, he was not without a few petty vanities. For example, when he was made an honorary member of the collegiate honor society of Phi Beta Kappa, he loved to wear and display his "Phi Bate" key on his watch chain.

But these minor imperfections detracted little from his basic charm. On the contrary, they seem, if anything, to enhance it. Those who recall them do so with a warm chuckle. There can perhaps be no greater testament to his character than that his faults and flaws, such as they were, appear to have added to, rather than detracted from, his fundamental appeal.

***

Lincoln Filene at home was much the same as he was at the office. His daughters in their eighties still treasured rich memories of the man who returned from work every day to take them skating on the Charles River or walking in the woods of suburban Weston. As for his wife, she almost certainly would have liked him to have had a better ear for music and a greater taste for the arts generally. But just as certainly, she must have appreciated the support he gave her in carrying out her cultural activities as well as the dutiful and devoted manner in which he discharged his own responsibilities as provider and parent. Lincoln eventually wrote two books and dedicated both of them "to my wife."[3]

Since Therese Filene was very attached to her mother, the young couple first set up housekeeping in an apartment on Newbury Street just a block or two from her family's home. With the birth of Catherine they moved to a larger apartment on Bay State Road, still less than ten blocks away. Here in 1899 their second daughter Helen was born.

The family lived on Bay State Road for several years. When the girls reached school age, Lincoln would walk them to school and then would continue on his way, traversing on foot the rest of the Back Bay, the Public Garden, and the Boston Common before coming into downtown Boston and the Filene store. (Edward also walked to work, crossing the Common from the foot of Beacon Hill.)

In the early 1900's, Lincoln and Therese bought a home in Weston, a suburb situated about 15 miles west of Boston. For the first few years they used it mostly as a weekend and summer-time retreat, but gradually it became their principal residence. Lincoln loved the outdoors and with the advent of the auto he found he could commute between his new country home and the store quite easily.

Lincoln also loved to entertain and his new capacious and commodious home permitted him to do it well. However, it was not in the large living room with its enormous cathedral ceiling that he loved to play host, but in a fireplaced family room in the basement. Here with logs crackling in the hearth he would sit with his guests exchanging experiences, ideas, and jokes. Each new male guest received a corn cob pipe to smoke and when he left, his pipe was assigned a number and placed on the wall. The number was then written in a book opposite his name. When the guest came again, his number was looked up in the book and his pipe taken down from the wall so that he could smoke it again. Such was the hospitality of Lincoln Filene.

Who were the guests who enjoyed themselves at his friendly fireside? They included Filene's managerial staff and, on occasion, rank-and file employees as well. They also included other business-men, public officials, and educators. He also entertained his wife's more cultural friends as well as his daughters' school companions. He especially enjoyed younger people and they enjoyed him. Later, one college graduating class would in a sense adopt him, formally making him an honorary member of their ranks.

Education was one of Lincoln's lifelong interests. He devoted great sums of money and time to its furtherance and in so doing would hold many public positions in the education field. But he had other outside interests as well. He would also do much to improve business practices, including labor management relations and, on a more personal level, he helped many young men start their own businesses. Unlike Edward, he took great care to separate his outside activities from store functions and to pay for them separately. (Edward was less scrupulous about this because of his firm belief that all of his activities, including his operation of the store, formed one combined effort to promote the common good.)

Lincoln did not share Edward's reading tastes. He knew no language but English and generally confined his reading to biographies, an occasional book on labor or social problems, and Westerns. About the latter he developed a lifelong passion. His eldest daughter would remember driving down in the 1950's to his Cape Cod home as a hurricane was coming. She wanted to make sure that the now elderly man was all right. She found him with the electricity out sitting by an oil lamp devouring the latest Zane Grey.

His appetite for Westerns reflects his appetite for adventure generally, an appetite that showed itself in a zest for sports and outdoor activities of all kinds. Lincoln was an enthusiastic golfer, squash player, horseback rider, swimmer, ice-skater, hunter, and fisherman. At the last-named sport, he became quite proficient, but remained somewhat mediocre at most of the others. Though he played a great deal of golf, for example, he never became a good golfer. Yet this never seemed to bother him, and if many of his drives turned into slices, then he never threw his club down in annoyance or disgust. Instead, he cheerfully continued to slice his way around the course, unperturbed by the usually better performances of those who played with him. Such was Lincoln Filene.

***

Lincoln Filene was destined to spend his lifetime in the shadow of his older brother. Even though he survived Edward by many years, he never fully escaped from his brother's presence. When most people think today of the many innovations associated with the store, or of the many other projects and proposals associated with the Filene name, they think of Edward A. and not A. Lincoln.

To what extent are they right in doing so? To be sure, Lincoln lacked the dynamism and multi-faceted ingenuity of his brother. Few people ever equaled Edward in this respect. But by the early 1900's Lincoln had already left his own imprint on their joint enterprise. Many of the Filene store's innovations, especially those concerning employee relations, were at least in part and sometimes in whole the product of Lincoln's less fertile but more sensitive mentality. And as Lincoln grew older he showed more and more independence and initiative in suggesting and pursuing ideas of his own both within and without the retailing profession. As a thinker and a doer he deserves his own place in the pantheon of America's businessmen-benefactors. And if his pedestal should not be as high or his niche so large as that accorded to Edward, then he did possess in abundance one talent which his more famous brother would always woefully lack. This was his talent for handling people, a talent spawned and sustained by a great gift for human fellowship.

If the two brothers were separated by many distinctive differences, they were at the same time joined by some striking similarities. We should bear these similarities in mind as we follow the Filenes on their roughly parallel but increasingly separate pathways through life.

On a superficial level, both were short and neither was physically attractive. Moreover, although they would lead long and active lives, both were plagued by bouts of illness. (In Edward's case, these may have been largely psychosomatic.) Both also smoked cigars. Edward rather characteristically chose foul-smelling, three-for-a-dime Italian stogies. Lincoln preferred Havanas, though he smoked pipes as well.

Both loved and respected their parents. Though Edward was extremely close to, and considerate of, his mother--he would write her every two or three days when he was out of town--Lincoln was also a warm and thoughtful son. He paid for most of his mother's medical care and, as indicated earlier, she would spend many weeks with him and family every summer in Weston. Both brothers also spoke and wrote of their father with deep affection and respect, and Edward always made some gift or contribution to a worthy cause each year on his father's birthday.[4]

Both brothers were frequently accused, although only behind their backs, of repudiating their Jewish background and of trying to pass as Gentiles. Lincoln especially was subject to such a charge since he never used the name Abraham--in fact, he legally dropped the name when he became older--and also because he contributed to the Unitarian Church of Weston and, at one time, to the Old South Congregational Church of Boston as well.

But the charges do not really hold up. In matters of religious faith, Lincoln followed in his father's footsteps. Like the elder Filene, he felt little affinity to Judaism. As a matter of fact, he knew little about the family's ancestral religion, and when a Jewish holiday arrived he had to ask one of his Jewish employees what it meant. At the same time Lincoln felt little affinity for any other organized religion. He consistently told his daughters and any others who asked him that he worshipped at a "seven-day church." In other words, he believed religious values and ideals were for every day and not just Sundays.

His church contributions are easily explained. When the family moved to Weston, his daughter Helen began attending the local Unitarian church with her friends. Furthermore, since it was the only church in town, and since the town itself had few public facilities, the church's building also served as something of a community center. For these reasons, then, Lincoln felt obliged to support it.

His other daughter supplies the reason for any contributions he made to the Old South Congregational Church in Boston. When Catherine was about eight, and the family was still living in Boston, the young girl developed an interest in religion and asked to go to Sunday School. Lincoln enrolled her in the one at Old South Congregational. Every Sunday he would walk his daughter to the door and leave her, returning to pick her up at the door later. He never, so she recalls, ever entered the building.

Usually, if a person is trying to conceal or cancel out his ethnic identity, he takes care to distance himself as much as he can from those who conspicuously bear that identity. This Lincoln never did. In fact, his closest friend in later years would be his business associate Louis Kirstein, and Kirstein was one of the most identifiable Jews in Boston. He headed up many fund drives for Jewish charities and some considered him the most prominent and generous supporter of Jewish causes in New England.

Edward's relationship to religion in general and Judaism in particular was much the same. He rarely contributed to Jewish charities but then, as we have seen, he gave little to any other charities. He never sought to create Jewish connections but he never sought to avoid them either. He ascribed his attitude toward Judaism to his father for when asked once if he had ever attended services in a synagogue, he replied, "I never went except out of curiosity--perhaps one or two or three times in my whole life--to Jewish services...There was no question of any Jewish rites on me because my father was a liberal before I was born."

On another occasion Edward answered the charge of assimilationism more directly. "I should be ashamed of myself," he said, "if I had even a secret desire to conceal or deny my Jewish origin, but it must be as clear to every thinking man as it is to me that I cannot have belief in any organized religion or any organized theology thrust or forced upon me; that I am bound to defend myself against any effort to do so." But Edward added, "I am proud of having come from a race that led the vanguard for monotheism and whose record through the ages has been of furnishing great leaders in the arts and sciences and literature as well as the more material fields of business, finance, and politics."

Developments abroad during the 1930's would cause both brothers to draw closer to the Jewish community. But while they accepted a responsibility to aid their fellow Jews, they never considered them their co-religionists. In religious matters, they were their father's sons and would remain so all their lives.

***

As one might expect, when it came to principles and precepts, Edward and Lincoln tended to think alike. Their differences were more of shading and tone. Edward became an active Democrat while Lincoln remained, at least until the 1930's, a nominal Republican. However, both supported the same local causes and in national affairs Lincoln confined his activities to supporting issues, not people. Generally, the issues Lincoln involved himself with were those that Edward would have backed had he not other things to occupy his time. So far as can be ascertained, the two brothers never found themselves for long on opposite sides of any serious political controversy.

Their attitudes toward retailing also did not conflict. Edward wanted to create cooperative enterprises and also reduce the country's distribution costs. These two goals would for him become a virtual obsession. Lincoln was less concerned with cutting distribution costs but would always be deeply, if less radically, interested in employee involvement, as well as in employee welfare generally.

Even when it came to implementing their ideas, the brothers shared one significant trait. They each possessed an almost uncanny ability to select able associates. Into their employ came men who would subsequently go on to hold such positions as these: President of Dartmouth College, President of the University of Wisconsin, Dean of the Harvard Business School, co-founder and chairman of the Sheraton Corporation, President of Prince Matchabelli (a prominent perfume maker), publisher of Who's Who, partner in the leading Wall Street banking firm of Lehman Brothers, and President of People's Broadcasting Corporation.

That Lincoln could attract and retain, for a fair amount of time, men of such caliber is not surprising. But that Edward could do so seems strange given the peculiarities of his temperament. However, Edward always recognized and appreciated ability, and though he might fly into rages with those who worked for him, he would at the same time heed what they had to say and respect what they did when they proved to be people of capacity.

Edward could sometimes show the same knack for recognizing ability when it came to rank-and-file employees. He once hired a slovenly and shiftless-looking fellow named Pillsbury to work in the store's shipping department because, as he afterwards said, "I thought there was something in him." His expectations regarding Pillsbury's potential were not speedily realized. The young man, when sent on an errand, would disappear for hours only to be found curled up asleep in an empty crate. But Edward refused to sanction the indolent employee's dismissal. Pillsbury later became the chess champion of the United States. His most spectacular stunt was to play 20 men simultaneously while blindfolded and to checkmate each of them in a few moves.

But if many of the outstanding men who joined the Filene firm managed to endure and even benefit from Edward, most were only too glad to leave when the time came to do so. Working with the older brother could be stimulating but never ultimately satisfying. And this may help explain why the partnership of Edward and Lincoln lasted as long as it did. For only a man like Lincoln could work so long and so closely with a man like Edward. Eventually, Lincoln would also rebel. But his rebellion came much later, and before it occurred both brothers would go forward together, leaving their mark on their profession, their community and their world.

Chapter 5
GOING PUBLIC
WITH BRANDEIS AND STEFFENS

1900

The new century has ushered in far more than a new page on the calendar. It has also signaled a sea change in the American perspective. For the forces that had begun gathering steam during the last decade of the 19th century are now sweeping through the country, bringing about a fundamental re-examination of certain basic American values and a reordering of the nation's priorities.

Heretofore, the country's creed had called for every man to stand on his own two feet. Now, a growing legion of reformers, such as Jane Adams in Chicago and Jacob Riis in New York, are championing institutional support for the downtrodden. Formerly, the government was to keep its hands off commercial relationships between private parties. Now, Congress has begun enacting such laws as the Pure Food and Drug Act, the Meat Inspection Act, the Narcotics Act, and the Employees Liabilities Act. Moreover, a constitutional amendment will soon allow the federal government to tax the income of the rich at higher rates than that of the poor.

Previously, American business had enjoyed the esteem accorded to society's acknowledged leaders. Now they find themselves confronting increasingly militant trade unions, a rapidly rising socialist movement and, in Theodore Roosevelt, a president who enjoys calling their more successful members "malefactors of great wealth" and who seems intent on smashing every substantial business conglomeration he can. As a perceptive Princeton University professor named Woodrow Wilson has pointed out, "This is nothing short of a new social age, a new era of human relationships, a new stage setting for the drama of life."

This new social age seems tailor-made for such socially minded businessmen as Edward and Lincoln Filene. It will serve as both a setting and a springboard in launching them on a lifetime involvement in social and economic reform.

* * *

Traffic congestion had begun to throttle many of the country's larger cities during the 1890s, and while the new electric street railways that had started to spring up seemed to offer a solution, many of these street car lines had fallen into the hands of selfish and rather swashbuckling interests; moreover, these interests were expending enormous amounts of money and influence to make their large and lucrative enterprises larger and more lucrative still.

Up until 1897, Boston had managed to hold such forces at bay, for the city had kept the franchises for street railways in its own hands. But in that year the Boston Elevated Company, thanks to an all-out and free-spending lobbying effort, secured near permanent franchises on many of the city's principal arteries. Individual citizens had protested the grab, but no concerted effort arose to combat it.

Two years later, as mounting traffic congestion made an additional line on Washington Street imperative, the company struck again. It introduced a bill into the state legislature that would give it the right to build and operate such a new line for as long as it wished. What's more, it could also charge its users as much as it wanted.

The company wooed and won the support of some highly respected citizens, and since it was also prepared to spend lavishly for favorable newspaper publicity and legislative votes, it reckoned on a fairly easy and speedy passage for the measure. However, as a later writer would note, "The sponsors did not count on Edward A. Filene, a bantam fighting cock [who]...insisted on the public's right to determine whether the track should be laid down."

Edward had become distressed over the situation and had decided to do something about it. But he knew he needed a shrewd, personable, and courageous lawyer to spearhead such a fight. He went from one attorney to another, only to be turned down. They were all afraid of tackling the powerful traction interests. All of them, that is, but one. The exception turned out to be his store's own attorney, Louis D. Brandeis.

At the time, the 41-year-old Brandeis was one of the most successful advocates in Boston. He had been retained by the store as its counsel only a year or two before. He would naturally appeal to Edward for he was, like him, a German Jew whose parents had emigrated in 1848. More important, Brandeis had great abilities, including an aptitude for handling figures. He shared Edward's belief in arithmetical analysis, saying on a later occasion, "If you can't solve it by law, you can solve it by mathematics."

Up to now, Edward had regarded Brandeis as a brilliant business lawyer but not one interested in public causes. He was delighted to learn that he had been wrong. Brandeis was as upset as Edward over the Elevated's high-handed methods and goals and shared Edward's eagerness to teach the rapacious railway a lesson. But before agreeing to take on the task, he subjected Edward to a barrage of questions to make sure that Edward's motives or at least his objectives were as public spirited as his own. Once assured that this was the case, he agreed to serve as attorney for the group which they would organize to oppose this harmful venture.

Their partnership would prove spectacularly successful. They enlisted not only some prominent businessmen but some prestigious bearers of distinguished Brahmin names, such as Richard Henry Dana and Robert Treat Paine, Jr. Working closely and competently, the anti-Elevated forces persuaded (or pressured) the state's governor into calling for a public referendum on the Elevated's take-over bill.

Having succeeded in this important initial skirmish, the Filene-Brandeis group now mobilized to win the war. Their task, as they saw it, was to educate the public into rejecting the bill. This would be far from easy, for the transit line was spending prodigiously for publicity and had lined up nearly every newspaper in town on its side. Some newspapers even refused to accept advertisements from the Elevated's opponents.

The task of countering the company's control of the newspapers fell specifically to Edward. To make up for his group's near exclusion from the press he had circulars printed outlining their position. And to guard against the company finding out and sabotaging these efforts, he had the circulars printed in New York. Gradually the group's arguments began to take hold, and other organizations, such as the Associated Board of Trade, the Fruit and Produce Exchange, and some labor unions, enlisted on their side. The result was a resounding defeat for the railways in the referendum that Fall.

But the Boston Elevated was by no means ready to retire from the field. The next year it presented a modified proposal that would allow it to operate a Washington Street subway for forty years without compensation to the city. Although better than a license to operate such a subway in perpetuity, which it had sought earlier, the new bill would still enable the company to charge what it wanted without sharing any of its prospective, and prospectively handsome, profits with the city. Brandeis claimed that other parties were willing to build and operate such a subway and pay the city for the privilege of doing so. Why shouldn't the Boston Elevated do the same?

Once again, Edward's public interest group marshaled its forces, and once again it blocked the railway company's bid to fleece the taxpayers as well as its own passengers.

The next year, the company decided to lie low and submit no new proposal, hoping instead, perhaps, to defeat the governor, who had vetoed their bill the previous year in response to pressure generated by the Brandeis-Filene band. But this group had now formally organized as the Public Franchise League and had gone over to the offensive. It now began pushing a bill of its own that would only allow the company to lease the line for stipulated intervals and would require it to pay well for the privilege.

The League's bill was drafted by Brandeis. Edward was once again in charge of publicity and he kept churning out statements, circulars, press releases and the like with a will and skill which impressed his associates.

The press could no longer afford to ignore the anti-Elevated forces, but it continued to treat them coolly. This forced Edward to find new ways of getting their attention. He would, for example, schedule large public meetings which the papers would have to cover. On one dull Sunday night he dropped in at the office of one of the few newspapers that had showed a bit of sympathy for the League's cause and offered the city editor a choice item. The editor seized it eagerly and in gratitude he granted Edward's request for the galley proofs of the story. As soon as the proofs came up, Edward sped off to other newspapers, showing them the story which their rival was going to publish, thereby goading them to publish it as well.

Faced with the League's growing popularity and its own growing unpopularity, the Boston Elevated finally capitulated, agreeing to the essentials of the Brandeis bill. The League's long fight was over. Louis Brandeis and Edward Filene had proven to the world and themselves that they could enter the public arena and emerge with laurels. Undoubtedly, it sharpened their appetites for the numerous battles in the public's behalf which henceforth would characterize both their lives.

Since Brandeis had acted as the League's official attorney, Edward asked him on several occasions to submit a bill for his services. Brandeis had never done so, but when the fight was over Edward became insistent, saying that he would no more think of not paying for Brandeis' services than Brandeis would think of going into the Filene store and walking off with a suit without paying. "I'll take half of what you got out of it," Brandeis finally retorted. The answer surprised Edward who, far from deriving any profit from the endeavor, had actually spent much of his own money to sustain it. Brandeis then followed up his reply with an explanation. "If you have the right to give your money to the public service, Mr. Filene, I claim an equal right to give my time."

The bond which the Elevated fight had forged between Edward and Brandeis would last for many years and would never completely disappear. The year after their victory over the street railway company, they found a new cause to champion. Eight gas companies in Boston had decided to merge. In so doing, they were planning to "water" their stock in such a way as to force their customers to pay more for their gas. Brandeis and Edward reactivated their Public Franchise League and sprang into action. Once again they confronted a heavily bribed legislature and, in effect, a heavily bribed press as well. But again they triumphed. The merger came about but in such a way as to reduce, not increase, the price of gas to consumers.

Edward was not the only Filene brother to become a Brandeis ally. Lincoln soon joined with the increasingly eminent attorney on numerous public issues. One of these was savings bank life insurance; this was a cause which vitally concerned Brandeis, for he saw it as a way of reducing the costs of insurance to consumers, thereby making it available to lower income people. When Brandeis filed a bill to permit such insurance to be marketed in Massachusetts, Lincoln lobbied long and successfully to help secure its passage. One of his store's Irish-American supervisors had maintained good contacts with Boston's state representatives, and through him Lincoln was able to keep Brandeis abreast of the legislature's thinking and activities and even to act as his mediator while the bill successfully worked its way through the legislature.

Edward was on his round-the-world cruise at the time and so was unable to play any real role in the fight. But he was apparently sympathetic to the idea. He had earlier read and critiqued for Brandeis an article which the attorney had authored, entitled "Wage-Earners' Life Insurance," and when he returned from his cruise he sent off some material on such insurance to a Japanese statesman he had met in Tokyo.

Brandeis subsequently became deeply involved in another issue, and on this one the Filene brothers would initially take opposite sides. The New York, New Haven & Hartford Railroad had long cast a covetous eye on the Boston and Maine and had started to acquire some of the B & M's stock. Controlled by the Morgan interests, the New York, New Haven was embarking on a scheme to gain control of all the railroads in the Northeast.

The issue first surfaced in 1905 and waxed into a searing controversy the following year. Initially, the B & M's largest stockholder had retained Brandeis to fight the New Haven's take-over attempt, but as the fight developed, Brandeis decided to forego all his fees so that he could rally support on a public-interest basis.

An Anti-Merger League was formed by those who shared his views. Among them was Lincoln, who served as one of the League's directors. But Edward stayed on the sidelines, for not only was he then heavily engaged in organizing a national chamber of commerce, but, more important, he favored the merger. Edward felt that such a consolidation would benefit the public through improved service and lower costs.

The anti-merger forces succeeded in delaying and dragging out the take-over move for over a year. Finally, an attorney for the New York, New Haven, in an apparent act of desperation, accused Brandeis of being in the pay of another railroad magnate, H. H. Harriman. Harriman was trying to block the merger, said the attorney, so that he could acquire the B & M for himself.

The charge was essentially baseless. One of Brandeis' law partners had done some work for Harriman, but it concerned a completely unrelated matter and had terminated some time before. Brandeis himself had had no dealings with Harriman at all.

The false accusation dislodged Edward from his seat on the sidelines. He promptly fired off a long letter to all the Boston newspapers defending his long-time associate. In so doing, Edward compared himself to a spectator at a football game who could not bear to see a player dealt a foul blow in the back by an unworthy opponent. The destruction of an honest fighter's reputation when the fighter was someone of Brandeis' stature, he argued, would be a national calamity.

Since many sincerely wondered why Brandeis spent so much time and effort on the fight without payment, Edward sought to put their minds at ease. "If a man were to give $50,000 a year for some public cause, and many of our men do give such an amount, or a larger one, that would not create astonishment," Edward pointed out. "If Mr. Brandeis gives, as he does, his professional services for a cause which he believes he ought to assist in the public interest, the action is yet so uncommon as to lend itself to the arousing of suspicion of his motives, even as all uncommon things may be so used."

The letter, which appeared in one newspaper under the headline, "Cause of Leader of Anti-Merger Forces Defended by E. A. Filene," drew considerable attention and provided a good deal of sympathy and support for the embattled Brandeis. Edward himself eventually swung over to his cause and sent a check for $100 to the Anti-Merger League. He had come to the conclusion that this particular merger would be unwise.

But although the two men ended up on the same side in this fight, and although Edward would come to Brandeis' aid again, especially when the distinguished attorney would be fighting for his confirmation to the U.S. Supreme Court, their initial differences regarding the railroad merger reflected a basic difference in their points of view. Brandeis feared and distrusted both big government and big business, believing that large-scale governmental or business units threatened not only individual freedom but economic efficiency. Edward believed just the opposite. To him, large-scale operations opened up opportunities for increased efficiency. And he saw no danger to liberty as long as each sector became large enough and strong enough to hold the other in check.

This basic division in philosophy, in addition perhaps to the peculiarities of Edward's personality, would prevent the two men from ever becoming close friends or steadfast allies. But their relations would always remain cordial, for they would continue to respect each other's honesty, intelligence, and fearlessness in fighting for those causes in which each sincerely, if sometimes separately, believed.

***

While the early 1900s saw a great growth in trade unionism, it witnessed no commensurate growth in worker wages. Held back by the tidal wave of immigrants who were flocking to the United States, and who were willing to work for existence-level wages, the average real earnings of the American worker largely remained stagnant. In some years they actually slipped below the level of the 1890s.

This condition obviously caused much discontent among the country's work force. But a more important factor in fostering worker dissatisfaction was the basic attitude of management. The capitalists of that era considered themselves the sole sovereigns over their property and fiercely resisted any attempts by their employees to influence their policies and practices. One manufacturer went so far as to fire all his employees one morning and then hire them back in the afternoon just to show them who was boss.

Such an attitude only fueled the flames of unrest which had started to break out during the last years of the previous century. Violent and often prolonged strikes were the frequent result. Given the nature of their work force as well as their advanced labor policies, the Filene brothers remained largely immune from such unpleasantness. But given their own personal attitudes and principles, Edward and Lincoln wanted to help.

In the late spring of 1903 they gathered together a handful of other progressive businessmen in Boston to form what they called the Industrial League. Brandeis was unanimously chosen president. Lincoln assumed the post of treasurer, while Edward headed up the group's executive committee. The League described its purpose in its awkwardly-worded preamble:

> To promote the investigation and study of, and to provide instruction as to, economic and industrial questions, and to aid in improving the relations of employees and employers, and to provide and maintain places for reading rooms, libraries or social meetings for such employees.

The League never became more than a talking shop. Its activities consisted, for the most part, of monthly dinner meetings where the 15 or 20 members present would discuss an industrial question. Brandeis and the Filenes sought to get some of the more able and broad-minded local labor leaders to join the League, but their efforts apparently failed and the League eventually languished.

The Filenes continued, however, to involve themselves in labor problems and to support progressive measures to resolve them. In 1904 a long and bitter strike at the National Cash Register Company in Dayton, Ohio startled the nation's entire industrial community. The firm was thought to be a leader in employee welfare, having given its workers health insurance,, pensions, and other benefits. After the strike ended, Edward journeyed to Dayton to find out what had gone wrong.

He soon had his answer. It was not what the company did but the way it did it. All its impressive welfare work had remained completely within its executives' control, with its workers denied any real say in this or anything else the company did. The company president, William Patterson, was so autocratic that when, in following his doctor's orders, he went to Hot Springs to take the baths, he lay in bed and made his male secretary take the baths for him!

Edward reported all this in two perceptive and well-written articles which he wrote for *The Echo*, a monthly publication which the Filene Cooperative Association had launched. Privately, he reported that in interviewing Patterson, he had given him a copy of the latest edition of *The Echo*. Edward had brought it along with him but had not had time to read it himself. The cash register head opened it up and saw on the front page a leading article attacking his handling of the strike and his labor relations in general. He then proceeded to read the article aloud to his embarrassed visitor from Boston.

The following year Edward made another attempt to spread his ideas in the Midwest. This occasion was a speech which he delivered to the Cleveland Chamber of Commerce. His address, from the vantage point of nearly a century later, seems strikingly prophetic. As the 19th century had brought many changes in business methods, he said, the 20th century would bring many changes in the economic and moral responsibilities of business. Among them would be a recognition of the worker's right "to have a definite voice as to conditions under which he works, including pay, hours, rules and environment."

Edward had sent the speech to Brandeis before he left, and the latter had returned it with a note saying he could "find in it nothing which it seems to me necessary to correct."

At home, Edward and Lincoln were generally supportive of labor unions. In a letter to an official of the International Ladies Garment Workers Union in 1905, Edward flatly asserted that "it is the policy of our business to give preference to goods bearing the union label." Both Filenes threw their support into the state AFL's battle to pass workmen's compensation and minimum wage laws for Massachusetts. Edward also gave some help to a rising young woman trade union leader named Margaret M. Fitzgerald. He would rent a car for her so that she could travel from one factory gate to another distributing handbills calling for a 48-hour week and a minimum wage.

Fitzgerald was also a suffragette and this cause also elicited Edward's sympathies. However, when it came to women's issues, he was more directly interested in the problems and plight of the new and growing class of working women. Their condition was the subject of his first published article, which appeared in the May 1906 edition of the *Annals of the American Academy of Political and Social Science*. In this article, he called attention to the fact that more and more women were entering the labor force and were faring poorly as a result of inadequate preparation. "...great numbers of women and girls are forced to work who have never been trained to work-who do not know how to work--who do not know how to keep themselves well-- who lack the qualities necessary to enforce their rights," said Edward. After describing their problems in detail, Edward went on to call for more vocational education, more effective organizations, and more understanding as well as support for working women. Their predicament, he said, requires "more real democracy--expressing itself in work for the common good, more neighborliness and wise, progressive and remedial legislation."

In the course of his somewhat discursive article, Edward observes how "democracy cannot live if class distinctions grow and multiply constantly. But that is what in the natural order of things has come about in our country from things that were done with good motives." The passage is of interest not because of his observations about democracy which, as he himself elsewhere observes, are rather trite, but because of what he says about motives. That good motives do not necessarily make for good action, that some of the worst mischief is done by the best of men acting from the best of intentions, had already become one of his basic beliefs. We will see this conviction continually at work as we watch Edward engage in the numerous battles that will mark the remaining 30 years of his life.

The conclusion of his article, which was really a reprint of a speech he had delivered at the Academy the previous month, also offers some further insights into Edward Filene. It ends with a poem, and while his verse can scarcely be called great or even good literature, it does afford an additional illustration of the unusual mentality of this most unusual businessman.

Entitled "How to Make a Poet," Edward's poem reads as follows:

> First get a good piece of land.
> Build a factory.
> Govern it wisely,
> That is, with knowledge plus sympathy.
> Make it a business success,
> Make the factory and the village beautiful.
> Make conditions just;
> And then more just;
> And then more just;
> And one of the sons of one of the workers will be a poet.

***

The highlight of Edward's round-the-world cruise in 1907 occurred when he left the ship in Bombay and picked it up again in Calcutta. In the interim he made his previously noted 1200-mile auto trip through the heart of Bengal. Even today such a journey can provide plenty of challenge and one can well imagine the difficulties it posed at a time when cars, drivers, and roads had only barely been developed. But with a former British official to act as companion and interpreter, the 47-year-old Boston retailer set out on his trek with his customary gusto.

The inhabitants of most of the villages through which they passed had never seen an auto and therefore looked upon it as a god. The Englishman turned this belief to advantage, using it to secure native labor to tow the car through riverbeds and other difficult passages by telling the villagers that in rendering such service they would acquire merit with the four-wheeled deity.

There were other occasions as well when the two travelers had to call on the natives for help. Their driver turned out to be a devout Muslim, and whenever the car's engine faltered he would react by saying, "Allah will provide." He would then sit patiently behind the wheel awaiting Allah's assistance. Since Allah usually declined to intervene, the Hindu villagers obtained additional opportunities to gain merit with the new god.

The trip yielded consequences far more important than the diverting and occasionally dangerous incidents which marked its passage. The Englishman who accompanied Edward had formerly been in charge of organizing the cooperative credit societies which the British were setting up in Bengal to protect the poor peasants from their native moneylenders. During the trip he told Edward how these poverty-stricken villagers had previously paid 24 to 40 percent interest when they needed to borrow for a wedding or funeral. All too often they never managed to pay anything on the principal but continued paying the exorbitant interest all their lives. The British had greatly eased their plight by persuading them to form their own credit associations and loaning them the money to get started.

This deeply impressed Edward, and when he later reached the Philippines he saw an opportunity for the United States to help its colonized people in the same way. On his return to Boston he wrote to President Theodore Roosevelt suggesting that Roosevelt introduce such a system into the then American colony. Roosevelt replied briefly, expressing interest and asking for more information. Edward promptly sent it to him but received no further response, probably because Roosevelt had become preoccupied with the forthcoming presidential election.

But this did not end Edward's connection with such credit societies. Unbeknown to him at the time, a movement to start up such associations was already forming in North America. It was a movement in which he would eventually become the central figure and which would provide the crowning success of his multi-faceted career.

A French-Canadian journalist named Alphonse Desjardins had started organizing such mutual credit societies in his own impover-ished province of Quebec. His work attracted the attention of the Massachusetts Commissioner of Banks, Pierre Jay, who despite his first name was actually a Yankee blue blood and a descendant of

America's first Chief Justice, John Jay. Commissioner Jay brought Desjardins to Boston in November 1908 and invited a group of progressive Boston businessmen to meet him. Edward immediately became an enthusiastic supporter, and when Jay drafted and submitted a bill to the state legislature authorizing the formation of such associations, Edward appeared at the hearing to speak warmly in its behalf. He also promised Jay that if the bill passed, he would "see to it that the advantages of such associations are made known throughout the state."

The principle of the legislation was simple. Groups of employees would be allowed to incorporate, contribute money to a general fund, and then make loans to each other from this common fund. These loans could be offered at low interest since the members themselves would run the association largely on a volunteer basis. Also, since the borrowers would be fellow employees of the lenders, their credit worthiness would be well known and, in any case, they would be under constant pressure from their fellow employees not to default.

Many sneered at the proposal. "Do you expect plumbers and mechanics to go into the banking business?" was a frequent reaction. But Edward and the other supporters whom Jay had mobilized continued to lobby for the bill, and on April 15, 1909 Massachusetts became the first state to pass a general statute for the incorporation of credit unions.[5]

That the credit union concept should have aroused Edward's ardor should come as no surprise. As we have seen, he fervently believed that people should participate in and accept responsibility for all matters which affected their own lives. The credit union movement offered an ideal vehicle for advancing such a concept.

Edward had also acquired some first-hand acquaintance with such schemes not just during his stay in India but in Boston. Employees of *The Boston Globe*, for example, had formed a savings and loan association in 1892 to take deposits and make loans to one another. Filene's itself had also begun operating a sort of informal bank where employees could deposit their savings and earn interest. When business turned down in 1908 and sales commissions fell off, several of the store's employees fell into the hands of loan sharks. The store, at the behest of the FCA, began using the deposited funds to make loans to some of these employees so that they could escape the exorbitant interest rates which they were then paying. This had led the store to call its bank the Deposit and Loan Bureau and to involve the FCA more closely in its operations.

But beyond all these considerations, still another factor was motivating Edward's enthusiasm for and involvement in the budding credit union movement. The loan sharks of those days were customarily called "shylocks," and although most of them were probably not Jewish, many were. Furthermore, much of the agitation against such moneylenders carried strongly anti-Semitic overtones.

Edward was quite sensitive to this issue. He was also quite explicit in acknowledging how it had helped stimulate his own efforts. As he later stated, he was propelled into the forefront of the credit union movement partly "because I wanted to fight an age-old prejudice that all Jews were usurers."

Thus, a variety of factors prompted Edward to become, in a sense, the father of credit unionism in the United States. But his involvement with the movement in its earlier years remained somewhat marginal. He did speak out in its behalf on all suitable occasions, distributed its literature, and sought to interest a popular magazine of the time, *Survey*, in doing an article about it. But his real commitment would come later, for by the time the Massachusetts credit union bill became law, he had plunged deeply into still another area of public activity.

***

A little wispy man with a goat-like beard had begun to cut a large figure on the American political horizon in the early 1900s. He would also be a strong influence in the life of Edward Filene.

Lincoln Steffens had never held and never would hold political office. But his name was known and his pen was feared, or at least respected, by politicians everywhere, for his journalistic exposés of municipal and state corruption had alerted and alarmed progressive-thinking citizens throughout the country.

One of these citizens was Edward Filene. Edward's early experiences in fighting the traction, utility, and other interests had introduced him to the seamy underside of Boston politics. To be sure, he and those other public-spirited citizens who had fought alongside him had won most of their battles but, as Edward was all too painfully aware, they had not fundamentally altered the basic pattern of municipal behavior. Corruption and inefficiency continued to characterize large sectors of the local body politic.

So Edward wrote to Steffens urging him to come to Boston to investigate the municipal mess he would find there. Steffens was intrigued. As he later put it, he "had long wished to go there to study, at their source, the American ideals which did not 'work' in the rest of the country..." He was also somewhat intrigued by Edward himself, who seemed to Steffens to be cut of a different cloth than most of the successful businessmen he had encountered in his long march through the corridors of municipal power. When Edward sent him a copy of the public letter he had released in behalf of Brandeis in the New Haven Railroad fight, Steffens wrote back, "Your appeal for fair play for Brandeis was very, very good; moderate, earnest and plain. It must have done its work. But isn't it strange that such obvious things have to be said?"

Nevertheless, the journalist did not immediately jump at the businessman's bait. Steffens had become a little weary of muckraking and needed some additional inducement to bring him to the New England metropolis.

Edward was prepared to offer it. Come not just to expose but to propose, said Edward in effect. He would arrange a year's stipend for Steffens to enable him not just to probe Boston's problems but to develop a plan to resolve them. Five years earlier Steffens had bewailed the fact that "So far there has been no market for municipal experts in this country." Now he was being given the chance to don just such a mantle himself. In Boston he would not merely describe but decide, thereby moving from a front-row seat to the middle of the political stage.

This was an offer which Steffens could not refuse, and arrangements for his new assignment were soon completed. They called for the journalist to receive, as he later put it, "a small but sufficient sum to pay my expenses." As it happens, the sum amounted to $10,000 a year, which was exactly double the pay of a U.S. Senator. It enabled Steffens to install his household, consisting of a wife, mother-in-law, three servants, dog, cat, bird, and 17 large trunks, into a commodious house on Beacon Hill located only two or three blocks from Edward's home. The money ostensibly came from a group called the Good Government Association, but whether anyone besides Edward ever contributed to financing Steffen's stay in the city remains doubtful. As Steffens himself later noted, "E. A. Filene was my sole boss in Boston."

Both men were highly enthusiastic about their unusual joint venture. Edward had earlier written Steffens that their project "bids fair to be one of the most important ever done in this country, and might well rank in importance with anything that has been done either nationally or in any state or city, within our memory at least." Steffens called it "the biggest piece of work I ever attempted" and, he continued, "I have a dim hope that it may lead to the establishment by me of a new profession, a new calling: that of a city manager or municipal architect."

Edward set up a press conference to announce the undertaking, and while some newspapers showed skepticism, others reacted with positive fervor. One paper hailed Steffens as the messiah come "to save Boston from the pit which our own people have dug for our city."

As he got to work, Steffens began to see that much of the exposing and proposing had already been done. What was needed was a plan to tie all these proposed reforms together into one master blueprint for the city. Moreover, a time limit should also be set for this master plan's implementation.

Edward called a group of leading citizens to hear Steffens propound his proposal. The famed muckraker said the city needed a vision of the future sufficiently grand to stir the spirit of its citizens and goad them into taking the sweeping measures needed to attain it. As matters stood, he said, "Boston was partly a place to live in, partly a place to live on." It was finally decided to set 1915 as the year when Steffens' yet-to-be-completed master plan would be fulfilled, and a special committee consisting of some of the more distinguished men in Boston was formed to oversee its design and execution.

Steffens eventually produced a plan and, along with it, a book detailing Boston's problems and his proposals for correcting them. But the plan was never widely publicized and the book was never published. Just what stymied the project remains unclear. Steffens himself later said his plan portrayed a city so mired in the muck of selfishness and sloth as to be too unpalatable for even its would-be reformers to accept. To him, Boston was in a "later, lower, worse stage of the same growing system which gripped all the other cities I had studied." Also, some of his proposals, such as one for workmen's compensation insurance, had sensitive ramifications which went beyond the bounds of mere municipal reform.

But Steffens would also admit, at least indirectly, that his own efforts may have left something to be desired. If the Boston 1915 Committee declined to published his book, so did all the publishers whom he contacted personally. Furthermore, he came away from his Boston adventure feeling that men of ideas, such as himself, might not make adequate men of action. An intellectual, he would recall in a later reference to his work in Boston, is a person "who can't do a damned thing."

But if Edward failed in his ambitious attempt to use Steffens to make over his city, he did succeed in forming a valuable friendship. Though Steffens, like most people who dealt with Edward, frequently found him tedious--"the man is a bore but not his life," he would say of him years later--he found him fascinating too. In his famous autobiography he describes Edward as "a big businessman" who "seemed to be a democrat, a thinker, who said things like an intellectual, but who went and did them like a practical man of business." The two would remain in fairly close contact all their lives and eventually they would collaborate on a more successful, if far less sweeping, venture than their effort to rehabilitate Boston.

***

Edward's subsequent forays into the field of municipal politics did not turn out much happier than his Boston 1915 movement. Hardly had Steffens left town in the fall of 1909 than Edward became immersed in the mayoralty campaign of his friend, James Storrow. Storrow was a prominent investment broker, a graduate of Harvard and the Harvard Law School, and a former president of the Boston School Committee. His opponent was John Fitzgerald, the congenial and corrupt incumbent whose grandson and namesake, John Fitzgerald Kennedy, would become the country's first Catholic president. Storrow promised faithfully to clean up the city and his supporters, including Edward, worked devotedly to elect him, but Fitzgerald eked out a narrow victory and things continued pretty much as before.[6]

The Fitzgerald election convinced many that the Irish now firmly controlled Boston and any new, crusading mayor would have to come from their ranks. For a time, Edward and his fellow reformers thought they had such a man in a bright, silver-tongued politician named James Michael Curley. The reformers eventually helped install Curley into the mayor's office only to see him engage in the same patronage ploys which they had hoped he would eliminate. By this time, however, Edward's attention had turned to the national and international scene and here, ironically enough, he would exercise more influence than he would ever wield in his own city.

***

One last, strictly local endeavor of Edward's remains to be noted. His immersion into Boston politics over the past decade had brought home to him how deeply his city was divided. The biggest and most bitter schism was the one separating the Irish and the Yankees. But there were others as well. The Irish looked down on the Italians and sometimes refused to let them worship at their churches. Both groups, meanwhile, were hostile to the Jews. Economic divisions only exacerbated these ethnic ones. Businessmen disliked labor leaders who, for their part, tended to distrust them. Far from being a melting pot, Boston was a constantly simmering stew of antagonistic ingredients.

Disgusted and dismayed at this picture of endless intergroup rivalry and rancor, Edward had asked Steffens to suggest a solution. Steffens had thrown out the idea of a city-wide club where leaders of all these groups and factions could get to know one another in a relaxed social atmosphere. The journalist had spun the idea off the top of his head and meant it only half-seriously. But his businessman friend at once saw its potential. After drawing out any further thoughts Steffens could come up with, Edward set to work.

He knew that he lacked not only the time but the temperament for organizing such a club on his own. Consequently, he started out by making inquiries for a popular and able organizer. Once he found such a man, he offered him a good salary plus the prospect of a lifetime career. The organizer was to compile a list of all the going clubs in Boston, find out who were the leading members of each club, and then meet with these leaders to tell them, privately and separately, what he was trying to do. Together, they were to scout out an inexpensive and convenient location which would serve as the site of the future Boston City Club.

As Edward envisioned it, the club would hold no meetings, draw up no programs, and take no action on any extraneous issues. It would serve solely as a place for its members to meet, eat, and converse. Any camaraderie or bonhomie which might result among the leaders of the various groups would, so Edward reckoned, be achievement enough.

For the club to succeed, the food would have to be first class. But it would also have to be inexpensive so that trade unionists and other less affluent leaders could afford to come without being the guests of others. Edward therefore set out to find a chef who could meet these somewhat conflicting criteria. Whenever he ate a good meal, he talked to the person who cooked it until he finally found an "undiscovered genius" in a third-class restaurant in New York and engaged him on the spot.

Edward also saw to it that those who were invited to join not only constituted a cross section of the community but were also men who had made their own clubs. However, he kept himself in the background as much as possible, even going off on his annual summer trip to Europe when the club was getting ready to open.

With James Storrow as its president, the Boston City Club became quite successful. By the 1920s it would boast a membership of 7,000. To what extent it succeeded in infusing any increased amity among the city's divergent elements remains more difficult to determine. However, the sharp acrimony which had marked their relationships during the early 1900s did subside during the next few decades, and Edward's club may well have helped speed this development along.

***

Boston's fragmented character was reflected within the city's business community itself. At the beginning of the decade there was a Merchants Association, a Board of Trade, and numerous other business organizations, all of them more or less acting separately from each other and none apparently accomplishing much.

This situation also bothered Edward, and well before Steffens had come to town he had embarked on a program to correct it. Although hindered not only by his deficiencies in diplomacy but also by his maverick ideas on various social and economic issues, Edward, with the help of Storrow and others, did manage to unite three of the leading groups into one potentially powerful chamber of commerce. At the same time, he sought to broaden the base of this new organization in order to democratize it.

Edward then went on to help organize similar chambers of commerce in other American cities and to play a primary role in establishing the first U.S. Chamber of Commerce in 1911. Here too he was keenly conscious of the need for a broad-based and active membership, and it was at his suggestion that the new national chamber included in its bylaws a referendum requirement stipulating that all its members have the right to vote on its major positions and policies. As Edward later explained, "It is better to get the opinion of all the businessmen of the country than to have our opinion determined for us by an executive committee, however wise."

From the U.S. Chamber of Commerce Edward went on to help establish the first International Chamber of Commerce and to serve as its first American vice-president. Here too he succeeded in getting his referendum rule written into the organizational bylaws so that the rank and file and not any ruling elite would make or at least ratify all major decisions.

Such a string of successes should have provided Edward with a deep and abiding source of contentment. Such, however, was not to be the case. All of these business organizations, despite and perhaps even because of their referendum requirements, turned into reactionary organizations and Edward would end up feuding with and finally disowning what were in effect his own children. As Brandeis, who was skeptical of Edward's efforts from the start, would later say in reference to the chambers of commerce, "Yes, Filene is forever making weapons for the enemy."

***

While Edward was busily expanding the scope of his public activities during the first decade of the 1900s, Lincoln largely concerned himself with running the store. But largely does not mean exclusively, for the younger brother was also starting to feel and respond to the pull of public service. Although he would never turn into the public figure which his older sibling would become, he would play a part, and often a vital one, in many a cause and crusade.

Lincoln's debut in the public arena came during the fight to bring Savings Bank Life Insurance to Massachusetts. This sounds like a most minor issue, but it was not so to its supporters who saw in it a chance to substantially reduce insurance rates and thereby make insurance available to working people. Since there was no welfare state at the time to protect workers against the vagaries and vicissitudes of misfortune, cheaper private insurance could benefit them greatly.

Brandeis passionately believed in such insurance and when he filed a bill to bring it to Massachusetts, Lincoln along with a few other socially minded business and professional men rallied to his side. The state's young and still relatively weak trade union movement gave what support it could, and together the backers of the Brandeis bill overcame the resistance which the entrenched insurance interests had manifested toward the measure.

Under the provisions of the bill, almost any organization could file as an agent for accepting applications for insurance and annuity policies. The Filene Cooperative Association became one of the first to do so.

The two other areas of public activity which aroused Lincoln's greatest interest and involvement during this period were education and worker-management relations. In 1906 he became a member of the National Society for the Promotion of Industrial Education and also of the Massachusetts Committee on Industrial and Technical Education. His concern with vocational education soon led to further commitments. In 1908 he joined with a few others to set up the Vocational Bureau of Boston and two years later helped sponsor the nation's first Conference on Vocational Guidance. In the interim he had been appointed to the Massachusetts Advisory Board of Education, a position he would hold for over a quarter century.

The industrial strife which he had seen in Lynn as a child, and in the nation generally during the 1890s, and which had only seemed to increase in the early 1900s, continued to shock and sadden him. He had evolved a theory that the violence and bitterness which a labor dispute engendered was often inversely related to the importance of the issue or issues which had created it. In other words, the more trivial the cause, the more costly the consequences. As an example, he liked to cite the case of a shoe manufacturing company in Lynn which had only one grindstone for its leather cutters. The cutters had asked for a second grindstone so that they would not have to stand in line so long to sharpen their tools when their workday was over. The company's owners said no. The result was a turbulent, prolonged strike which, before in ended, had taken two lives and caused widespread hardship.

As his continual citing of this incident indicates, Lincoln blamed the selfishness and shortsightedness of management for most labor discord. This helped make him so sympathetic to unions that he actually assisted their efforts to organize. Trade unionists, for example, had no place to meet but in saloons. Lincoln often invited them to hold meetings at his home. His ability to empathize with the workers while at the same time enjoying, as a successful businessman, the trust of management would enable him to play a major role in resolving one of the great labor disputes of the prewar era.

***

Lincoln had become increasingly close to Brandeis, and the two had formed a warm and firm friendship that would last until Brandeis' death. The attorney had moved to Dedham, a Boston suburb then dominated by upper-class Yankees. There he found himself virtually isolated, since, despite his accomplishments and wealth, his attractive appearance, and his social graces, his Jewishness caused most of his neighbors to exclude him from their social life. He took to visiting Lincoln, whom he called "my social-minded friend," at the latter's Weston home, and the two men spent many a Sunday afternoon rambling through the woods discussing various issues.

Brandeis held advanced views regarding the rights of workers. He felt, for example, that their right to steady work equaled the right of stockholders to receive steady dividend payments. His progressive ideas struck a sympathetic chord in the younger man, who was already inclined to support employee interests and who in any case had come to hold the brilliant, highly educated Brandeis almost in awe. (Throughout his life Lincoln would always speak of Brandeis in tones of respect bordering on reverence.)

For all these reasons it was natural for Lincoln to become quite concerned when a strike shut down the New York City garment industry in June 1910 and for him to write the vacationing Brandeis about it. When Brandeis returned, Lincoln came to his Dedham home and asked him to go with him to New York to look into the situation. He was certain that Brandeis with his vast prestige and impressive abilities could successfully mediate the dispute.

The major issue in the strike was the union's insistence on a closed shop, meaning that members of the International Ladies Garment Workers Union could be hired. The manufacturers adamantly refused even to confer with the strike leaders until they dropped such a demand, since on this issue Brandeis sided with management. He therefore declined Lincoln's request to intervene, saying, "I'll have nothing to do with any settlement involving a closed shop."

Upset but undeterred by his friend's refusal to join him, Lincoln boarded the train for New York to see what he could do. He took with him his wife's cousin, a settlement house director named Meyer Bloomfield. Bloomfield had helped the International Ladies Garment Workers organize in Boston and so could approach the labor side of the strike equipped with contacts and credibility. In New York they were joined by a Dr. Henry Moskowitz, director of the city's Ethical Culture Society.

As Lincoln and Bloomfield soon learned, the city's entire Jewish community had become involved in, and virtually obsessed with, the strike. Bearded Orthodox Jews could be seen and heard passionately discussing it on almost any street corner in the lower East Side, while the city's dominant Yiddish newspaper, *The Jewish Daily Forward*, spoke of little else on its front page.

Despite the highly charged atmosphere, Lincoln immediately saw possibilities for a settlement. The ethnic confines of the dispute favored a solution, for virtually everyone involved, from the leading manufacturers to the lawyers and trade union leaders to the lowliest pants presser, shared a common culture. They spoke the same language, read the same newspaper, and in some instances worshiped in the same synagogue. Such a commonality of background and basic belief, so Lincoln reasoned, provided a pathway to compromise.

He still felt that Brandeis could play the pivotal role in bringing such a compromise about. As he had previously written to Edward, who was off on his annual summer visit to Europe, "It does not seem to me to make very much difference which side has him so long as one side gets him. I think he will succeed in bringing about an adjustment much better than is at present possible."

After consulting with both sides and receiving their approval or at least their acceptance of Brandeis' participation, he returned to Boston and this time persuaded the noted lawyer to return to New York with him. Brandeis conferred with all parties to the dispute and came up with a compromise suggestion for the biggest stumbling block, the closed shop. He proposed what he called a preferential union shop which would permit management to hire non-union members but would require such employees to join the union once they had been hired. After offering his suggestion, Brandeis returned to Massachusetts, where he spent the rest of the summer vacationing on Cape Cod.

Lincoln, however, continued to come to New York every weekend, forsaking the cool woods of Weston for the steamy summer city. As Brandeis' representative, he soon became the major mediating force as both sides continued to deliberate the union shop proposal. Thanks to his own reputation as a successful pro-labor businessman and, as a result of his winning and conciliatory personality, he managed to maintain cordial relations with all the parties involved. Gradually he prodded them to move closer together.

By the end of August a settlement seemed in sight. The major obstacle was the opposition of the Forward or *Vorwarts*, as it was called. The newspaper was socialist in orientation, and its reporters and editorial writers persisted in fanning the flames of discontent. But the flames were dying nonetheless. On August 31 Lincoln could report back in a letter to Brandeis, "We, Dr. Moskowitz and myself, were on the East Side until one O'clock this morning, talking to a group of East Siders... They all feel that if the *Vorwarts* could be brought around, the strike would be over."

The newspaper remained recalcitrant, but the strike ended in the next few days. The union accepted the union shop while the manufacturers agreed to grievance and arbitration procedures. Lincoln's long, hot summer was over.

But all strikes end sometime. To what extent, then, can Lincoln be credited with helping resolve the great Garment Workers' Strike of 1910?

Brandeis willingly accorded his friend the major role in resolving the dispute. In a letter to social worker Jane Addams, who had written to congratulate him on his accomplishment, Brandeis replied, "The success obtained in New York was due in very large measure to the admirable teamwork of A. Lincoln Filene, Meyer Bloomfield, and Dr. Henry W. Moskowitz. Without their careful work of preparation, their patient watchfulness and excellent judgment it would have been impossible for me to accomplish anything. Indeed they are entitled to far more credit than I am." But since it was Lincoln who recruited Bloomfield and Moskowitz and paid their expenses, he was the obvious leader of the mediating team and therefore deserves the major share of the credit.

This raises still another point. Why did Lincoln Filene go to so much personal trouble and expense to take on this task? What prompted him to forsake the family and home he enjoyed so much to spend nearly every weekend of the summer and a good many week days as well on New York's sweltering East Side?

Lincoln later sought to explain it by saying that his store had a distinct interest in ending the strike for it depended on the goods which the garment industry produced. However, this rationale does not really stand up. He could have easily and cheaply purchased goods from non-union operators as well as from abroad.

One of Brandeis' biographers, in speaking of the strike, points out that "as for Filene, the strike situation hurt his business far less than it troubled his conscience. He was in a position, as one of the country's largest retailers, to obtain merchandise despite the stoppage, but he did not want to buy goods made under repulsive conditions complained of by workers. Retailers bore a responsibility to them but none was lending a hand." In such situations, Lincoln Filene would always be willing to lend a hand.

One final note of interest is the impact the strike had or failed to have on its two principal resolvers. Brandeis, a German Jew like the Filenes, had had little experience in dealing with groups of non-German Jews. He came away impressed by the way both sides to the dispute had at almost all times put their principles before their pocketbooks. To quote again from his biographer, "He recognized his own passion for justice as an identical spirit in the two camps. Before that he had regarded his heritage as simply a historical fact." The experience prompted Brandeis to identify more fully with the Jewish community and eventually to become an active Zionist.

But the immersion into Yiddishkeit which the strike provided failed to have the same effect on his friend Lincoln. The latter would calmly continue to "worship" at his "Seven-day Church" by being a friend to people of good will everywhere.

***

If it was Lincoln who induced Meyer Bloomfield to become involved in the great Garment Workers strike, then it was Bloomfield who introduced Lincoln's wife to public service.

Thanks to her mother's guidance and her husband's sympathetic support, the shy violinist had become a capable homemaker and hostess. But the death of her mother in 1905 plunged the young woman into a deep depression. Bloomfield, who was then operating a settlement house in Boston's North End, suggested to his cousin that she organize a music program for the children of the neighborhood. The proposal immediately ignited a spark in 30-year-old Therese Filene, and she embarked on a series of activities that eventually gave the country its first settlement house devoted primarily to music.[7]

In creating the country's first music-oriented settlement house, the once terribly shy girl and still somewhat shy young matron had demonstrated an organizational ability that neither she nor those who knew her had suspected. Soon thereafter she found a still greater opportunity to put this long-latent talent to work.

One Palm Sunday evening when the family had returned to their Back Bay apartment after a weekend in Weston, Therese, in glancing out the window across the Charles River, saw to her horror a sheet of flame shooting up into the night sky. The neighboring city of Chelsea was burning. The great Chelsea fire of 1908 would become the third worst such blaze in American history, taking 19 lives, destroying 6,000 buildings, and leaving 17,000 homeless.

After getting her family off to work and school the next morning, Therese set out to see what she could do. For the next month her family hardly saw her as she took on a major role in aiding the fire victims. She raised money, set up relief stations, and helped arrange new housing and jobs for the dispossessed.

Although she would always retain a certain reserve which would cause some to call her a snob, the former Therese Weil had proven herself in the public arena. With her husband's and brother-in-law's record in mind, one might say that she had become a true Filene.

Chapter 6
THE FLOWERING OF FILENES

1912

On the Tuesday after Labor Day in 1912 huge crowds poured into downtown Boston and quickly formed block-long lines on Washington Street. They came not to take advantage of the unprecedented half-price sale which Jordan Marsh, the city's largest department store, had so extensively advertised over the weekend. In fact, this throng of men, women, and children had not even come to shop, but only to stare. They wanted to be among the first to inspect the twentieth century's most modern and most spectacular store. They wanted to share in the latest and, in some respects, culminating triumph of the merchants Filene.

**

By the early 1900s the two brothers had evolved the three basic principles which would govern and guide their retail operations. These principles were permanency, profit, and service.

Permanency came first since it provided the basis for the other two. Both brothers wanted to build an enduring enterprise, one that would continue to serve society--and they firmly believed that a well-run store would serve society--long after they had departed. Both were quite explicit and emphatic on this point.

"It has long been thought," Lincoln later wrote, "that one of the primary duties of a serviceable business is to see to this perpetuation of itself. It is economical to society--and that means all of us--to keep a settled business going; it is costly to society to be forever financing new experiments."

Edward, rather typically, took a more profound perspective. "Business is a public trust... We have no right to build a business upon principles and procedures that will not be valid and workable after we and our sons are dead and disabled." He would further point out that "a businessman is a failure, although he makes millions of dollars, if he creates a business so dependent upon his personal administration that it disintegrates after his death."

Since a business which lost money could not last, profit was essential to permanency. Filene's had to operate in the black. Moreover, the greater its profit, the more it could do. Edward and Lincoln Filene never sought to mask their belief in the legitimacy of maximizing their store's income. On the contrary, they would frankly and freely affirm, to a world that often viewed their innovations and experiments with suspicion and scorn, that such ventures were undertaken primarily to bolster the store's balance sheet.

If sound and secure profits provided the key to permanency, then service supplied the basic and enduring source for profits. Satisfied customers would ensure the health and survival of the Filene store. They adopted as their maxim, "the right goods at the right time in the right quantity and at the right price", and they made every effort to live up to such a standard so that William Filene's Sons would continue to flourish long after the sons had faded from the scene.

***

Permanency meant setting up a sound organizational structure and then staffing it with people who could sustain it. In reviewing their retail operation, they came to the conclusion that its activities naturally divided themselves into four distinct divisions: merchandising, advertising and publicity, administration, and financial control. Such departmentalization seems logical and even obvious today, but at the time it marked still another Filene foray into the yet largely unexplored terrain of retail management. Of particular interest was their separation of the merchandising and advertising functions, for although advertising is part of merchandising, i.e., the buying and selling of goods, Edward in particular insisted on keeping the two separate. This was to prevent the merchandising head from trying to cover up purchases of slowly moving goods by over-advertising them, thus depriving other wares of their rightful share of the advertising budget while concealing mistakes in buying which should be made known.

The brothers grouped all the store's operations into these four basic divisions or, as they called them "pyramids of authority". Many other large stores would later follow the Filene lead in this respect and organize their operations in a similar manner.

Having set up the structure, they now set about finding the staff to head it up. They were looking for four exceptionally able men to serve not just as subordinates but as colleagues and associates. As a subsequent scholarly study of their store would report, "While from the first, the Filenes recognized the necessity of maintaining enough power in the business to give their ideas a fair trial, they saw no merit in monopolizing it. Quite the contrary, they saw serious limitations in doing so... They wanted associates who would compete with and challenge them, not subordinates. They wanted the broadest practical base of abilities on which to build their business."

They further realized that in order to secure such men, and to extract from them the best their abilities afforded, they would have to make them their partners. As Lincoln put it, "Your helper is not a real helper until he is also bound to the risks as well as the gains. If he has a genuine desire for success and something to contribute to it, nothing but a genuine partnership will get it out of him." So the capitalization of the store was increased, the number of shares was expanded, and eventually the number of individual shareholders was increased from two to twenty-two, allowing not only the four division or pyramid heads to own stock in the store, but eighteen lesser executives to do so as well. Furthermore, a certain number of shares were given to the FCA, enabling the employee-run organization to obtain financial support directly and automatically in the form of dividends, without having to request such funds from management.

Gradually, too, a profit-sharing plan came into being covering all executives, buyers, assistant buyers, and other specialists. Since salespeople received commissions, it was felt that they were, in a sense, already included. To be sure, most of the profit was being plowed back into the store, and so the distributions to those employees covered by the plan were fairly meager during these years. However, the brothers believed that since all these employees would benefit from the growth of the business, which would be reflected in increased value for their stock, such a plowing back of profits did them no disservice.

***

The first two division heads the brothers appointed were Thomas K. Cory and John R. Simpson. Both were long-time employees whom they had developed into capable executives. Carey, a chunky and affable man, was put in charge of store administration. His nickname was "Dan," but many employees called him 'Dad" because of his benevolently paternal attitude. Simpson, longer, leaner, and more suave than Carey or, for that matter, than Edward or Lincoln, became advertising and publicity head. As an urbane Yankee, he functioned well as Filene's outside man.

A later and, as it would turn out, more important appointment came in 1906 when Edward J. Frost was named chief finance officer. Orphaned at the age of 9, Frost and his younger brother had been raised by an aunt who had given up her school teaching job to take care of them. By the age of 12, Edward Frost had become the breadwinner for this struggling household, working as a janitor and errand boy in a local bank. He nevertheless managed to finish high school in his spare time. A devout Protestant, he had by the age of 18 also become superintendent of his church's Sunday school.

In demeanor Frost often seemed the stereotype of a finance man-- humorless, austere, and skeptical of costly experiments. As he would later say, "No business can be successful without one top-level son-of- a bitch and I'm the son-of-a-bitch here."

Although, as might be expected, Frost never became amiable to or even appreciative of Edward, he did develop a strong, lifelong loyalty to Lincoln, who found his facility with figures helpful to him personally as well as beneficial to the store. That Frost would maintain a lifelong membership in a country club where Lincoln, as a Jew, could not even enter as a guest, apparently never struck either of them as odd.

By far the most important as well as interesting appointment came in 1911 when Louis E. Kirstein took over the last remaining pyramid, that of merchandising. A great gorilla of a man who could polish off an omelette consisting of two full-sized lobsters, he had had an unusual life for a Jewish clothing merchant. It included, among other things, a stint at playing professional baseball.

Born in Rochester, New York in 1867, Kirstein was the son of an optical goods dealer. Although his family was far from poor, he had celebrated his 16th birthday by running away from home, choosing to see the country by riding the rails as a hobo.

His most notable experience occurred in St. Louis, where he earned his keep working as a janitor in a brothel. While trying to earn some money on the side by selling a fraudulent patent medicine, he was arrested and fined five dollars. When the judge gave him a few hours to try to raise the money, Kirstein had immediately gone to the local rabbi, only to be turned down. He then went to the madam who employed him. The woman, who had lost an eye in a fight with one of her girls, cheerfully advanced him the sum. The incident made a deep impression on Kirstein, who, in relating the story years later, liked to point out that he had found a one-eyed whore to be more charitable than a man of God. The woman, he said, saved him from the life of crime he would have inevitably followed had he gone to jail.

He eventually returned to Rochester where, after playing some professional baseball and then managing a semi-pro team, he met and married Rose Stein, the daughter of a prominent men's clothing manufacturer. His in-laws frowned on the marriage but reluctantly took him into the family firm.

From the start Kirstein showed an exceptional flair for the clothing business. He also proved to be adept or lucky in investing his money. When, for example, Ben Forman, his wife's semi-literate tailor, wanted to start his own clothing company, Kirstein, at his wife's urging, loaned Forman $10,000. Forman's firm became a speedy success and soon Kirstein was receiving his $10,000 back every year as a return on his original investment.

Louis Kirstein was thus a well-established and quite wealthy man when Lincoln met him in 1907. The two took an immediate liking to each other. Since Filene's at the time was planning to start a men's clothing line, and since the position of merchandising head had still not been filled, Lincoln offered him the position and begged him to take it. Inasmuch as Kirstein was not getting along with his brothers-in-law in the family's business, he was tempted. However, he first made sure that Filene's was on a firm financial footing and then insisted on a chance to buy heavily into the business which so badly wanted his services. Negotiations dragged on for two years, but eventually provisions were worked out allowing him to invest $250,000 in preferred, nonvoting stock. He was also promised an opportunity to acquire some of the common or voting stock at a later date. Finally satisfied, Louis Kirstein became the fourth and final member of the top-level Filene management team.

The hiring of Kirstein was largely Lincoln's doing. Edward at the time was heavily involved in other activities and took little part in the whole matter. He would have cause later to deeply and bitterly regret his failure to do so, for Louis Kirstein would be instrumental in dealing Edward the most agonizing blow he would ever suffer in either his private or public career.

The four pyramid heads and the two brothers made up a management board which decided all major store policies. "Under the forms of our organization," said Lincoln later, "no direct order is given in our business to our partners by my brother or myself." This particular policy was undoubtedly easier for Lincoln to follow than for Edward, although the latter, at least initially, sought to adhere to it. At the same time, the two brothers continued their own practice of swapping the positions of president and general manager. They also continued to share the same office, sitting back-to-back, taking separate offices only when the new store opened.

One policy which the brothers had previously adopted, and which their partners had accepted, was a strict rule against nepotism. Family members of the partners were not to become employees. Admittedly, this rule posed few problems for Edward and Lincoln, since neither seemed likely to have any sons to bring into the business. Yet its adoption was motivated by their desire to make their store a permanent institution. Both had seen too many businesses disintegrate when the original founders turned them over to their own children. Thus, in later years, when Kirstein's younger son George showed a distinct knack for retailing, he went to New York to make his career. So would one of Lincoln's sons-in-law, who would later become president of the largest store in Providence, Rhode Island. The prohibition against nepotism was inflexibly and universally applied.

To groom younger executives for succession to the management board, and also to lighten some of its burdens, the board set up what it called the Operating Committee. This committee was made up of the partners' own top-level subordinates. It handled most of the details of implementing the management board's decisions. "The expectation," as Lincoln later explained it, "was that in placing them next to the practical issues of the whole business, they would learn the principles and practices that guide it, and while they thus learned under our eyes, we had a constant opportunity of judging their ability."

The whole thrust, then, of the Filene operational style was to secure the best people and develop their abilities to the utmost. As Lincoln bluntly put it, "I always believed that if the store had the right people it would grow, and if it didn't have the right people, it wouldn't grow."

This concern for employee development was not confined to the level of upper management. It colored and conditioned the brothers' attitude to their entire staff. Out of it would come the innovations which during this period would make their Boston clothing store a world leader in the emerging field of human organization.

When we last viewed the store's employee relations activities, we saw Edward and Lincoln setting up a board of arbitration to decide whether a cashier should be penalized for a shortage in her accounts as noted. The board found in favor of the cashier, and the brothers not only accepted the finding but decided to make permanent use of such a dispute-handling device. Henceforth any employee assessed a penalty for shortages, breakage, or damage could appeal to an arbitration panel.

Gradually, the board's membership was increased and its jurisdiction extended. It became the final arbiter in all kinds of disciplinary matters, including dismissal. This bold and unprecedented step set a new standard in American business practice.

The question then arose as to whether the board could challenge and overturn any of the store's rules and regulations. What should they do, asked some of the board members, if, in adjudicating a conflict between employee and employer, they found that the rule the employee was accused of breaking was itself unjust? Edward agreed that this presented a problem, but he pointed out that giving the Board power to change or challenge such a rule would trample on the powers and prerogatives of the Filene Cooperative Association itself. When it came to dealing with store policies, he said, the entire employee membership should decide.

The Board saw the logic of his argument and agreed. So the power to change any store rule was given to the FCA membership, with the Arbitration Board having the right to suspend any rule it deemed unjust pending FCA action.

By this time, a written FCA constitution had come into being to incorporate and formalize this rather startling devolution of managerial authority. The constitution was drafted by Brandeis, who had become and who would remain an enthusiastic backer of the Filene experiment.

"The Filene Cooperative Association," wrote Brandeis in the constitution's preamble, "is established to give its members a voice in their government, to increase their efficiency and add to their social opportunities, to create and sustain a just and equitable relation between employee and employer." This was certainly a tall order, but the Brandeis document detailed how it was to be filled.

Every store employee would become a provisional member of the FCA immediately on joining the store's payroll. Full-fledged membership would go into effect automatically after 90 days. There were to be no dues or other restrictions or qualifications for membership.

The members would elect an executive council of 18, one from each department or unit of the store. The FCA's new charter provided for management to appoint the council's executive secretary since this officeholder would serve as management's liaison with the Board. But even here the council usually ended up nominating its own candidate, and management almost invariably went along.

In the words of the charter, "the Council shall have the power to initiate, amend or cancel any store rule affecting the discipline, work, or conditions of work of employees." To be sure, implementation of such a major step would not be easy, yet it definitely could be done. What was required initially was a two-thirds vote of the employees. Management would then have 48 hours to veto their action, but such a veto could be overridden by a second two-thirds vote. The brothers were a bit uneasy over going this far, but eventually decided to do so. As it developed, this provision would never create any serious problems.

Each of the store's eighteen subunits was also to elect a member to the panel of arbitrators. As each case came up, names would be drawn from a hat of those who were to judge it. As a result, no grievant would ever know in advance just who would sit on his or her particular case. Also, there would always be enough members around to constitute a twelve-member hearing panel. Service on the Arbitration Board was limited to one year.

The employee arbitrators were given the right to "hear, determine and have final jurisdiction over grievances or disputes and working conditions..." Management would appear before them only as a defendant, usually in the person of the store's personnel director. No witness appearing before the Board could have his character or credibility impugned. The deliberations and votes of all arbitrators were to remain secret.

The machinery of the great Filene experiment in employee participation was now in place.

During these initial years and, in fact, as long as it lasted, this machinery worked quite well. Employee involvement reached a level unparalleled in any other successful business and attracted attention from all over the Western world. Observers from Europe joined those from various parts of the United States in coming to Boston to observe the Filene experiment at work.

In its first three years of operation, the Board of Arbitration heard 85 cases. Of these, it favored the employee in 42 and management in 31. In the remaining 12 cases, it arranged a compromise.

Many of the appeals brought before the Board did not involve major problems except to the employee involved. Not atypical was the petition of R. M. Jackson, the store's sign painter. The store had started giving prizes to employees who could spot errors in either its advertisements or signs. Jackson found this upsetting and unfair. In a scrawled plea for justice, the irate sign painter protested that he was under great pressure. He had no office of his own but had to work in the shipping and supply room which, he claimed, was one of the noisiest places in the building. What's more, he was also being constantly badgered with questions by those entering or leaving. "My room is a Bureau of Information," he groaned. He further pointed out that much of the copy he was sent had errors in it already, that he had no college education, and that, unlike the advertising people, he had no proofreaders to check his work. It was therefore unfair to embarrass him by offering prizes to those spotting errors in his work.

The Board promptly agreed and management stopped rewarding employees for reporting mistakes in Mr. Jackson's signs.

Not all the cases represented such easy-to-resolve issues as those posed in the above incident. Especially sensitive were those involving employee dismissals. But even in these the Filenes found they had nothing to fear as long as the store could present a full and fair case. Of the six dismissals appealed during the Board's first two years, the employee arbitrators upheld management in five. In the one they lost, the brothers readily acquiesced and reinstated the discharged employee.

Holding hearings and airing charges and countercharges in themselves often produced a salutary effect. One man who was fired for being lazy and incompetent appealed to the Board, but as he heard his case discussed, he began to see it in a new light. He persuaded management to give him another chance and promptly became one of the store's most capable and loyal employees. In fact, he eventually won election to the Arbitration Board himself. Other dismissed employees petitioned only to seek vindication and to clear their record. The store regarded this as quite right, for as Lincoln like to say, "No employee has left us with the complaint that he had appealed to the established machinery for justice and been refused."[8]

As the Board continued to function, it elicited increased attention and approval from those within and outside the store. One anonymous jurist (possibly Brandeis) who went over its records in later years compared it favorably to a court of law. "Here," he wrote, "there was nothing but an earnest, and yet not too tragic, endeavor to turn up the truth, all of it, let it hit where it would. There was no jockeying, no sophistry by attorneys; no browbeating of witnesses; there were no personalities, no impugning of character." Long before the U.S.Supreme Court began extending due process of law to the states, the Filenes had begun extending it to their own employees.

Giving their employees the right to sit in judgment over them in deciding employee grievances represented a significant and probably unprecedented conferral of power. But giving them the right to change store rules and policies went even further. In effect, the Filenes were placing their business in their employees' hands. How would these sales clerks, shipping clerks, elevator operators, etc. respond? What would they do?

The first move to utilize this authority came in June of 1902. The Fourth of July would fall on a Friday that summer and some employees began calling for the store to close on Saturday as well, thus giving them three full days of rest. Since this was the era of the six-day week, such a move could be considered a substantial step. When the FCA voted for the Saturday shutdown, the Filenes contacted the other major Boston stores to see if they would follow suit. They all stoutly refused to do so. To their fellow merchants it was not just a case of foregoing a day's business but of spoiling their own employees. They were aghast at the Filenes for even considering such a measure.

Edward and Lincoln briefly mulled over the situation and then agreed to do what their employees wanted. Filene's would be closed for business on Saturday, July 5. Surprised and grateful, the FCA voted at its next meeting to thank management for deferring to its wishes, but one of the brothers who was present--it was probably Edward--suggested amending the motion to read, "Thanks for the system which made the vote possible."

During this time, the FCA had also been preparing to launch its own newspaper. *The Echo* made its debut on July 1. The new employee organ heralded its organization's fresh triumph in a front page report. "The Association recently voted to make July 5th a holiday," said the newspaper, "thus giving us a chance for three days of recreation. Our house then asked the other houses to join us before we advertised the same, in order to give them an equal chance in the matter, but all refused, so we shall stand alone." And stand alone it did as downtown shoppers on July 5 found the city's largest clothing store closed.

The issue of closing hours continued to dominate the FCA's deliberations when it came to invoking the organization's rule-changing power. It had become customary for downtown stores to shorten their hours during the summer, resuming their regular schedule in mid-September. But in 1903 one FCA member moved to extend Filene's summer schedule to October First.

The motion provoked a heated debate at the meeting called to discuss it. For if it meant 13 hours less work a year for the average employee, it meant approximately one and a half less days a year for the store to do business.

During the heat of the debate a senior executive blurted out, "I want to warn you people that the way you vote here will have a decisive importance on your future as far as the store is concerned." Edward, who has been listening but not participating in the discussion, immediately rose to his feet. He assured the assembled members that no vote which they would ever cast at their meetings would have the slightest influence on their careers in the store. He was certain, he said, that the previous speaker has not intended to threaten them personally but had only wished to suggest that extending the summer schedule would weaken the store and this would eventually harm them all.

In speaking as he did, Edward showed that he could on occasion be a smooth diplomat. His remarks conveyed the message to his workforce that they could and should vote as they pleased without fear of reprisals from management. At the same time, he saved the face of the executive who had raised the issue by deliberately misinterpreting what the fellow had said.

Edward went on to say that while he had not studied the extension of the schedule, he was willing to give it sympathetic consideration. He did not know but what the loss, measured in terms of sales lost when the store was closed, might not be offset by the good will and favorable publicity which this pioneering step might bring.

These ruminations brought store manager E. A. Cory into the fray. Taking the floor, Cory proceeded to take exception to what his boss was saying. "I'd like to see E. A. bring some facts and figures to support his point that the advertising that would come from closing the store early would make up for loss of sales. I'd like to see it figured in dollars and cents," said Cory.

Edward handled this statement diplomatically as well. He pointed out that he had not thought the matter through but had merely suggested that such publicity might compensate for the loss. The FCA finally decided to adopt the proposal and Filene management extended the shortened schedule until October First.

Starting the summer schedule earlier or extending it into the fall continued to preoccupy the FCA for the next few years. But the employees often showed a surprising sensitivity to management's concerns. In part, of course, management's concerns were directly their concerns since many were sales personnel who depended on commissions as well as salary to support themselves, and closing when other stores remained open had an immediate impact on their pocketbooks. Consequently, the following spring some 80 FCA members petitioned to have the store's summer schedule brought in line with that of the other downtown stores. The membership approved this move, although they did vote to close on the Saturday after Bunker Hill Day, which that year fell on a Friday.

In 1904 another effort was made to extend the summer schedule, this time by starting it earlier. The motion was carried and implemented, only to be rescinded by the employees themselves the following year.

Still more surprising than this conservative approach by the employees with regard to shorter hours was their general reluctance to tamper with other store regulations. Although the Filenes had pledged themselves in writing to heed their employees' requests in all such matters, no requests other than changes in closing hours were ever made.

***

While Filene employees showed no particular zeal for overturning management policies, they did demonstrate a remarkable zest for utilizing other opportunities which their new charter provided. Soon their organization was sponsoring a wide variety of self-help and recreational programs. These included a band, a theater group, a dance group, and many others. A girls' club was formed to assist its members primarily in matters of personal hygiene, and before too long found itself undertaking other activities as well. And when some of its members felt they had outgrown it, they organized a women's club whose stated purpose was "to provide for the women of the store an opportunity for an exchange of ideas and to promote individual efficiency and group spirit." Later a men's club was launched.

Edward and Lincoln welcomed and encouraged these initiatives. They provided the FCA with club rooms and office space, purchased advertising space in *The Echo*, and bought rows of tickets to the "Filene Follies" and other employee-organized events. Clara also helped by giving the employee organization dishes and furniture and sending in a check from time to time. But generally, management sought to make their assistance as indirect as possible so as to avoid the taint of paternalism. Such an approach had become a near obsession with Lincoln, who liked to refer to the store's entire staff as "my work associates."

Lincoln had learned his lesson regarding the perils of paternalism when he set up a medical clinic staffed with a part-time doctor and a full-time nurse. As we saw earlier, most of the Filene workforce boycotted the facility, fearing that any health problems they might have would be reported to management. Only by getting the FCA involved in its operation, as well as agreeing to keep no medical records on any employee, did the clinic finally catch on. (Eventually, it would employ three full-time nurses and service about 200 employees a day.)

Edward summed up the attitude of both brothers when, in speaking at an FCA dinner in 1904, he acknowledged that "in the beginning we tried to do the work for our people under well-meant but still despotically benevolent principles. But grown wiser and more democratic by our failures, we agreed to do nothing for our people, but to try to help them with all our minds and strength to do everything for themselves."

As noted earlier, Filene's pioneering labor policies had begun to attract attention and acclaim throughout America and Europe. Numerous articles had appeared in magazines concerning the brothers and their unique store, and many professional and amateur sociologists had arrived at their offices eager to observe the Filene phenomenon in action. Most of the articles published were laudatory and most of the observers were impressed. Most, but not all. Some of those who examined the store's operations felt otherwise.

Many of their fellow merchants viewed the Filene brothers, especially Edward, as crackpots whose experiments were not just silly but even dangerous since they might encourage their own employees to seek similar reforms. Such criticism did not greatly bother the brothers, for they knew that their efforts were not only paying off in terms of growing profits but were eliciting warm approval and applause from some of the country's more progressive thinkers and leaders.

That some of their own employees shared their competitors' skepticism, however, disturbed the brothers much more. Edward, for example, was terribly hurt when he heard that an observer who asked an employee about the FCA had elicited the answer, "Oh, some fad of Mr. Filene's." Still, most of the employees, as judged from their participation in FCA activities, seemed to take a more positive view of the Filene fad.

Other criticism came from the Left. The brothers were accused of using the FCA to manipulate their workers and divert them from joining militant trade unions. According to this view, the store's labor relations program amounted to a counter-revolutionary sham. As might be expected, Edward was especially sensitive to such attacks. At an FCA meeting in 1906, he suddenly blurted out, "How many of you realize that men and women all over the country, whose opinions are worthwhile, charge my brother and myself with insincerity and with lack of decency in this FCA work?"

A more benign and constructive critic was Frank Parsons, a popular lecturer, economist, and advocate of worker participation. In a letter to Edward, in which he addressed him as "My dear Co-operator," Parsons raised two quite pertinent points. First, he felt that employees should be given representation on the firm's board of directors; second, he felt that the firm should plow less of its profits back into the business so that more could be distributed to the employees.

The brothers were not unsympathetic to the points Parsons raised. But regarding the plowback of profits, they felt that this enabled the employees to share some of the risks, along with the rewards, which the greater profits generated through the store's expansion would create in the future. The policy of plowing back profits to finance growth would encourage employees to stay with the store and help make its expansion plans succeed.

As to having employees on the board of directors, they had given a good deal of thought to the idea and felt it should some day be done. But that day was not now, since the store's workers had evinced little desire for or interest in such representation. As we have seen, the employees were far from eager to change store policies or to suggest new ones. This was actually a source of sadness to the brothers, who insisted that they were willing to give their "work-associates" as much responsibility as the latter would accept. They were even willing to make arrangements to turn the entire business over to the employees if they really wanted it. The trouble was they did not seem to want it.

One outsider who had a chance to see and experience this situation first-hand was Lincoln Steffens. During his stay in Boston, Steffens happened to glance at an issue of *The Echo* and saw a front-page article written by Edward. In his piece Edward was taking his employees to task. But he was doing so not because they were demanding too much but because they were demanding too little! We have granted you enough power to take over the store and run it yourselves, lamented Edward, and all you have done with it is to secure a few petty benefits such as shorter hours and an occasional half holiday.

Steffens read the article with amazement. "Do you really mean it, E. A.?" he asked. Assured that he did, Steffens then asked to address the employees and Edward brought him to the next FCA meeting.

The journalist began his talk by entertaining them with stories of the political scandals he had unearthed in various American cities, including Boston. He then proceeded to tie this problem to their situation in the store. The real fault, said Steffens, lay in the refusal of intelligent, well-meaning citizens to use the power they possessed to do things better.

Pointing to Edward, who was sitting in the front row, Steffens said, "There he sits. He will stop me if I say anything untrue. He asked me to come here and see if I could not lead you to see the chance you have to take and govern this great business. He says he can't make you believe it. He says that he, the boss, is a democrat and that you, the workers, are not; that you want to be bossed; that all you want is a little more pay and a little more time to play. I say that you here are a fair test of democracy and that if you don't want to take over this offered shop, it means that the people don't want to govern their cities, states and--themselves."

Steffens stopped, awaiting the response. It took the form of a thundering silence, for no one spoke. Thinking that Edward's presence may have intimidated some of his hearers, he asked Edward to leave the room. Edward did so, but again no one rushed to seize the bait Steffens had flung to them. The silence continued.

Afterwards the dumbfounded Steffens and the downcast Edward discussed the situation. The journalist suggested hiring some professional agitators to stir the workers up. The businessman replied that the store already had some. "They do not agitate for power; it is they who start the demands for petty privileges."

***

For the Filene firm overall, the early 1900s were years of enormous expansion and growth. In the spring of 1901, the store moved from 445 to 453-63 Washington Street, a shift that tripled its selling floor space. Two years later the Filenes re-leased 445 Washington Street for a new "Baby-to-Miss" annex. Only a music store separated the annex from the main store, and the following year Filene's took over this store as well. Walls were taken down and the three buildings became in effect one. Still more space, including an office in Paris, was leased in succeeding years as the store's offerings and clientele continued to increase.

Sales, as might be expected, fully matched this growth. They passed the half-million-dollar mark in 1900 and swept well beyond the million-dollar level two years later. By 1906 they exceeded $2-1/2 million, representing a fivefold increase in just six years. During the same period, the gross income of R. H. Macy in New York and

Marshall Field in Chicago, America's two leading department stores, had only doubled.

The following year, a depression slowed down business activity throughout the country, but William Filene's Sons kept on growing. By 1912 Filene's, with a payroll of 900, had become the largest clothing store in the world, as well as one of the largest stores of any kind in the country. Its annual sales, which were now approaching five million dollars a year,, had increased by nearly 1,000% in just twelve years. The "crackpot" brothers seemed to have hit a jackpot.

While much of the store's success can be attributed to the policies and programs already mentioned, other, though not unrelated, factors also contributed.

One of these was the store's training program. In a sense, it began on Christmas Eve, 1902, when Edward, exhausted at the end of another hectic Christmas selling season, expressed dissatisfaction with the amount of time the store's management had to spend correcting the same mistakes over and over again. Out of his complaint evolved the first employee training program in American retailing. Initially made a part of the welfare director's duties, its topsy-like growth soon prompted management to make it a separate department with its own director.

The early classes were simple affairs, consisting largely of short talks on textiles, store policies, etc. But the appointment of a dynamic new Education Director named Ernest Hopkins in 1909 brought some explosive changes. With Edward and Lincoln's encouragement, Hopkins organized systematic courses in various retailing subjects which employees could take during business hours, that is, on the company's time. The courses were open to any member of the workforce, so that a stock boy who wanted to go into selling or a clerk who aspired to become a buyer could enroll.

The training program as it evolved thus offered a convenient ladder for able and ambitious employees who wanted to rise. And rise they did. Many women took advantage of the training to become buyers and even executives, with the result that many began earning "thousands of dollars a year." These were quite unusual earnings for members of their sex at that time.

While opening up unique opportunities for their own employees to work their way up, the store also began recruiting outside employees from among the rising ranks of college graduates. Many other Boston store owners laughed at the idea, saying the Filenes were trying to turn their personnel into a "bunch of college professors." But the brothers characteristically ignored the taunts and, as with so many other of their innovations, they would live to see the other stores eventually follow in their footsteps. Hopkins would later leave Filene's to become president of Dartmouth College, but the policy of recruiting college graduates would remain a fixture of the Filene system.

Meanwhile, the systems approach which Edward had inaugurated in the 1890s was also expanded and refined. By 1912, the store had been divided into numerous subunits, each of which was required to fill out daily forms on actual sales, sales to date for the month and year, stock on hand, and so forth. All told, the subunit heads had to fill in 28 columns of data on every selling day. Each fashion department was set up as an individual shop, and in its ads the firm often described itself as a "store of shops". A half century later, many smart stores in New York would come around to adopting a somewhat similar approach.

Since Edward was an early believer in planning, each of the four basic divisions was required to work out six-month plans listing in detail its projected costs and accomplishments. Here too the store was blazing a trail that others would eventually follow. Such, or similar, procedures would become common business practice a generation or so later.

In the fall of 1911 Filene's began placing advertisements in local newspapers offering five dollars--a far from insignificant sum in those days--to anyone other than one of its own employees who could spot a piece of merchandise being sold at a lower price by any other Boston store. During the ad campaign's first two and a half years, the store made only seven such awards. This indicates its success in keeping its prices down while giving its customers above-average service and its employees above-average salaries and other benefits.

Nevertheless, Edward was far from satisfied. The high costs of distributing goods disturbed him. Of each dollar received by Filene's or any other store, 55 cents was on the average absorbed by the store itself and only 45 cents went to the manufacturer. "This is disgraceful," he had told Lincoln Steffens. "I would like to lower that percentage."

Of especial concern to Edward was the vast amount of goods that were wasted. Perfectly sound items that people could use were often thrown away thanks to minor imperfections in their manufacture or an oversupply in their markets, or for some other reason. He once bemoaned to Steffens how a piano manufacturer had recently destroyed a batch of pianos which had turned out to be non-saleable. Surely, he complained, there must be some way to stop such wanton waste.

In pondering the problem, Edward eventually came up with a solution. It would become his best-known, though by no means his most important, innovation.

Bargain basements were already quite common in the early 1900s, but the one Edward conceived would be quite different. For one thing, it would, in conformity with Filene's overall decentralized system, have its own buyers. They would scour not just the country but the world, looking for distressed merchandise which could be obtained and sold at well below its customary price. As a further enticement to manufacturers and wholesalers to sell such goods at bargain prices, the buyers were authorized to offer cash payments within 48 hours.

But it was what would happen to the goods once they were on the store's shelves that would spell out the real difference between the bargain basement Edward had in mind and those of other stores. Each item would be tagged not just with its price, which would always be at least 10 percent below what any other store was selling it for, but also the date it was put on sale. If it remained unsold after 12 days, its price would be lowered by 25 percent. If after six more days it still had not sold, the price would come down another 25 percent. Six more days on the shelf would bring still another 25 percent reduction. Finally, if it had not found a buyer at the end of 30 days, it would be given away to charity.

Edward's unprecedented, indeed, unheard of scheme, like so many of his other innovations, initially provoked a good deal of doubt and derision. Many retailers sneered at his new brainstorm, dubbing it Filene's Folly. They reasoned that customers would simply wait for the wares they wanted to reach their bottom price before buying. What they failed to see was the danger inherent in doing so. Filene's new bargain basement would function as a reverse auction, and, as with any auction, hesitation could prove fatal. A would-be purchaser waiting for the price of a wanted item to be reduced ran the risk of losing it altogether. Shopping in Filene's Basement would be a bit of a gamble.

Called the Tunnel Bargain Basement because it was connected with the station of a new subway line which ran under the store, Edward's new adventure in merchandising was launched on January 4, 1909. The store took out large ads in the local press to announce its advent. "A new kind of store! The new Tunnel Bargain Basement opens Tomorrow!" So their headlines heralded. In the body of the ads the store spelled out the markdown features while assuring customers that the goods being offered still carried "the Filene Guarantee." The merchandise would consist of manufacturers' surplus, discontinued lines, odds and ends, including "seconds," but "nothing will be bought for or sold in this new store that is not up to our standard." Filene's had from William's day built a reputation for quality, and the brothers did not intend to let any false notion regarding their new venture destroy it.

Pursuant to this end, the basement sought to persuade its suppliers to let it retain the supplier's original label. The customer could then see the provenance of the article he or she was interested in. At the same time, the store promised that it would indicate clearly whether the garment was a second or irregular while still affirming that it harbored no defect which would affect its wearability.

As a further aid in holding down prices, the basement offered as little service as possible. Everything was done to enable the customers to wait on themselves. Alterations, gift wrapping, charge accounts, elevator service, free delivery --none of these was provided and only a few fitting rooms were set aside for customers. But the key to the basement's operation lay in the scheduled markdowns. Edward knew that such automatic price reductions would not be easy to carry out on schedule because of the reluctance by buyers to admit their errors. So the store began offering prizes to customers who could spot an item that had remained at its original price beyond the expiration date. With such an inducement, the markdowns generally occurred on schedule and the new "store" functioned well.

It was not, however, immediately profitable. Despite its attractiveness and uniqueness, the basement operated in the red for several years. However, accounting, as anyone knows who has investigated it, is far from the cut-and-dried operation that it seems to most outsiders. Technically, the basement may have lost money during these years, but how can one figure its contribution to that hard-to-pinpoint but very real asset called "good will"? The Automatic Bargain Basement, as it came to be known, generated a lot of publicity, brought many new customers into the Filene building, and facilitated and improved the store's contacts with manufacturers, wholesalers, and even other retailers, many of whom found they could use the basement as a convenient dumping ground. Perhaps more creative or sophisticated accountants than the store then employed would have found it to be a profitable venture from the start.

In any case, the failure of the basement to show a bookkeeping profit did not deter the Filenes from seeking to expand and enhance its operations. They retained their faith in the concept, though probably not even Edward anticipated that it would one day be the biggest money-maker in the entire Filene operation.

One major boost to the basement's later growth and development came in 1912 when a young Yale graduate named Harold Hodgkinson joined the Filene staff. Hodgkinson had studied engineering in college but had decided to become a newspaperman instead. Unfortunately (rather fortunately, as it turned out), he wrote poorly and the first editor he worked for had finally fired him. Aware of the young man's basic capabilities, however, his boss had suggested that Hodgkinson go to Boston to seek a job with the up-and-coming Filene's store.

Edward was recovering from the flu when Hodgkinson came to town, but the enterprising young man located his home address and knocked on the door. He told the housekeeper that he was from the Associated Press. The increasingly publicity-conscious Edward, on hearing this, immediately called for Hodgkinson to come in. He soon found a gangly, six foot-three-inch fellow with protruding front teeth standing over him.

With the Filene knack for picking winners, Edward sensed almost right away that the unprepossessing-looking young man had something to offer. More amused than angered at the questionable ploy the young man had used to gain entrance--Hodgkinson had after all worked for the Associated Press and so, in a sense, he was "from the A.P."--Edward sent him up to the store's personnel director. Hodgkinson's first job was to sort out overshoes in the basement. He would spend the next thirty years with the basement store, helping to pilot it into profitability and eventually piloting himself into the Filene presidency.[9]

***

By the end of the decade Filene's was again experiencing growing pains. Despite its amalgamation of three leased buildings and some other rental space, it desperately needed more room. The brothers decided that it was time to erect their own building.

The site they settled on was an area bounded by Washington, Summer, and Hawley Streets. The land involved was all in the hands of one family, but the site was occupied by fifteen different structures with nearly 25 separate occupants. All of them were under leases, and many of these leases had many years to run.

Negotiations to clear and lease the land for their store went on for two years. Finally, the other occupants were compensated and moved, and in February 1912 construction of the Filene building got underway.

To design their new structure the Filenes had called on Daniel Burnham, the country's premier architect, who was known almost as much for his famous maxim, "make no little plans" as he was for his architectural creations. It would be Burnham's last project, for he would die before its completion. Nevertheless, his design would be fully fulfilled.

Buyers were sent around the world to bring back fetching merchandise with which to stock the structure, while construction at home proceeded apace. In digging out the site, workers unearthed an unknown graveyard containing 23 skeletons. Otherwise the work proceeded according to plan, and by September it was ready. It cost seven million dollars, which translates into over 100 million 1995 dollars, but its eight floors, basement and sub-basement gave the firm five times as much selling space as their former quarters, plus ample room for offices, FCA activities, employee and customer restaurants, etc. Thirteen elevators stood ready to carry as many as 10,000 customers an hour.

The huge throng of sightseers who showed up on opening day found it to be all they expected, and more. A giant doorman stood ready to usher them in, and once inside they could inspect the new water curtain--a progenitor of the sprinkler system--gaze at the 17 models parading in fashionable new gowns, and breathe air that was ventilated every six minutes. This marvel of modern merchandising, whose various departments were all arranged as separate shops, would draw nearly three-quarters of a million people, more than the entire population of Boston, during its first week.

Retailing experts were also impressed. One commentator called it a veritable "temple of commerce," while a prominent business magazine noted how, with its Italian Renaissance motif, "the building has a peculiar effect of dignity and orderly beauty, yet it has nothing of the solid heaviness that characterizes many other structures devoted to a similar use."

And so, with a precedent-setting structure to house their pioneering enterprise, Edward and Lincoln, now 52 and 47 respectively, could face the future with confidence and hope, unaware that their most severe strains and stresses lay ahead.

Edward Filene and Roy Bergengren (Courtesy, Research Division, Boston Public Library).

Lincoln Filene (Courtesy, Research Division, Boston Public Library).

Harold Hodgkinson (Courtesy, Research Division, Boston Public Library).

Edward Frost (Courtesy, Research Division, Boston Public Library).

Louis Kirstein (Courtesy, Research Division, Boston Public Library).

**Edward Filene and Dorothy Warner, sister-in-law- of Robert Moore.
The Boston merchant met the 28-year old widow on a ship bound for
Europe in 1924.**

Chapter 7
EDWARD: SEEDLING STATESMAN

1911

As the year drew to a close, America's politicians were preparing for an important presidential election. It was with this in mind that on December 28, Senator William Gibbs McAdoo, a leading member of the Senate as well as of the Democratic Party, wrote a letter to his party's prospective presidential candidate, Governor W. Woodrow Wilson of New Jersey, saying, in part,

"Mr. Filene of Boston (a very prominent merchant over there and one who stands high and is an admirer of yours) feels hurt because he sent you an invitation some weeks ago to speak in Boston on one of several occasions, and that he never had a reply. He is going to send another invitation. Before you decline it, I wish you would let me speak to you about it."

As McAdoo's letter indicates, Edward had achieved a measure of national prominence. As the letter further indicates, Edward wanted to use this prominence to help elect the next President of the United States.

***

Edward's entrance into national politics actually occurred some four years earlier when he returned from his round-the-world tour. He had hardly re-established himself in Filene's presidential suite when he wrote an article for the Boston American on U.S. policy toward the Philippines. Under the title "We Must Rule the Philippines Until They Are Educated," he argued against granting the Islands immediate independence for such a step would leave their mostly impoverished inhabitants at the mercy of a despotic dictatorship imposed by their own elite class. The U.S. had already done more for the Filipinos in ten years than their native leaders had ever done for them, said Edward, and we should continue to govern the islands until they were ready for self-rule.

Edward's point of view did not set well with doctrinaire anti-imperialists, many of whom had been his allies on previous domestic issues. But his views in this instance, as on most other such issues he would later confront, were based on strictly pragmatic grounds. He did believe in home rule for Mexico and Ireland, and a few years later he would even go to Ireland to attend a convention called by Lady Aberdeen to further Irish independence.

As it so happens, 1907 was, like 1911, also a pre-presidential election year, and a few weeks after Edward's return, William Howard Taft, the prospective presidential candidate of the Republican Party and a former governor of the Philippines came to Boston to speak to the local merchants association. Edward met with Taft and the two discussed the Islands as well as other matters including the Filene store. Taft showed an interest in Edward's ideas for the country's new colony and requested more information which Edward gladly sent him. Taft in turn sent back a copy of his own report on the Philippines which he had drafted some years earlier.

In the meantime, Edward had already begun to communicate his various ideas, including the earlier mentioned suggestion for Credit Unions, to President Theodore Roosevelt. As we have seen, he received a rather perfunctory reply, expressing interest and gratitude but no more. With an election in the offing, the President apparently had other things on his mind.

But in May, Edward wrote Roosevelt again, this time on a completely different matter. Reports had begun circulating that the often bold and brash president was considering another bold and brash move: naming Louis Brandeis to be America's first Jewish cabinet member. Edward quickly dispatched a letter to the White House giving Brandeis his enthusiastic endorsement. On May 28 Roosevelt wrote back, saying "I thank you for your letter about Mr. Brandeis. I believe in him; and I am particularly pleased to get what you say."

Edward, meanwhile, had already initiated contact with Lincoln Steffens, and while trying to persuade him to come to Boston he also sought to have him put in a word in Brandeis' behalf. Steffens had gotten to know Roosevelt through covering the president's stormy career as a New York police commissioner many years before, but Edward, in soliciting the muckraker's support for a Brandeis appointment, only showed that he still failed to understand the proper role and functions of a journalist. Steffens replied that what Edward had requested "isn't the thing I can do, not and write as I do about

Roosevelt, Taft et. al." He also thought it would be a pity to remove Brandeis from Boston where he had accomplished so much, though he admitted that "he would make a corking good cabinet officer." The appointment never materialized.

It was through Steffens that Edward two years later made his first contribution to a national political figure. This was a $100 dollar donation to the campaign fund of Robert La Follette, the Wisconsin Senator who had become an outspoken opponent of the trusts and , so it seemed, of big business generally. Edward sent the check to Steffens in June, 1910, asking that it be listed simply as "from a friend." (Campaign laws did not then require that contributors be listed by name.)

That Edward would support a Senator who seemed so hostile to business does not mean that he himself had lost faith in capitalism. Although he felt that some of the activities and antics of the big businessmen of his day were undermining the system, the system itself, he believed, was still far superior to socialism. Writing to Steffens from Europe two months later, Edward spoke of the government-run railroads as "wasteful to an extraordinary degree of peoples time--except the rich who can afford the comparatively few fast cars--and serve the masses very badly as to light in the cars, etc..." At the same time, he demonstrated a flexible outlook that was rather extraordinary in one whose own personality tended to be so rigid, for in a later letter he noted, "If I lived in Germany, I would be with the Socialists and I approve of their emphasis on class distinctions here just as much as I am not with them at home and disapprove of their emphasis on class distinctions in the United States." What made sense in Germany simply did not,in his view, make sense in America.

***

That Woodrow Wilson should have ignited Edward's interest to the point of propelling him into presidential politics should come as no surprise. Wilson had shown himself to be a brilliant scholar, an adept administrator and a most practical exponent of the liberal approach to public affairs. Thus, he incorporated all or almost all that a thinking and progressive capitalist of that era could have desired. Consequently, as McAdoo's letter indicates, the Princeton professor turned governor had already evoked the Boston businessman's enthusiasm.

The McAdoo letter apparently succeeded in stimulating Wilson's interest in Edward for he subsequently came to Boston to attend a lunch in his honor at the Boston City Club. He met with Edward privately before the event and the pair formed an alliance that would endure until Wilson's death.

Edward attended the Democratic convention that summer as a Wilson delegate and continued to aid the New Jersey governor through the ensuing campaign. Since he was now a successful and well-known businessman, and since most business leaders were backing Taft, Edward's support proved valuable. For example, when New York store owner John Wanamaker made an appeal in the influential *New York Herald* for Taft's re-election, Edward responded with a multi-column article in the same newspaper calling on all business men to rally to Wilson instead. "Governor Wilson alone of all the candidates," wrote Edward, "has taken a consistent position for the preservation of the individual in the business world, he alone of the candidates is pledged to legislation which will prevent such financial confederacies as now control the business and credit of the nation."

Following his election, Wilson named McAdoo as Secretary of Treasury, and McAdoo began considering Edward for the post of Collector of Customs for the Port of Boston. He wrote Brandeis, among others, to ask about the merchant's fitness and availability for a government position. Brandeis promptly wrote back describing Edward as "an ideal citizen' whose character, standing and qualifications equip him "for any post in any department." But, Brandeis added, "I should not think there is the slightest possibility of his accepting office."

Brandeis was certainly correct on this last point, since as it so happened, Edward was already busy trying to get a cabinet appointment for Brandeis! Wilson manifested far most interest in the idea than Roosevelt had shown and even sent a friendly magazine editor to Boston to gather information on the controversial lawyer. Edward compiled and turned over to the editor, whose name was Norman Hapgood, various letters, clippings and memoranda about Brandeis and later wrote Wilson concerning the one charge against Brandeis that had seemed to have some substance, that he was sometimes unfair in fighting his enemies. "Never in my experience with him" Edward wrote, "has he allowed any personal assault on him to distract him from considering the just rights of his opponents, however slanderous they may have been. This has been true even when the victory was his and he had in his hands the power to dictate the conditions which his opponents must accept."

Despite Edward's efforts, and those of many others as well, the president eventually decided that the appointment would arouse more antagonism than his new administration could then bear. Edward on reading press reports of the decision not to appoint Brandeis, immediately joined with five other Brandeis backers to dispatch a telegram to the White House. "We firmly believe," they said, "that the great mass of men who voted for you in Massachusetts are wholeheartedly in favor of Mr. Brandeis as representing the fundamentals on which you were elected."

Despite the indignant tone of the telegram, Edward remained on good terms with Wilson. Before too long he would see his faith in both Wilson and Brandeis fully vindicated.

***

Edward's annual summer trip to Europe had evolved into a rigidly-observed ritual. Only the most dire and decisive circumstances would keep him home. And so the Spring of 1914 found him once again boarding an ocean liner en route to the continent. Accompanying him was John H. Fahey, a former Boston newspaper publisher who had become, and who would remain, the nearest thing Edward would ever have to a truly close friend.

The pair's first stop was Paris where Edward attended the convention of the International Chamber of Commerce. As the Chamber's American Vice President, he offered a plan for setting up a full-time permanent bureau in Brussels. He also proposed a rule requiring a mail referendum of the organization's membership before the Chamber could take a stand on major issues. The American delegation supported him on both proposals and the convention in its closing hours gave them tentative approval. The convention proceedings had generally gone smoothly and few apparently suspected that in two months the delegates now sitting so amicably side-by-side would be frantically trying to destroy one another.

His convention agenda successfully completed, Edward proceeded with Fahey to Carlsbad for a cure. Taking the waters at the mineral spa had also become part of Edward's summer routine. His regimen required him to spend three weeks at the famous resort drinking five glasses of hot mineralized water every day and walking for at least 15 minutes between each glass as well as walking a mile or two before breakfast.

On June 28 came the assassination of the Austrian's Archduke followed by rapidly rising tension throughout the continent. Fahey became uneasy, wanted to depart and soon did so. But Edward had already started on, and paid for, his cure, and out of stubbornness, or stinginess, or courage, or perhaps all three, he insisted on staying until it was completed, managing to get back to France before the border closed. Instead of going home, he went to Paris. As hostilities broke out and the Germans, following their successful sweep through Belgium, began closing in on the French capital, Ambassador Myron Herrick summoned all the American businessmen and professional men left in Paris to an urgent meeting. They were to decide on whether to evacuate all Americans from the city. The U.S. was as yet neutral in the conflict but if the Germans started to shell the city, as was expected, American lives would also be endangered.

Edward argued, along with some others present, that evacuation would indicate that the Americans had lost faith in the French armies, and this would badly shake the morale of the city's population. The group agreed to stay.

They then decided to divide up the work that such a decision now made mandatory. To Edward fell the task of marking all American property and of locating shelters for his fellow countrymen to take refuge when the shells started to fall. He had lined up a host of cellars in the neighborhood of the embassy and had printed up posters to identify them when the French suddenly halted the German advance in the famed Battle of the Marne.

With the threat to Paris over, Edward departed. But once again he did not go home. Instead, he took advantage of his status as a neutral to visit the other side. He entered Germany via Switzerland, and after looking around at how the nation was coping with the war, he engaged a private car and chauffeur to take him to Belgium which was now under German occupation. In Brussels he conferred with bankers and other business men as well as government officials about plans for resuscitating the moribund Belgium economy. He then left for neutral Holland and from there returned to the U.S.

Although Edward's parents were German Jews, and although the Jews of Germany were participating patriotically and even enthusiastically in their country's war effort, Edward Filene came away from the conflict with strong sympathies for the allies. He was especially censorious of the way the Germans had handled Belgium. As he noted in his journal when he reached neutral Holland, "I am feeling, as never before, what an atmosphere of law and order and justice and liberty means in contrast with militarism, martial law and force."

On arriving back in Boston Edward wrote up his experiences for the local press and then hurried to Washington where he met with President Wilson. He told the President that the U.S. could not escape involvement in the war and urged him to take steps to prepare fur such an eventuality. Wilson tacitly agreed with his premise but not his proposals. The American President felt duty-bound to resist intervention until it was thrust upon him. Edward accepted this reasoning and went on to solidly defend the President against the latter's rising chorus of critics.

Edward soon found another issue on which to rally to the president's side. Having backed off from naming Brandeis to his cabinet the President was now preparing to appoint him to something higher: the U.S. Supreme Court.

Wilson announced the appointment in January, 1915. The news created such a sensation that it temporarily pushed the war in Europe off the front pages. The country's business community reacted not just with rancor but rage. Brandeis earned the unofficial title of "People's Lawyer" but to most business men he was a socialist if not an anarchist. And the fact that he was Jewish scarcely added to his appeal.

The business community was not alone in opposing the nomination. In Boston the President of Harvard, A. Lawrence Lowell, headed up a committee of 55 distinguished citizens in decrying the nomination of one of Harvard's most brilliant sons——Brandeis had graduated Harvard Law School at the top of his class——to the nation's highest bench. However, a former Harvard President, Charles W. Eliot, came out in support of Brandeis as did numerous other leading figures. The battle was thus joined.

Edward at first advised Brandeis to turn down the appointment for it would remove the "People's Lawyer" from the political arena where he had served so effectively. But, as Brandeis told him, "No one declines an invitation to the Supreme Court." Furthermore, his appointment would breech an important barrier since he would be the first Jew ever to serve on the nation's highest bench.

Brandeis' arguments easily convinced Edward who promptly plunged into the fray. He did so with his customary zeal and gusto, sending out letters, issuing statements and writing articles in Brandeis' behalf. Along with some other Wilson-Brandeis supporters he planned to sponsor mass meetings in Boston and New York to rally support for the appointment. However, Brandeis, as well as his law partners, asked them to refrain from going that far.

The fight, though successful, was an ugly one which opened wounds and left scars. Not the least of these unpleasant developments was the amount of anti-Semitism that it generated or rather unearthed. Edward retained in his possession a Star of David which some anti-Brandeis forces had put out. It consisted of concentric circles superimposed over triangles bearing the names of prominent Jews who were supporting the Jewish lawyer. As might be expected, among the names was his own.

***

Edward, by this time, had so fully earned the ear of the President that he could on occasion even change Wilson's mind on a particular issue, or at least modify the President's tactics for pursuing it. Sentiment was rising for the establishment of a commission to review the nation's tariffs. As an internationalist and free trader, Wilson opposed it, fearing it would lead to more and higher tariffs. Edward fully shared his views on free trade but nevertheless he joined forces with Senator Robert Owen of Oklahoma in seeking to persuade the President to sign the legislation setting up such a commission. Edward pointed out that most business men favored the measure so strongly that a Wilson veto might wreck the Democratic Party's election hopes the following year.

Wilson saw the wisdom in Edward's words and signed the measure. Edward's advice turned out to be sound for the commission effectively neutralized the tariff as an issue in the 1916 presidential election.

Partly through his ties with the White House but mostly through his own achievements as an articulate business leader, Edward was also earning the ear of the business community. To his great delight he found himself in increased demand as a speaker before business groups. In September, 1915 he addressed simultaneously the

Providence, Rhode Island and San Francisco Chamber of Commerce, this unique event being accomplished by having him appear in person in Providence while having his remarks conveyed simultaneously by telephone to San Francisco. It was believed to be the first time such a stunt had ever been staged and as such it constituted another "first" for the head of William Filene's Sons.

The next year, his dual role of business leader and Wilson advisor resulted in his being named Executive Committee Chairman of a group called the Business Men's National League. Despite its neutral name, the group had been formed by the Wilson forces to aid the President's re-election. In his new capacity Edward campaigned extensively for Wilson and the Democratic party. When Congress passed a law during the campaign giving railroad workers an eight-hour day, he issued a statement through the Democratic National Committee praising the measure and calling for employers in other industries to adopt its principle. Edward was now deeply embedded in the Democratic Party, and he would remain there for the rest of his busy life.

***

America's re-entry into the war on April, 1917 made Edward a nearly full-time resident of the nation's capital. "Washington is the Mecca for Americans who are doing things," he wrote back to his mother. "If I didn't have to work, I'd stay here constantly until the war was over." As it was, he was now spending more time in the city then in Boston and was expending far more energy on the war effort than he did in running the store.

He became a great admirer of Newton Baker, a scholarly lawyer who, following a successful stint as a reform mayor of Cleveland, had become the nation's new Secretary of War. He offered Baker his services as a dollar-a-year man but finally decided he could better serve the administration by heading up two important committees of the U.S. Chamber of Commerce. These were its Shipping Committee and its Committee on Financing the War.

Despite his role as a spokesman for business, he showed no qualms about taking his fellow capitalists to task. On May 29, *The New York Times*, under the headline DECRIES THE SLOGAN "BUSINESS AS USUAL", published a lengthy interview with Edward in which he excoriated those business men who were showing too much caution in expanding production to meet the national emergency. Such a policy would only prolong the war, said Edward.

He especially urged his fellow business men to spur ship production to counteract the losses which the deadly German U-boats were now inflicting on the Allied merchant fleets. In a speech to the Merchants Association of New York, the following year, he called for two shifts a day in all the country's shipyards and noted that ship production would not catch up with the losses already suffered through submarine warfare until the Spring of 1919.

His last remark was picked up by the Germans who sought to use it as propaganda. A German admiral cited it in a speech to the German parliament as proving that Germany was winning the war on the seas. As he chose to interpret it, Germany was sinking ships faster than the allies could replace them.

When the admiral's speech was reported back in America, Edward became furious. He promptly issued a statement denouncing the distortion of his remarks. He had given the Spring of 1919 as the time when all the losses would have been recouped, not as the time when ship production would match current levels of destruction. *The New York Times* published an editorial supporting his stand." The Admiral dodged the context," said the *Times*, "which made it plain as a pikestaff that Mr. Filene was speaking not of current tonnage loss month by month but of total tonnage losses."

As the leading liaison man between American business and the government, Edward also became embroiled in a host of other issues. Once a group of corset manufacturers asked for his aid. The government had banned all further production of corsets as a way to save the thousands of tons of steel which the garment's manufacture consumed. The corset makers claimed that their products were a necessity and that many women simply could not work without them. Edward helped them persuade the government to repeal the ban but he remained somewhat in the dark as to the validity of their case. As he noted in his journal, "I am inclined to think they are right. Are they?--a bachelor, so I don't know."

Edward had returned home from Europe in 1914 not only convinced that America would eventually be drawn into the conflict but concerned with its eventual impact on all the countries involved. For the next ten years the effect of the war on the world economy, plus the possibilities it offered for lasting peace, were never far from his thoughts.

In 1915 concerned citizens from the Boston-Cambridge area set up an organization which they called the League to Enforce the Peace. Their ranks included Senator Henry Lodge, Alexander Graham Bell and Harvard President Lowell. Former President Taft later joined them. Edward also joined the group, and as the only one experienced in fund-raising, he became chairman of its Finance Committee.

Edward considered a fellow-Bostonian named Charles Ward to be the best fund raiser in the country and attempted to get him to take over the day-to-day chores of the League's money-raising efforts. However, Ward was in St. Louis raising half-a-million dollars for a local charity and he insisted that he could not abandon this assignment. Undeterred, Edward called a half dozen rich men he knew in the St. Louis area and, explaining the situation, asked them to guarantee the remainder of the sum that the local charity needed. They at first protested but finally agreed. Edward then called Ward back and told him to come to Washington immediately.

Ward was to raise $250,000 for the League and at the outset he said he could not be expected to produce such a sum in such a short time unless he could start with ten percent of it already in the kitty. So he put Edward down for $25,000. Edward grimaced and grumbled but agreed to go along.

Not content to depend on Ward alone, Edward went after a few likely prospects on his own. One was the internationally-oriented steel magnate Charles Schwab. When Schwab offered him $500, Edward dismissed it with contempt and demanded more, much more.

"Have you brought me here to rob me?" protested Schwab.

"Yes," said Edward "in a way, you will thank us for the rest of your life. Will you give what I gave?"

"You won't catch me that way," said Schwab when he learned the amount of Edward's contribution.

"Well, will you give half as much as I gave?" Asked the persistent Edward.

"I'll give ten thousand dollars," said Schwab.

Through enterprising tactics such as these the quarter million dollars was soon raised and a dinner to highlight and publicize the League's goals was scheduled. The principal speaker was to be Senator Lodge. Edward called on Wilson and pleaded with the

President to attend and say a few words in support of the League's program. At Edward's insistence Wilson did so but the unforeseen consequences were immense. Lodge, who was not friendly to Wilson, immediately ceased his connections with the League and after the war led the move to block America's entry into the League of Nations.

Edward's post-war concerns also carried over into his Chamber of Commerce activities. In 1916 he induced the Chamber to hold a national membership referendum on whether sanctions should be used to back up international decisions on disputes. This was the position of the League to Enforce the Peace at the time and he was pleased to see his fellow business men vote "yes" on the use of economic sanctions, although they backed away from the use of military ones.

Edward was less successful in January 1917 when he attempted to get the Chamber, at its annual convention, to support the President's peace plan. The country was not yet at war and Wilson's ideas were as yet only a set of broad principles which seemed in concordance with positions the Chamber had taken. However, the assembled delegates were more concerned at the time with a threatening rail strike, as well as with a proposed new Washington headquarters for their organization, and so they failed to pay much attention to post-war policy.

The following year, Edward proposed a referendum to the Chamber which upset his President considerably. Edward wanted the members to vote on the desirability of economically discriminating against Germany after the war if such a step should be necessary for self-defense. "I must say to you," the president wrote to Edward, "that I am exceedingly sorry that this was done without first consulting me. No matter which way the vote turns, it will embarrass my handling of international affairs and the policy of the government." Edward saw the President soon after and patched matters up.

On subsequent issues they were more fully on accord. When Edward opposed a proposed Chamber referendum regarding Russia, Wilson warmly approved. "I entirely agree with you," Wilson wrote him, "that the handling of such questions as you refer to by referendum within the Chamber of Commerce of the United States is more apt to lead to embarrassment than to a clarification..." And the President showed his respect for Edward's counsel by requesting his advice. "I shall be interested to know what steps you suggest that will be likely to greatly reduce the danger of such moves...I am going to beg your indulgence and ask you if you would be generous enough to send me a brief written memorandum..."

A week or two later Edward elicited another favorable response from the President when, with the war drawing to a close, he urged him to support the early establishment of a reconstruction commission to "forestall the formulation of a number of separate and conflicting class programs." Wilson speedily replied "your instinct is right. It would be hurtful to have a number of competitive and class schemes for reconstruction after the war..." The President would frequently look to Edward for aid and assistance in implementing his own post-war policies and his Boston backer would not fail him.

With the end of the war came the issue of whether the United States should join the League of Nations which was being formed to protect and preserve the peace. Edward fully shared Wilson's belief that the country should, indeed must, do so. Edward also enjoyed giving speeches and holding press conferences. So when he was asked to go on a speaking tour in behalf of the League, he accepted with alacrity. The other member of the tour was Henry Van Dyke, a popular non-fiction writer. Together the duo swept through the Midwest and West seeking to stir up public support for American participation in the proposed World organization.

Edward reveled in his new assignment. "I am being converted rapidly from a shopkeeper into a speaker," the 58-year old man wrote back to his mother as he proudly reported how on one occasion he had given three speeches in a single day.

His bliss was crowned in Salt Lake City when formed President Taft joined them on the speaker's platform to address a crowd of 8,000. Unfortunately, neither their speaking tour nor the ill-fated one undertaken by the president himself later managed to persuade the U.S. Senate to approve, by the necessary two-thirds majority, American's entry into the world organization.

But although his country failed to follow his, and his president's, exhortation against isolationism, Edward steadfastly tried to steer the nation toward a more pro-European policy. He was now in demand as a speaker and he could command a certain amount of attention from the press. So in speeches to such groups as the International Lyceum and Chataqua Association, the American Academy of Political and Social Science and the Atlantic Congress for the League of Nations, as well as in press conferences and signed articles in such publications as *The New York Times Sunday Magazine,* he continued to harp on the necessity for helping Europe get back on its feet.

In his comments on these occasions he showed a great deal of prescience and perspicacity for he advocated aid somewhat along the lines which America would undertake with singular success after World War II with its Marshall Plan. Had the country only been ready to hear such suggestions from Edward Filene a quarter century earlier, the course of world history might well have been altered for the better and the catastrophe of World War II possibly averted. (Of course, Edward was not the only person advocating such approaches.)

Edward also correctly foresaw the peril which an impoverished Germany could pose. In a letter to Lincoln Steffens he stressed the need to "understand the danger to the peace of the world that will come from a Germany whose masses are without work... For many years to come it seems to me probable there will be monarchist and military groups openly or covertly trying to re-establish their power, but they can only become dangerous if they get the support of the middle bourgeois (sic) classes made desperate by continuous critical labor troubles." Thus in 1919 Edward Filene wrote a near scenario for what would occur in Germany a few years later.

In 1921 Edward got an opportunity to move from advocate to actor on the international scene. As the year was drawing to a close, Germany, caught up in a runaway inflation, abruptly announced it was suspending reparation payments to France. The French reacted by occupying the Ruhr, and the miners of that coal-rich region reacted in turn by going on strike. The result was a situation foreboding catastrophe for all concerned.

The U.S. government appointed a commission headed by Chicago financier Charles Dawes to see what could be done. The commission recommended that the U.S. give Germany a loan on easy terms. Germany was then to use part of the money to pay France a portion of its reparations bill; it would use the rest of the loan to shore up its shattered economy. France, for its part, would evacuate its troops from the Ruhr.

France and Germany sent delegates to London to work out the details of the plan with Dawes. But the talks soon deadlocked. Each European delegation was bound by rigid instructions from its government, and the instructions for each were so far apart that no accord seemed possible.

Edward, in London at the time, talked freely with both groups.(He was, it will be recalled, proficient in both German and French.) When he counseled the French to return to Paris and seek further, more flexible instructions, they responded negatively. "If the government gave us new instructions, it would be swept out of office tomorrow. Every newspaper in Paris but two is fighting the Dawes plan and public opinion is so inflamed that the government cannot move."

When Edward tried to point out that if the Dawes plan failed, the government would fall anyway, the delegates asked him to go to Paris and explain the situation. "They would not believe it from us, but they might from you since you have no official position and therefore nothing at stake."

Edward leaped at the chance to operate on the world stage and sped off to Paris, where he arranged a dinner for two dozen prominent guests including bankers, industrialists, newspaper publishers and government officials. With an impressive array of figures and facts, he persuaded them to soften their hostility to the plan.

Spurred on by his apparent success in Paris, Edward hastened to Munich where, at the home of a local industrialist named Kurt Wolff, he set up a similar meeting and made a similar plea. The Germans proved harder to convince than the French—the Dawes Plan, after all, did not really reduce their burden but only made it more immediately bearable—but eventually they too conceded the correctness of his case. Edward's efforts helped to get the Dawes plan accepted, thus sparing Europe from catastrophe—at least for a while.

The next year Edward scored a similar though smaller success in helping Europe rebuild when he had introduced into the U.S. Senate a resolution lifting some liens that the United States had imposed on Austria. The move permitted that nearly destitute nation to raise a new foreign loan to feed its people. "Mr. Filene," *The New York Times* reported, "said he was acting as an American, keenly interested in the rehabilitation of a world now torn by the peace as it was formerly by the war..." The paper noted that Edward's resolution had drawn the support of the Federal Council of Churches and several other humanitarian groups.

Edward's efforts in behalf of post-war Europe did not go unnoticed or unappreciated. The Austrian, Italian, Czech, and French governments all gave him decorations. The French government made him a Knight of the Legion of Honor, the award representing, in the words of the French ambassador the United States, "the appreciation of my government for your friendship towards France and your efforts in view of the establishment of that definite peace which is the desire of my countrymen."

But Edward had received another memento from France which he treasured even more. During his activities abroad he had met Edouard Herriot, a former Prime Minister who, after Clemenceau, was the leading political figure of France. He found Herriot deeply depressed. His government had just fallen and he felt that he had lost all influence over the course of events. All his life's work, so Herriot told him, had been destroyed and he was thinking of emigrating. Edward offered to bring him to the U.S. and pay him $10,000 a year while he learned English. Herriot could then work with him on various projects. Herriott actually gave the proposal some serious thought. But he finally decided that whatever future he might have lay in France. (He would, in fact, be prime minister again.)

Like most prominent French statesmen, Herriott had been given the largely honorary post of Mayor of his home city. In saying good bye to Edward he took out his card, scribbled something on it and smilingly presented it to his American friend. In glancing at it, Edward saw that under the printed message "Herriott, Mayor of Lyon' the former French Prime Minister had written, "Head employee of Mr. Edward A. Filene."

***

Although Edward reaped much attention and acclaim for his speeches, writings and efforts at diplomacy during this period, the most recognition and renown he received came from a project of his own making. This was a plan to offer prizes in four different countries for essays on the theme "How can Peace and prosperity be restored in Great Britain. (or France or Germany or Italy, depending on the country) and in Europe through international cooperation?"

The project's guidelines allowed anyone to submit a theme of no more than 5,000 words on this topic. Some $10,000 would be made available to each country for prize money plus $2,000 for administrative expenses. The entire project would cost Edward almost $50,000 but he was apparently not only ready but eager to pay it though it represented a substantial sum in 1924 dollars.

With the help of a member of the Secretariat of the League of Nations, Edward managed to set up impressive panels of judges in each of the four designated countries to determine the winners. In France a former president of that nation's Senate headed his panel. In Italy, the current president of that nation's Senate accepted the honor. The German panel chairman was the Cchief Justice of the German Supreme Court while the British chairman was the noted classical scholar and essayist, Professor Gilbert Murray.

Even many of the ordinary panel members were far from ordinary. In Germany, for example, they included a former minister of justice, a Prussian count and two prominent industrialists.

Announced early in January, 1924, the project received widespread newspaper coverage not only in the four countries designated for the awards but in America as well. Those wishing to enter the contest were to first file an application and receive a number which they would then use to identify their proposals. This was to keep the judges from knowing any contestant's name. Within three weeks nearly 100 applications a day were being filed in France alone.

The prize money for each country was divided up to insure a large number of winners. In Great Britain about five percent of the 700 who eventually submitted essays received an award of some kind.

Interest naturally focused on those who won the major prizes. In France a night watchman won the top prize; a high school instructor walked off with the second while a government clerk placed third. In Great Britain an Irishman won first prize, a decision which drew some whimsical editorial comment in *The New York Times*. In Italy three persons, two of them professors, shared the number one prize.

The German peace plan awards attracted the most attention. In a front-page story headlined PRIZE PEACE PLANS SHOW GERMAN TREND OF THOUGHT TODAY, The *Times* gave the full text of the two top-winning German plans and summarized in detail many of the others. Most of the contributions condemned the Versailles Peace Treaty but supported the League of Nations. (Most of the contributions from the other three countries also made the League the centerpiece of their proposals.)

The question now arises as to what the whole project actually accomplished? This remains hard to gage. However, it did generate interest in the problems of World peace while it also generated a lot of favorable publicity for its sponsor. With both these results in mind, Edward Filene probably considered his $50,000 well spent.

* * *

Although world affairs were absorbing more and more of Edward's energies during these post-war years he still found time for domestic concerns. The war's end coincided with the off-year elections and Wilson was hoping for a Democratic sweep to strengthen his hand in the coming peace negotiations. Edward heavily supported the successful election bid of Wilson Democrat David Walsh of Massachusetts for the U.S. Senate, and his efforts in Walsh's behalf not only pleased the President but also Brandeis, who sent Edward a letter of congratulations on Walsh's election.

Edward was continually worried about Wilson's safety and had urged him to take more precautions when going out in public, especially when attending the theater. The president had shrugged off the matter by saying he needed some relaxation in order to do his job and so he simply could not allow fear of assassins to constrain him.

The next year the President was struck down, not by an assassin's bullet but by a stroke suffered while trying to whip up public support for America's entry into the League. A genuinely grieving Edward hovered about the White House while the stricken president sought to fight his way back to health. After the inaugural of Warren Harding in 1921, Edward, at the invitation of Newton Baker, joined the small group of Wilsonians who welcomed the president and Mrs. Wilson to their new residence.

Remaining a staunch Democrat, Edward gave his now valuable support to his party's presidential candidate in 1924. Under the headline FILENE ATTACKS COOLIDGE'S RECORD, *The New York Times* two weeks before the election published a six-column story presenting Edward's position. "I shall vote for John W. Davis," said Edward. "I shall vote as a businessman who unselfishly wants to see his country prosper and (who) selfishly knows that his own business cannot prosper unless our citizens are at work at good wages and good salaries." He flayed "the reactionary policies of the present administrations" and called for a new political leadership that would be "liberal and fearless." Although few would ever call Davis, who was a corporation lawyer, a liberal, he apparently seemed so to Edward who had found Coolidge's leadership both as President and previously as Governor of Massachusetts sadly wanting. The Boston merchant little suspected that five years later he would, in effect, be calling upon Davis to support him in a much more personal matter.

Although his duties as President of William Filene's Sons necessarily suffered considerable neglect while he was bustling about Washington and Europe, he nevertheless managed to attend some business conferences, particularly when he had been invited as a speaker. In one address to the National Retail Dry Goods Association in 1923 he prophesied the creation of chains of department stores. The association's managing director, Lewis Hahn took issue with him, saying, in effect, it could and would never happen. Yet, a mere six years later Hahn himself would be heading up a chain of 40 department stores.

In 1924, in a speech to the annual convention of the U.S. Chamber of Commerce, Edward called on the country's individually-owned department and other stores to form joint purchasing syndicates. This would enable them to reduce prices, and thereby meet the coming competition. He warned such proprietors that the growing chain stores would eliminate single enterprises such as theirs unless they banded together into chains themselves. He saw a great future especially for chains that would operate individual departments within groups of department stores. In other words he wanted, and was predicting, the formations of specialty chains, such as a chain of shoe departments, within chains of overall stores.

As these statements indicate, Edward had not lost faith in capitalism. He maintained his support for the system even though its failings, both real and alleged, were coming increasingly under attack. The strikes and disruptions which were playing havoc with the economies of the western world, coupled with the seemingly bright dawn of communism in the East, had caused many a thinking person to look to socialism for society's salvation.

One of these was his former comrade-in-arms Lincoln Steffens. The one-time muckraking journalist had visited Russia soon after the communists had seized power and had sent back his famous telegram "I have seen the future and it works." Steffens wrote Edward from Berlin the following year condemning the way European businessmen were crushing the revolutions which had broken out in Germany. "There seems to me at the moment," said Steffens, "very little hope in your class, E.A. They are going to do in the world at large what they have been doing in Boston and in your Chamber of Commerce."

Edward, however, continued to affirm capitalism's essential appeal. "Civilization did not begin," he wrote in a Colliers magazine article in 1922, "until man began to have something left over after providing for himself and his family. Communism represents an effort to prevent a man having anything left over. Taxing away wealth does not necessarily help the community; it mostly curtails the rich man's ability to be of service."

But having put in a plug for business, he then proceeded, in effect, to pull the plug on some of its misdeeds. Watering stock, capitalizing expenses to create illusory profits, paying substandard wages—such practices as these, so Edward claimed, not only flouted the public interest but even damaged business' own long run interests. He also called for more regulation of the securities industry. This suggestion, like his call for increased aid to Europe, might also have spared America and the world much grief, for had it been accepted, it might well have forestalled or at least limited the crash that would come only seven years later.

Writing for the same magazine the following year, Edward bewailed the "loneliness of the liberal in business circles." He maintained that "business liberalism will be one of the essentials of big business success during the next twenty-five years," but he admitted that most of his colleagues had failed to grasp this fact. He put part of the blame for their failure to do so on the narrowness of both their training and their contacts.

The succeeding year found Edward becoming increasingly disappointed and even somewhat desperate over the failure of his fellow businessmen to get his message. "One of the social tragedies of our time lies in the fact that we rarely deal with discontent until it has been captured by doctrinaires and demagogues," he wrote. "If as businessmen, we cannot meet this responsibility, we deserve to see our leadership superseded--*we shall be superseded*." (Edward's emphasis)

If the mood of these last two statements, the lament for lonely business liberals and the warning to businessmen about being bypassed by history seems out of keeping with Edward's usual enthusiastic tone, then we need not look far to find a reason. While traveling throughout Europe in his role of World statesman he had also been telling his fellow businessmen to quit trying to resurrect the good old days of pre-war capitalism. Instead, they should find a middle way between unbridled capitalism and socialism. Their response to his exhortations, which were undoubtedly delivered in his unpleasantly hectoring manner, is described by Lincoln Steffens in a letter to Steffens' sister. "E.A. has just been dropped from the Directorate of the International Chamber of Commerce, his place being given to a reactionary of the Rightist Type! He told me last night and I laughed until I cried with joy, and he with rage."

One can well appreciate Edward's consternation at being repudiated by an organization that to a great extent owed its very existence to his efforts. And one can imagine how Steffens exacerbated such feelings with his mocking, "I-told-you-so" reaction. But neither the right-wing tending Chamber of Commerce or the left-wing heading Steffens would enjoy the last laugh. Future events would vindicate neither reaction nor radicalism but rather the moderate, middle-way approach of Edward Filene.

As Edward later reflected on the experience, he began to see that it was not so much his ideas as his way of presenting them that annoyed his Chamber colleagues. This is quite evident in his speeches and writings during the next two years as on several occasions he notes how "liberal businessmen" often become too wrapped up in their beliefs to observe "the normal courtesies and amenities of human relations." Such statements coming so soon after his rebuff, lead inescapably to the conclusion that the liberal business man he was chastising was Edward Filene.

The setback which Edward had suffered at the hands of the International Chamber of Commerce did no great damage to his position either nationally or internationally. As we have seen he went on to play a key role in various important public issues. It did not even keep him from being asked to address the U.S. Chamber of Commerce two years hence. But it probably spurred him on in fostering two organizations which he had recently set up on his own.

The first of these was the Twentieth Century Fund which he organized in the Spring of 1922. The Fund was really an outgrowth of the Cooperative League which Edward and Lincoln has initially established in the early 1900's but which had never gotten off the ground. The new organization was to be more soundly structured and more broadly based.

To guide the Twentieth Century Fund Edward chose, beside himself, two Massachusetts friends, newspaper publisher John Fahey and a progressive business man named Henry Dennison, plus three distinguished national figures: Newton Baker, James McDonald who headed the Foreign Policy Association and a New York newspaper executive named Bruce Bliven. (Bliven would later become editorial director of *The New Republic*). Roscoe Pound, Dean of the Harvard Law School later joined them.

The Twentieth Century Fund, as Edward and the other directors conceived it, was to be essentially a study group. But it was not to engage in largely academic exercises. Instead it was to uncover all the available and necessary facts on particular and pressing public issues, then, basing itself on these facts, it was to offer practical proposals for action. It was also intended to give assistance, financial as well as moral and intellectual, to other organizations which were usefully engaged in carrying out the fund's objectives. To enable his new organization to do this, Edward made over to it several thousand shares of his preferred stock in William Filene's Sons.

Provided with able leadership and a substantial endowment, the Fund set about to fulfill its ambitious goals. Its first major grant went to the newly organized League of Women's Voters, then struggling to establish itself following the extension of the voting franchise to women a few years before. The women's group found the $25,000 award most helpful. Other early grants included two to the women's college Bryn Mawr to develop an economics department, a sizable gift to the International Labor Office in Geneva to devise ways and means for "increasing and cheapening production and bettering the relations between employees and workers," and a smaller grant to the same group for studying the potential effects of an American boycott against nations resorting to war. In addition, some financial help was given to the credit union movement.

This list of early beneficiaries might seem to indicate that despite its blue-ribbon board of trustees, Edward did most of the deciding. After all, most of these projects represented causes which he had long supported. (It will be remembered from Chapter 5 how he aided an early Massachusetts suffragette leader. Also the use of economic sanctions against aggressive nations had long evoked his warm approval.) But this would be to over-simplify and over-generalize. Edward had purposely set up the board so that he would have only one vote among seven. He insisted that he wanted the Fund to acquire an identity and a stature of its own so that it could speak with greater authority, and those he had invited to give it guidance were hardly people who would rubber stamp anyone's proposals.

As it so happens, Edward did not always get his way. For example, when Harvard finally decided, despite the bitter opposition of much of its faculty, to establish a business school, Edward wanted the Fund to give the new venture some support. Such a school, he argued, would not only lead to improved business practices, but to broader business thinking. The other trustees, however, maintained that the projected business school could and should find other donors and so no grant was ever made.

Edward accepted this as well as other occasional refusals of his fellow trustees to go along with his wishes. The experience with the International Chamber of Commerce had taught him something, and though it came too late to alter his basic behavior, it did succeed in softening, in at least some situations, his approach to opposition. In so doing it probably better prepared him for the challenges that were to come.

***

The other organization which Edward established would prove to be much more socially significant as well as more personally satisfying. It would provide its progenitor with the most tangible and lasting to his active, achievement-oriented life.

The Massachusetts Credit Union movement, despite its impressive start, had failed to flourish. By 1913 only 334 Credit Unions had come into existence in the entire state. This bothered Edward and early in 1914 he joined with a few other businessmen, all of them Jewish, to organize the Massachusetts Credit Union. As its founders envisioned it, the new organization would act as a credit union for credit unions. Individuals could join it, but so could entire credit unions as well.

A few months later the new organization's founders met with some leaders of the Boston Chamber of Commerce to seek their assistance. The Chamber leaders expressed sympathy and support but suggested that "the work should be contributed to by a more interracial set of financiers and businessmen." More specifically, they urged Edward and his associates to expand the board of directors to include "a number of people of other than the Jewish faith."

Their motive for making this suggestion was not, they indicated, the result of any racial prejudice on their part. In fact they expressed high regard for the "philanthropic and intelligent work of the gentlemen now constituting this organization." But making its leadership more diverse would help "to make the work general and to reach the outside public."

The Chamber of Commerce leaders had put their collective finger on a formidable problem. For the real impetus behind the credit union movement so far had come from Jewish businessmen seeking to overcome the image of Jews as usurers.

Edward, as we have seen (Chapter 5) fully shared these concerns. Indeed this is why he had chosen other Jews to help him set up the new organization. As he later expressed it in explaining his activities of this period:

"...Now some of the loan sharks were Jews, and some of the agitation against them was anti-Jewish propaganda. It should be recorded, then, that the first promoters of credit unions in America were also Jews. They were not thinking of themselves as Jews in doing the work they did. They were simply citizens sincerely interested in rescuing other citizens from the jaws of the loan sharks; but the fact that they were Jews, I think—and thought at the time—was strategically important. So when I broached a plan for the organization of a society in Massachusetts to promote the credit union idea, I saw to it that the Jewish citizens became its first organizers and directors."

Edward, however, quickly saw the wisdom of the Chamber leaders' advice. So did the organization's other directors and soon they had added some Yankee and Irish names to their board's roster. Meanwhile, the pace of credit union growth began to pick up and by the following year 50 were in existence. In April the Massachusetts Credit Union held its first state-wide dinner meeting and both the Governor and the Mayor of Boston attended. The Mayor, James Michael Curley, told the gathering that he had ordered all city employees either to get out of debt by the end of the month or to go to a credit union to get their affairs straightened out.

Prospects for the movement thus looked bright in the Spring of 1915 and Edward, ever the ambitious optimist, immediately began thinking of going national, that is using the Massachusetts organization "to bring all the possibilities of the movement before the state and national officers of the big organizations of the country." He even began dreaming of an international credit union movement consisting of 15 million credit unions placed throughout the world.

Unfortunately, while Edward was dreaming his grandiose dreams—he even had a detailed plan drawn up for organizing credit unions nationally—the movement was beginning to sputter to a halt in its home territory. Ten credit unions went bankrupt in Massachusetts in 1915 and their failure was not fully offset by the creation of 12 new ones.

In March 1916 Edward gave a dinner for the other directors at which these problems were discussed. Their discussion led to the formation of a new organization which would not serve as a credit union itself but would primarily "disseminate information with respect to the benefits of credit unions." Felix Vorenberg, a Boston jeweler who had headed up the old organization, would also head the new one while Edward would serve as one of its three vice presidents. At Edward's urging they hired a former government official with impressive credentials to be their operating director.

This new effort to energize the movement failed to make much heading. Only seven new credit unions were organized in 1917 and a mere four were set up in 1918--all of them in Massachusetts. Meanwhile, four existing ones collapsed.

Instead of becoming disillusioned by all these defeats, Edward characteristically decided to set his sights higher. In May 1919, he began, almost single-handed, to organize the National Committee on People's Banks. He persuaded several illustrious, and non-Jewish, Americans to lend their names to his new organization. They included a former governor of North Carolina, the head of the Brotherhood of Locomotive Engineers and the country's leading historian, Charles A. Beard. But the organizing action remained, in the words of two credit union historians, J. Carroll Moody and Gilbert Fite, "little more than a list of impressive names on stationery." Its finances depended largely on three men, Edward and another Boston Jewish businessmen each of whom contributed $12,500, and a local, non-Jewish oil company president who contributed $5,000. Furthermore, a national credit union bill filed in Congress that year died before it reached the floor of the House.

Edward assigned an aide to review the situation and the aide's report accurately pin-pointed the problem. Most of those connected with the movement did not regard it as important enough to give it much more than lip service.

"In light of these discouraging reports," write Moody & Fite, "Filene might reasonably have abandoned the credit union movement. But he abhorred defeat. More important, he believed deeply in the principle behind cooperative credit. What he needed was the right man to carry out the organizational work."

As it so often happens, the right man appeared at the right time or at least soon thereafter. He came in the form of a 40-year old lawyer from Lynn, Massachusetts named Roy E. Bergengren. A graduate of Dartmouth and the Harvard Law School, Bergengren had spent much of his time in Lynn defending working people who had gone deeply into debt and who stood in danger of losing everything they had to loan sharks and even banks. He had also helped lead a campaign to reform Lynn's creaky and corrupt city government, and subsequently served with conspicuous success as the city's Commissioner of Finance.

When America entered World War I, Bergengren although married and with children, volunteered for the army. Discharged as a captain he tried his hand at private enterprise but was unsuccessful. He did not, however, want to go back to defending clients trying to escape from the coils of their creditors for he had become convinced that such legal assistance provided no real solution to the working-man's credit problem. So in the Spring off 1920 he showed up at Edward's office to apply for the then vacant post of managing director of the Massachusetts Credit Union Association.

Edward, with his Filene knack for spotting ability, hired him ten minutes after he came through the door. The two men would enjoy, or perhaps endure, a stormy but surprisingly successful association that would produce what many consider the crowing achievement of Edward's career.

Chapter 8
LINCOLN: MINDING THE STORE

1916

A bright afternoon in May finds 18 limousines belonging to some of America's leading retailers parked at or around New York City's Aldine Club. The retailers themselves are inside attending an unusual luncheon. Most have traveled a considerable distance to be present but then their host is a well-regarded and well-liked Boston merchant who is not an easy man to turn down. Moreover, he has assured them that the event would open up a new era of possibilities for their separate enterprises. So with anticipation they have come to hear what Lincoln Filene has to say. They would not be disappointed.

***

In setting up their new store in 1912, the Filenes also set up a new pattern of ownership to insure its long-lasting survival and growth. With Edward now over 50 and Lincoln in his late 40's, and with their management team now complete, the brothers felt that the time had come to make their managers full-fledged partners in their enterprise.

So Edward and Lincoln formed a new corporation, bearing the same name as the old one, William Filene's Sons, but including four non-sons among its owners and directors. The new firm issued 100 shares of common stock. Each brother received 26 shares, giving them control over the corporation so long as they voted their shares together. The other 48 shares were divided equally among the four pyramid heads.

At the outset none of the new shares had more then a nominal value for the brothers gave themselves preferred i.e. non-voting stock for the assets of the old corporation. Their preferred stock, together with the preferred stock already given to the FCA or sold to employees, including the quarter million dollars worth purchased by Kirstein, meant that a lot of dividends would have to be paid before the common shareholders could receive anything at all. But the store seemed almost certain to grow and such growth would basically benefit the common stock shareholder who would realize all the surplus after the preferred stockholders had received their fixed return. Of course, Edward and Lincoln would hold a majority of the common shares as well but that too would eventually change.

The Associates Agreement, as the formal document outlining all these provisions was called, stipulated that on January, 1928 the Filene brothers would end their connection with or at least their control over the family firm. Of their 52 shares, four were to be transferred to the four pyramid heads while the remaining 48 were to be allocated to "other employees of the corporation or the Filene Cooperative Association."

Thus, in a little over 15 years, the Filenes would let go the reins completely. Their store would be totally owned by their employees, and while the four top employees would have the controlling interest, they could exercise such control only if they voted unanimously. In any case, other employees and the FCA would hold the remaining 48 percent of the voting stock and thus would constitute a formidable force in determining the store's practices and policies.

The agreement, however, left many loose ends. While it stipulated that the a stock of any pyramid head who died or left the company must be sold back to the corporation, it did not say what the corporation should do with these repurchased shares. Also, just how would the transfer of Edward & Lincoln's 48 shares to other employees or the FCA be effected when the time for doing so arrived, and what if Edward and Lincoln were to disagree on basic policies? These were some of the questions that went unanswered and even unnoticed at the time but they would emerge to haunt the two brothers, especially the eldest, in the years to come.

Hardly had the four new Filene partners received their voting shares when they faced the possibility of seeing them become worthless and seeing their jobs disappear as well. In building, stocking and operating the new store the firm had run up enormous debts. Paying off or even paying the interest on these new debts, plus meeting the expanded payroll and other increased expenses of the new facility, were eating up so much of its receipts that it was falling increasingly behind in paying its suppliers. The latter, as a natural reaction, were slowing down and even stopping their shipments. While crowds of enthusiastic shoppers continued to throng the spectacular new store, the store itself was teetering on the brink of bankruptcy.

Thanks to their reputation as astute and honorable businessmen, and thanks as well to their connection with financier James Storrow, the Filenes had earned the respect of Boston's biggest bank, the First National Bank of Boston. Now, confronted with calamity, the Filene brothers and their four partners went to the bank with a desperate plea for help.

The First National was amazed at the amount of debt and expense which the firm was carrying. But it was impressed with the amount of business the store was doing and this, plus its respect for the Filenes, stirred it to respond favorably and fast. Saying "We will back you to the limit," the bank promptly took the unusual step of placing ads in the relevant trade publications announcing it would guarantee all of the firm's bills. Manufacturers and wholesalers resumed their shipments and disaster was averted. Sixteen years later, long after all its debts to the bank had been repaid, the store would find a way to show its appreciation for the First National's faith and support in its time of need.

William Filene's Sons lost $261,000 in 1913. It was the first unprofitable year in its history. It would also be the last one for despite depressions, recessions and wars, Filene's would never again fail to make a profit.

Its brush with bankruptcy did not squelch the store's aggressive and adventurous attitude toward innovation. Within a year or two after meeting with its bankers, it had installed the first air conditioning and the first public address system in the United States. It was also operating the only private telegraph system in Boston.

On a more serious and significant level, the store had adopted a new advertising policy. From now on, its ads would rarely use such words as "great, big, enormous" or "latest, finest, most elegant". A dress could not be called "gorgeous" unless the sales people genuinely felt that it met such a standard. Instead, Filene ads would concentrate on providing customers with useful information. The spirit of William Filene lived on.

This focus on giving its clientele information carried over into other fields beyond the selling of goods. In February 1915 the store sponsored a mother's conference at which a professor from the Harvard Medical School spoke on "How to Help Save 100,000 Babies in Boston" while the head of the city's new Children's Hospital delivered an address on "The Neglected Age of the Child." Filene's also gave Boston its first real look at the new Montessori method in education by offering a talk on the subject by Mrs. Ernest Hopkins, the wife of the store's employment director. Mrs Hopkins had been a member of Dr. Montessori's first teachers' class in Rome.

When Congress convened at noon on April 7, 1917 to declare war, Filene's chose the occasion to unveil on the side of its building the second largest flag in the United States. The company then went on to demonstrate its commitment to the war effort in more substantial ways. The Board of Managers voted to pay all store employees who enlisted in the armed services the difference between their military pay and their store pay, bonuses included. Among those resigning to enter military service was James Simpson, the head of the advertising/publicity pyramid. The move would have happy consequences for him though not such happy consequences for Edward and Lincoln.

The store also strongly supported all the country's war bond drives and its own employees had subscribed over a half million dollars in these bonds by the time the war ended a year and a half later. The Filene band, now consisting of over 40 amateur musicians, played at wartime rallies and parades, in addition to giving morning concerts on the balcony of the street floor. Band members received an extra ten dollars a month for such activities and for most of them this was almost the equivalent of an extra week's pay.

Seven months after America's entry into the war, the store sent a small delegation to Paris to buy presents for the men at the front. Both its customers and its employees took advantage of this unique service, which no other store in the country was offering at the time.

Not all the store's attempts at adjusting to wartime conditions proved successful. Business was brisk but costs were rising and in an effort to hold them down, Filene's began levying a fifty-cent fee on all credit accounts and a ten-cent fee on all deliveries. However, customers using these services protested while the majority who did not use them, and who would benefit by lower prices, showed no interest. So, when its competitors failed to follow Filene's lead, the store abandoned the new charges.

The war's end coincided with the end of a decade in which Lincoln had served as the store's general manager. The last time the brothers had swapped the title was in 1908 but Edward, with his growing involvement outside the store had never asked for it back. (He did, however, keep the more valuable title of President, a title he would not relinquish until death.) Consequently, although Edward had never ceased, and never would cease, to concern himself with the store, it was Lincoln who had piloted it through this difficult and, on one occasion, dangerous period. With the younger brother's bright but steady hand at its helm, Filene's was ready to weather the uncertainties, and take advantage of the opportunities, which the post-war era might bring.

***

The first major development of the post-war era proved a welcome one. In 1919, the Automatic Bargain Basement, or ABB as it was referred to in this store, celebrated its tenth anniversary by turning its first profit.

Bringing it to that point had been far from easy. It has been necessary, for example, not only to give the basement its own buyers but to give these buyers separate and special training. The store's regular buyers were instructed to look first for quality and then ask the price. The ABB's buyers were trained to look first at the price and then examine the quality. This did not mean that the basement was in the market for shoddy goods. Virtually everyone agreed that it would never succeed unless it offered decent merchandise. But unless it could offer such merchandise at highly advantageous prices, there would be no point to its existence.

High quality and low price still did not suffice to make an item worthy of a place among the basement's offerings. It also had to be something people wished to buy. The basement could not serve as a trash bin for unneeded and unwanted goods for its automatic price reduction plan could make purchases of such goods disastrous. Unfortunately, in its first few years such purchases had occasionally occurred.

On one occasion a buyer inspecting a few sample woolen overcoats purchased the entire lot of 2,000. The coats appeared to be of good quality and could be priced to sell for twelve dollars each. But the samples the buyer had inspected were misleading for when the coats arrived; most of them gave off a foul-smelling odor. Their price was cut to nine dollars, then 6 and then three at which level most of them finally sold.

On another occasion, a buyer bought 24,000 detachable linen collars, the remains of two carloads of such items from a manufacturer who was going out of business. They turned out to be mostly sizes 13 and 18, too small or too big to fit most men. However, while some had to be given away to charity, most of them sold and the entire operation made a small profit. This tempted the buyer a few months later to purchase a similar batch of collars from another manufacturer. Unfortunately, the first batch had saturated the market and so the store still had most of the second lot on its hands when the 30-day sales period ran out. It then offered them to the Salvation Army which had taken the leftovers from the first group but this time the Army turned them down saying it could not dispose of any more. Other charitable organizations responded in a similar vein. Edward then acerbically complimented the buyer for having set a new record in buying goods which not only could not be sold, but which could not even be given away.

But mistakes like these were becoming increasingly rare as the basement and its buyers gradually became more efficient in their purchasing efforts. What's more, they were starting to have some striking successes in disposing of goods that would seem to have been outrageous blunders. Once the basement found itself with a carload of shoes to sell. The shoes were well made and had been available on highly advantageous terms. The problem was that they were all for the left foot! The basement nevertheless bunched them in pairs, priced each pair at fifty cents and ended up selling the entire lot. They never found out what motivated those who snapped them up.

One major reason why it was getting easier even to sell ostensibly poor purchases was that the basement had ignited the fancy, and often the frenzy, of a growing number of shoppers. Though it offered no fancy wrapping or packaging, no free delivery, very little sales help and only a few fitting rooms, though its barren décor was broken only by rows of sales counters jammed in check-by-jowl, Filenes Folly had become a shopping Mecca not just for Bostonians but for many who lived far beyond the city's limits.

Spurring on its growing popularity was the Basement's increasing ability to make available attractive, and attractively priced, merchandise. Many of its initial buying mistakes could actually be interpreted as a healthy sign for they indicated the eagerness with which the Basement's staff was tackling their tasks. Inspired with an esprit de corps engendered by their feelings of rivalry with the staff of the main store, they were constantly ready to try something new.

In December 1913, the Basement took ads in the New York press to say that its buyers were coming to Manhattan and inviting manufacturers with suitable goods to sell to call at the company's New York office. As *The New York Times* subsequently reported, the ads provoked considerable comment in commercial circles for it marked the first instance anyone could remember of a major retailer advertising to purchase goods rather than to sell them.

The basement buyers discovered ways to create merchandise out of material previously considered junk. In Amsterdam, for instance, they had begun buying the leftover bits of precious stones from the city's jewelry makers. These chips, as they were called, sold well once they were sent back to Boston and offered at bargain prices.

Adroit processing techniques joined with aggressive purchasing policies in holding prices down. The basement staff had developed ways of simplifying and speeding up the entire sales mechanism. As one magazine commented in 1914, "the equipment and methods of this basement are reduced to such simplicity that many a visiting merchant, accustomed to the ponderous, slow-moving conventional store, has stood in amazement when he beheld it."

Thanks to such imaginative and innovative approaches, the basement had experienced some spectacular sales. On occasion it sold nearly 8,000 men's suits in a single day. On another occasion it disposed of 62,000 bars of soap in a mere three hours. Boston's Brahmins, long known for their frugality, had begun somewhat surreptitiously, to join the "hoi polloi" in sampling the basement's offerings. One popular story told of two dowagers accidentally running into each other in the aisle and each going to great lengths to convince the other that she was only shopping for her maid.

Customers sometimes became fierce and even ferocious. A bargain-priced grammarphone produced such a bitter fight between five would-be purchasers, one of them a clergyman, that the sales force had to remove the machine from the counter, interview witnesses and then later notify the winner. One battle between two women over a child's snow suit ended with one of them biting the other so badly that the victim required first aid. The bitten woman was taken off to the store clinic still clinging tenaciously, and triumphantly, to the disputed garment.

"Dollar Days" were proving especially popular, attracting as many as a half-million shoppers a day, or more than double the number that had showed up on the opening of the new store itself. Many mothers had begun purposely bringing their children who because of their small size could wriggle their way through the crowds and get to the counters. Zealous women shoppers could be seen trying on dresses and occasionally corsets in the aisles as they sought to make their buying decisions before the merchandise was gone.

On dress sales days the intensity and size of the crowds reached such a level that the staff developed the Filene Formation to re-stock the rapidly emptying counters. Under this plan stockboys would sally forth from the stockroom in groups of three. The first would run interference, the second would carry the stock and the third would hold off assaults from the rear.

Filene's Folly had thus become Filene's Phenomenon and as such was attracting attention well beyond the boundaries of Boston and of the business world itself. In 1921 a Hollywood studio chose the basement as the setting for a film entitled "One Flight Down." It was the first feature picture ever filmed in a store.

Harold Hodgkinson, the young ex-newspaper reporter whom Edward had hired in 1912, bore much of the credit for the basement's increasing success. Though still in his twenties he had now moved into a managerial position, and, working out of an office created from a former coal bin, he was developing imaginative and effective ways of promoting his boss's pet project. In a few years he would take over the entire basement operation and under his guidance it would do the largest cash business per square foot of any mercantile operation in the world. (The basement would relinquish this distinction in the 1960's to another Boston firm, a compact, 24-hour-a-day supermarket situated in the city's Prudential Center.)

***

Cooperative attitudes and approaches came naturally to Lincoln Filene. They not only suited his train of thought, as they did Edward's, but also his personality, as they failed to do with Edward's. Lincoln had, as we have seen, already made heavy use of cooperative techniques and tactics in running the store. Now he was starting to look for a larger stage in which to put them to work.

Lincoln had become intrigued with the possibilities he saw in fostering cooperation between stores that did not compete for the same customers. In trips throughout the country he had sounded out other store owners and had become convinced that what he had in mind would work. So in 1916 he invited a group of these store owners to a luncheon at the Aldine Club in New York.

His guest list included the presidents of some of the nation's leading mercantile enterprises such as Abraham and Strauss of Brooklyn, J.J. Hudson of Detroit, the Emporium of San Francisco, F & R Lazarus of Columbus, Ohio and several others. But only one store from each city was represented.

When the dessert dishes had been cleared away and the cigars lit, Lincoln rose to speak. His speech would open a new chapter in the history of American merchandising.

Lincoln proposed to his guests that they form a new organization to exchange information. Each store would report regularly its purchases, sales and profits. It would also report which goods were selling well and which were not, along with those retailing and operational practices which were working well and those which were not. All these reports would be sent to the headquarters of the proposed organization which would combine them into one consolidated report, copies of which would then be sent to each member store for use in its own planning and operations.

While Lincoln's idea may strike a present day outsider as innocuous and even obvious, it did not seem so to those who first heard it. Secrecy was considered such a vital necessity to retailing success that many store owners refused to tell their own wives and sons just how and what they were doing. Now they were being asked to open their books to other retailers, some of whom they hardly knew.

There was also an additional problem. Once an organization is formed there is no telling just what direction it will take and how far it will go. The big stores feared that the smaller ones would outvote them at meetings. The smaller stores, on the other hand, feared that the big ones would naturally dominate the organization and themselves as well.

Lincoln managed to overcome both objections. He persuaded his fellow merchants that they stood in no real danger from divulging the details of their business to one another. On the contrary, such a practice would not only provide them with much useful information, but also good contacts. They could call on one another for advice and assistance.

The problem of big store domination he solved easily by suggesting that all decisions be based on unanimous consent. Nothing was to be done that any individual member did not want to have done. Consequently, each store could feel sure of being able to protect its interests.

With such assurances as these, put forth in Lincoln's persuasive manner, most of the merchants capitulated. In November 1916, the Retail Research Association came into being. Despite its academic-sounding title it functioned solely as an information clearing-house for its nineteen member stores.

The new organization did not get underway without problems. In order for the members to make use of each other's figures, those figures had to be compiled in a uniform manner. In other words, each store had to figure its expenses, profits, etc. in the same way so that meaningful comparisons could be made. Yet some store owners used accounting techniques that were all their own.

One of these was B. Forman, the semi-literate former tailor whom Louis Kirstein had financed and whose subsequent success had now made him a member of the new organization. Forman did not use depreciation in figuring his net profits and when the Association's accountants asked him to take the wear and tear of his facilities into account, he became greatly upset and boarded a train for Boston. There, sitting in Kirstein's office and weeping uncontrollably, the confused man said, "Vunce, already, Lou, I paid for the building and now your meshuggene (crazy) bookkeeper says again a second time I gotta pay for it." Kirstein finally managed to explain the accounting concept to him and Forman returned to Rochester in a more tranquil state.

Aside from such difficulties, the RRA, as it was called, functioned well. The unanimity rule caused no significant obstructions for as the members became more at ease with each other they also became more compromising. As a result, the minority usually gave in to the majority after an issue had been thoroughly hashed over. As the Association's president, Lincoln chaired its meetings and his persuasive personality helped greatly in making the unanimity rule work.

From acting as an information gathering and dispensing organization, the RRA then went on to establish a central employment agency. This proved to be a great help to Filene's and the other members in finding personnel, particularly, specialists of various kinds.

The cooperative approach was working so well that in March, 1918 the members, under Lincoln leadership, took a still bolder step. They organized the Associated Merchandising Corporation to handle joint purchasing missions throughout the world. The new corporation set up offices on three floors of a building on lower Broadway in Manhattan and after the war established additional offices in Chicago and throughout Europe. This network of offices, which eventually expanded to Bombay and Tokyo, gave Filene's and the other members valuable foreign supply sources that none of them could have hoped to develop on their own.

There was no dispute as to who should head the new corporation. Lincoln was the unanimous choice. He had now firmly established himself as a trail-blazing leader in the field of American retailing.

***

With the basement now profitable, and with the cooperative mechanisms it had initiated with other stores working well, Filene's resumed the restless expansion that had marked its years prior to 1912. In 1920 the firm acquired additional space for its men's store, and still not satisfied, took over a new building for the men's wear department the following year. The company also erected a building in Cambridge to serve as a garage, free storage plant, print shop, etc. And notwithstanding the aid it was obtaining from Associated Merchandising, it opened its own New York office.

In September 1922 Filene's took out large display ads in the Boston papers to commemorate the tenth anniversary of its main store building. The firm proudly pointed out that it was handling 10 million sales transactions a year versus only one million, 600 thousand in 1912. Its number of employees had gone from a little over 1,000 in 1912 to almost 3,000 in 1922. When the new store was opened the average employee was earning only about 14 dollars a week; salaries now averaged about 26 dollars a week with most of the increase representing real (i.e. non-inflationary) growth. William Filene's sons were doing well, and so, apparently, were those who had cast their lot with them.

But the store's employees had benefitted from its expansion not just through increased salaries and promotional opportunities but through further advances in its pioneering labor policies. For in the new corporation which the brothers set up in conjunction with the move to their new building, they took what some considered their boldest step yet: they provided for direct employee representation on the firm's board of directors.

According to the corporation's new charter, the Filene Cooperative Association was to nominate a panel of six employees from which management would select four to be board members. The only requirement for nomination was five years of continuous employment with the store. The brothers wanted to make sure that anyone chosen for such a role should have demonstrated some degree of commitment to the store and acquired some measure of experience in its operation. Otherwise any employee would be eligible to be a director of the company.

A new minimum salary scale was also established. It was based largely on age with the minimum salaries set as follows: Under 18: $10 a week; over 18 but under 19: $12 a week; over 19 and with one year of experience: $14 a week. These minimums were somewhat above what other stores were generally paying but what made them more interesting and, within the context of the times, advanced, was their absence of sex differentiation. While in practice male employs did average more, this was mostly due to such factors as differences in the jobs they held, the increased effort many expended in order to feed their families and, in a few areas, unionization. The store itself made no deliberate attempt to pay its female employees less than what it paid its male workers. A scholarly study of the store done in the late 1920's by the Russell Sage Foundation would find no indication of sexual discrimination in any of its policies. This study gains increased credibility from the fact that it was headed by a woman, Mary La Dame, who at one time had worked as a sales clerk at Filene's.

In April, 1913 the store raised the discounts it gave on merchandise to its own employees from 15 to 20 percent. Since Filene's was basically a clothing store, and since clothing constituted a large portion of the working family's budget in those days, this generous discount policy was much appreciated. In fact, it became overly appreciated as some employees began using it to purchase items for friends, relatives and neighbors. Because of such abuses, the store canceled the discount policy the following year but later re-introduced it under tighter controls.

Store employees had always shown an understandable interest in shorter hours, particularly during slack times. Aware of such desires Lincoln in the Spring of 1913 urged the city's Retail Trade Board to adopt Saturday store closings during the slow Summer months. When the other Board members refused, Lincoln decided to go ahead on his own. The Filene Cooperative Association was naturally delighted. As *The Echo* jubilantly proclaimed, "Now the whole day is ours." Some years later the other downtown stores followed in Filene's footsteps and ended their practice of staying open half days on Saturday in July and August.

Some of these policies undoubtedly contributed to the financial difficulties which engulfed the store that year and which threatened its existence. But a more pernicious problem came from the over-expansion of its number of employees. In moving to its new building the firm had more than tripled its work force, going from a payroll of 900 to one of over 3,000. Retrenchment was required to restore solvency and several hundred employees had to be let go. (However, as we have seen, by 1922 the store would be doing enough business to warrant and, indeed, require such a large work force.)

The massive downsizing strained the machinery of the Board of Arbitration as many of the laid-off employees protested their dismissals. The Board processed 70 cases in 1914, far more than it had ever handled in the past or would ever handle again in a year.

The Arbitration Board's work load brought certain shortcomings in its operations to light and prompted Lincoln to revise its procedures. But far from curtailing the board's prerogatives or powers, the changes actually expanded them. The board was now given the right and even the duty to initiate inquiries on its own "to see that justice prevails". Thus it was transformed from an essentially reactive body, responding only to grievances brought before it, to a pro-active one, equipped and encouraged to ferret out failures in the firm's employee relations practices. Its procedures also became more formalized with provisions made for opening statements, cross-examination of witnesses, and a stenographic record of its proceedings.

As these changes make clear, Lincoln and Edward were still hoping to expand the FCA's involvement in the store's operation. In the Fall of 1914 Lincoln came up with the idea of an "FCA Day", on which the employee organization would actually run the store on its own. It was set for November 2 and went off smoothly. Encouraged,

Lincoln then offered the FCA $10,000 for its treasury if it could increase next month's business by ten percent over the previous December.

Since Filene's annual Christmas sales had steadily been going up, the goal did not seem inordinately high. The FCA eagerly took up the challenge but failed to meet it. Lincoln, however, was not discouraged, feeling that he had not given the association enough time to prepare for the challenge.

In 1920 another and more ambitious attempt was made to give the employees a greater role, along with greater responsibilities, in running the store. With Lincoln's encouragement, the FCA launched a drive to increase August business by fifty percent over the previous year. Since August was the slowest month of the year it would not take all that many new sales to reach the goal and the FCA succeeded in doing so. However, an FCA effort a few years later to raise store revenues by twenty percent fell short.

In the meantime the FCA was expanding its various service and recreation activities. Its library increased to 1500 volumes, its annual "Follies" moved to Copley Hall for its end-of-the year presentations, its band became larger and more proficient and several new recreational clubs emerged. The employee organization also worked with management to open up a dental clinic in 1919, another "Filene's First". And in 1920, the group's education committee went from sponsoring occasional lectures to offering entire courses in such things as needlecraft, singing, beauty-care and other subjects in which the members had expressed an interest.

But not all the education going on inside the store at this time fell into the category of recreation or general self-improvement. For Filene's was now operating one of the world's first schools of retailing.

Here again the development was spurred on by the move to the new store. But another factor fostering its growth was the appointment of a new, energetic training director, Joan Cannon. She was the first woman to hold such a post in an American store.

Each new employee was given three introductory talks plus a tour of the store. Once assigned to a department, he or she would join other employees in holding regular meetings to discuss how to organize and execute their department's work in the most efficient manner. Thus something akin to the quality control circle, a device which management began importing from Japan in the 1980's, was being utilized in a Boston specialty store before World War I.

In 1918 the store began offering more systematized and advanced instruction to those wishing to move into supervisory or specialist positions. These courses caught on so quickly that by 1922 the training department was employing a full-time "faculty" of 22. It was in effect operating a school of retailing. A few years later, Mary La Dame and her fellow researchers at the Russell Sage Foundation would credit Filene's extensive training program for the fact that over two-thirds of the store's managers and executives had come up from the ranks.

But despite these impressive advances, not all was smooth sailing on the Filene labor front during these years. For while the store's increasing size offered new opportunities, it also created new problems while compounding some old ones. And while Edward and Lincoln continued to push for stepped-up employee participation, they often ran into difficulties they had not expected, difficulties which sometimes caused them to differ from one another.

The two brothers had long wanted to set up a profit-sharing plan for the store's workers. This, so they felt, would advance their ideals and stimulate their employees to assume more responsibility. In 1913 they and the other four managing partners approved a draft plan for putting profit-sharing into effect. However, no profit can be distributed before it is earned and Filene's at the time was losing money. Even when the store returned to profitability the following year, there were still the accumulated debts plus the need to pay dividends on the store's preferred and common stock.

But by the Fall of 1916 it became clear that an earned surplus would be available and so Edward and Lincoln, along with Cory and Kierstein met with the FCA executive committee to discuss what to do with it. They decided to split the surplus fifty-fifty between the employees and management.

But further complications emerged. How was the employee share to be distributed? What factors should be figured in determining how much an individual received? Then, another drawback to the whole scheme arose. Filene's would have to pay taxes on the profit and this would reduce the amount available for distribution. But if it gave the money out in the form of bonuses, it could then be charged off as an expense to the firm and no taxes would have to be paid.

It was decided to follow the bonus route. But this still left the problem of deciding who gets how much. Sales people should be excluded, it was felt, since the commissions they received on top of their salaries already made them profit-sharers. The more business the store did, the more they earned. The surplus should go to the large and growing force of buyers, shippers, janitors, supervisors, etc. whose personal income did not automatically rise when the store's income did.

After several meetings with the FCA leadership, some sort of system was devised and put into effect. It did not work well. A cartoon in *The Echo* in early 1917 shows a "Miss FCA" as generally chilly to the bonus plan and another cartoon a week later offers some of the reasons. It depicts sales people, buyers, decorators, etc. all feverishly explaining why they should get a bonus.

The next year the newly-organized operating committee, consisting of the assistants to the six partners, began making the bonus decisions. This shifting of the decision-making process to the top or near-top seems to have reduced employee dissatisfaction. Unfortunately it also reduced employee participation as well.

The operating committee gave the lion's share of the bonus money to supervisors and specialists, claiming that such benefactions stimulated only upper-echelon employees to increase their productivity. Rank and file workers tended to look upon a bonus as a gift rather than as an incentive. Furthermore, while Filene's rank and file generally earned a bit more than their counterparts in other Boston stores, its managers and specialists generally made slightly less. Giving the latter group most of the bonus money, said the committee, would help rectify the balance.

Edward rejected this rationale and consistently voted against many of the operating committee's decisions. But Lincoln and the others accepted the committee's argument and approved most of its awards. So apparently did the FCA for no signs of discontent developed. Still, an effort aimed at increasing employee involvement had ended by reducing it. Power had gravitated to the top, not the bottom.

In reviewing the set back a few years later, Mary La Dame and her fellow researchers found they could not really blame management for the outcome. Profit-sharing through bonuses does demand some attention to such things as tardiness and absenteeism as well as some basic knowledge of accounting. Moreover, making such decisions involves a lot of work. Such factors as these, so the researchers concluded, made the operating committee a better vehicle than the FCA for assuming this responsibility. Also there was no gainsaying the fact that the operating committee's decisions seemed to provoke less employee dissatisfaction than had those of the FCA. Indeed, the employee group had not shown the slightest wish to further involve itself in this sensitive task. But the researchers expressed regret that this particular attempt at increasing employee participation had not worked out differently. Lincoln Filene undoubtedly felt the same way.

***

Despite the store's employee association and its advanced labor policies, some members of its work force had joined the country's growing trade union movement. One problem the unions presented was that those who belonged to them obtained benefits that FCA members did not enjoy while they continued to share in the FCA's benefits as well. For example, the members of the busheling department had won a reduced work day. Yet they also had their Saturdays free during July and August. These additional benefits, so Lincoln and the other management members reasoned, were unfair to other employees since it reduced the store's profits and thereby the bonuses it could pay.

In 1923 the store decided to deny trade union members certain benefits available to FCA members. The busheling department employees promptly offered to give up their union membership. The FCA passed on the offer to management, but management, interestingly enough, said no. As Lincoln wrote back to the FCA's leadership, "This corporation has no intention off taking action at any time to influence any employee to resign from his union."

A meeting between the various parties was soon scheduled but in the meantime the men stopped paying their union dues. This action annoyed rather appeased Lincoln who reproved them for not being good union members. There is no guarantee that you would be better members of the FCA, he told them, and he urged them to return to their union. They did so but although they were allowed to affiliate with the FCA they remained excluded from bonuses and other benefits until some years later.

The labor problem that bothered Lincoln most during this period was the same one that had grieved Edward earlier. The workers did not demand enough. They possessed potential power but they generally declined to use it.

To be sure they did participate in the working out of many minor matters. The FCA, for example, had made some suggestions for the new wage plan of 1919 and management accepted all of them. A few years later, when management tried to change the dress code for sales personnel, the FCA objected and the store quickly gave in. But this was not the kind of participation the Filenes had in mind.

When it came to nominating members for the company's Board of Directors the employees generally chose executives such as Employment Director Ernest Hopkins. While the Filenes did want board members who would understand what was going on and who would not divulge certain privileged information to the store's competitors, Lincoln realized that employee representation on the Board of Directors had not really brought the employees closer to the operation of the business.

In the Spring of 1921 an incident occurred which seemed likely to encourage the kind of employee participation the Filenes wanted. The store's drivers were working between 10 and 11 hours a day, and although this was about average for all store drivers in Boston at the time, the men asked for a shorter shift. The company granted their request on condition that the drivers assume responsibility for seeing that each of them give an "honest day's work." The drivers agreed on condition that the store give them the right to re-route their districts so as to insure equity and efficiency in apportioning the work.

Lincoln was delighted at the demand and quickly granted it. Two months later he checked on how it was working out. He found that the morale of the men had improved, the quality of the store's delivery service had improved, and, despite the shorter work day, the per package cost of deliveries had actually gone down!

This happy outcome seemed to confirm what he and Edward had been saying all along. But unfortunately, it failed to mark or spark any significant surge of a participatory spirit elsewhere within the store's staff. It remained an isolated, albeit encouraging, event.

More typical was what had happened with the suggestion committee. This committee had been set up under FCA auspices to solicit suggestions from employees which could improve the store's operations. But instead of the torrent of new ideas which the Filenes had expected, there had only been a trickle. And while some of them had proven useful, virtually none had demonstrated the depth or breath which the brothers had expected.

In late 1921 the Operating Committee decided to take over more of the Committee's work in the hope of stimulating more suggestions. As a further aid to this endeavor, the company, as part of the tenth anniversary celebration of the new store, held a special suggestion contest. It offered a total of $25,000 in prizes with a first prize of $15,000 for an idea "as valuable as the bargain basement."

However, the store management made clear that it was not promising "to award all or any of the prizes" for "awards will be made only for suggestions deemed valuable."

The contest lasted six weeks and did produce a substantial number of suggestions. However, the largest sum awarded was $2,500. There were two awards of $1,000 each, one for $500, six for $250 and a number of lesser awards of $10. Since even $10 was almost a week's pay for many employees, the sums could not be called paltry. Yet the total was less than a third of the maximum made available. Only one of the major suggestions ever became a prominent and permanent part of the store's operations, and it was modified considerably in the process. This was a proposal for a Bureau of Standards to test and evaluate new merchandise. Others dealt with such matters as replacing 60 watt bulbs with 25 watt bulbs in stock cases or erecting a sign at the entrance of the women's coat department. Moreover, most of these proposals had come from managers and specialists and not the rank and file.

Later that year, Lincoln called together a representative group of employees and asked them how much additional participation they wanted over and above what they already had. As he later summed up their reaction, "There was no real response. On the contrary, the members of this committee who were fairly typical of the rank and file, were frankly and unanimously of the opinion that their fellow employees had no desire whatever to meddle in management and control.

"I am sorry to have to admit this disappointment," Lincoln went on to say. "And the experiences of others who have made some such tender to their people is the same as ours. The truth has been brought home to us that the day of full self-rule in industry is still far distant."

***

Although guiding Filene's through the perils of over-expansion and then through the difficulties and the uncertainties of the war and post-war era had consumed most of Lincoln's energies during this period, he still found time to extend his outside activities. He would never compete with Edward for the public spotlight; he had no desire to do so. But he was gradually making his presence felt in public affairs.

Education had remained, as it always would remain, his prime public concern. In 1913 he became a member of the advisory committee of the Boston Industrial School for Boys. Two years later he was appointed to the Massachusetts Board of Education, and when his term ran out four years later, he accepted an appointment to the Board's advisory committee. He would serve on the committee for 17 years and would rarely miss a meeting.

Higher education had also begun to attract his attention. In 1913 Harvard University decided, after considerable controversy within the ranks of its own faculty and alumni, to set up a Division of Education. Lincoln contributed financially and in other ways supported the new division which would later evolve into a separate school within the university. Two years later when Ernest Hopkins resigned as Filene's employment director to become president of Dartmouth, he carried with him not only his boss's blessing but also his commitment to contribute to the college. The following year Hopkins showed his appreciation by arranging for Lincoln to receive an honorary Master of Arts degree.

In taking part in the festivities and rituals attending the event, this middle ages Jewish merchant and high school drop-out so captivated the largely Anglo-Saxon, blue-blooded graduating class of that year that in 1921 its members invited him to their fifth class reunion. Lincoln accepted, and when he showed up they took the most unusual step of making him an honorary member of the Dartmouth Class of 1916. Henceforth, he attended almost every reunion of his class, sometimes hosting the affair himself. He would remain a life-long friend and supporter of the New Hampshire college, eventually establishing a scholarship to help deserving students who needed aid.

In 1922 the College of William and Mary made him an honorary member of Phi Beta Kappa. Thereafter, he proudly and conspicuously wore his "Phi Bate" key on his watch chain, although Dartmouth continued to have first call on his academic affections.

Lincoln was pleased to see the protocol which he and Brandeis drew up to resolve the Garment Workers strike used, with few modifications, to settle a similar dispute in the "waist trades" in 1913. But in 1915 trouble once more broke out in the Garment industry and this time he and his brilliant friend would not be so successful.

Brandeis was in Washington when the new round of labor conflict developed. He immediately hurried back to Boston to confer with Lincoln on ways to end it. The pair designed a new plan which Brandeis then took to New York to present to a mediation board formed to restore peace to the industry. But the mediators watered down the Brandeis-Filene plan considerably, making it quite vague on various key issues. Consequently, labor trouble continued to plague the industry.

Soon after came the battle over Brandeis' Supreme Court nomination, and, as might be expected, Lincoln rallied to his friends' defense. He did his best to drum up support for the embattled Brandeis who corresponded and conferred frequently with Lincoln during this, for him, exhausting episode.

America's entry into the war brought new issues and involvements into Lincoln's life. He became an early supporter of Daylight Saving Time, then quite a controversial issue, and helped persuade both the U.S. Chamber of Commerce and the American Federation of Labor to support it. As Chairman of the Retail Research Association and an increasingly recognized and respected leader in the retailing field, he occasionally found himself in Washington serving as a spokesman for his industry. When Edward was also there, as was frequently the case during the war years, the two would get together. In one letter to his mother, Edward relates how he and Lincoln had both testified that day at a Senate hearing, then dined together and afterwards spent the evening with some "professor friends."

In 1921 *The New York Times* took its first notice of the younger Filene brother by publishing two stories about him. The first was a report from the annual convention of the National Retail Dry Goods Association where Lincoln had delivered an address. It was not the address itself, however, which caught the attention of the paper's correspondent but an interchange which Lincoln had with the then U.S. Secretary of Commerce, Joshua Alexander, who had also addressed the group. Although retail profit margins then, as now, were only averaging three percent of gross sales, Alexander, rather astonishingly, asserted that "the profiteering retailer is the only factor standing between the public and low prices." This drew the usually mild mannered Lincoln to his feet. "Nobody ever accused a five-and-ten cent store of profiteering," he retorted, "and yet isn't it a fact that they make as good profits as any other retailers." Lincoln then concluded by reaffirming his father's and his own retailing philosophy. "Selling simply means getting the confidence of the public," he said.

The second *Times* story published nine days later dealt with a far different matter. A bill had been filed in Congress to establish a Federal Department of Education. Known as the Smith-Towner Bill, it faced rough sledding for the Harding administration and the Republican party generally viewed with disfavor Federal incursions into such matters of hereteto local concern. In fact, the spirit of the country as a whole was hostile to all social welfare measures stemming from Washington. To counteract such attitudes the backers of the bill had set up a national organization to push for its enactment. This new nationwide organization had named Lincoln Filene as its president.

This development reveals two basic facts about Lincoln Filene in 1921. First, it shows that he had achieved some prominence on the national scene. Secondly, it shows that he, like his brother, was still well ahead of his time, for nearly a half-century would elapse before the country would be ready to recognize and sanction a Federal presence in the field of education.

***

Lincoln's devotion to his wife and daughters had rewarded him with a smooth and, for the most part, serene domestic life. During the war Therese had helped organize activities and services for locally-stationed soldiers and sailors. She had also taken on the additional hostessing duties which Lincoln's leadership of the Retail Research Association and Associated Merchandising had created. His daughters had grown up and off to college. But in 1918 his eldest one, Catherine, became a source of concern to both her parents.

A bright and exceptionally dynamic girl, Catherine had entered Vassar in 1914. On becoming ill she had returned to Boston where, after her recovery, she had entered a local women's college named Wheaton. There, as an undergraduate, she began organizing conferences on how to promote jobs for women. She was already showing signs of the initiative and imagination which would later make her the first woman to receive a Master's Degree in Education from Harvard, the first woman member of the National Democratic Committee, the editor of the country's first significant book on careers for women and, in later life, the primary organizer of the world-famed Wolf Trapp Music Festival in Virginia.

On graduating from college in 1918, Catherine took off for Washington where she promptly landed a job as assistant to the chief of the Women's Division of the U.S. Employment Service. The position called for her to spend half her time traveling throughout the country by herself. This was certainly a challenging assignment for a young woman of her day and she found it most attractive. But her parents, as expected given the fact that they grew up in the Victorian era, did not. For three months relations between daughter and parents virtually ceased. As Catherine put it, "they disowned me."

But the disowning, if such it was, was more Theresa's doing than Lincoln's and at his instigation the rift was finally patched up. No further disruptions in their relationship would ever occur but throughout his life, Lincoln would remain somewhat puzzled and mystified by his enterprising eldest daughter who in so many ways more resembled her uncle Edward than either of her parents. (This is probably the reason why she seemed to get along with Edward better than did any other member of the family. Fortunately for her, however, Catherine possessed far more tact and social grace than did her complex-ridden uncle.)

Catherine did give her father further cause for worry a few years later but this time Lincoln's concern took a more sympathetic turn. In 1920 he introduced her to a young man named Alvin Dodd at a dinner party at the family's Weston home. Dodd was a protégée of Lincoln's, having been picked by him to be executive-secretary of the Retail Research Association. Lincoln was quite pleased when, after a brief courtship, the couple became engaged. But his pleasure gradually turned to pain when he saw Catherine becoming overly nervous and upset as the wedding day drew near. He feared that she was having serious misgivings over the impending marriage. His fears proved well founded for the marriage did not last. Before it broke up, however, it produced a child, Joan, born in 1923. Lincoln thus became a grandfather.

No such problems developed with his more domestic and demure younger daughter, Helen. She graduated Skidmore College and shortly afterwards married a tall and handsome young Harvard graduate named George Ladd. The couple had met while Helen was still in high school and so their courtship had lasted five years. Consequently, when George came to Lincoln to tell him that he wanted to marry Helen and to ask if he had any objections, Lincoln merely looked up at him with the famous twinkle in his eye and said, "George, if I had any objections, don't you suppose you would have heard them by now?"

On the morning of the wedding Lincoln took the nervous bridegroom out to the golf course to calm him down. But every time George went up to drive, Lincoln, noticing how badly he was shaking, couldn't resist reminding him "there's still time to run, George, there's still time to run." George did not run and the marriage would last a lifetime, producing three sons and much happiness, not only for the couple themselves, but for Lincoln who not only enjoyed his grandchildren but became increasingly fond of, and close to, his son-in-law. The couple would be a great source of support and comfort to him in the difficult years which lay ahead.

Chapter 9
THE WRITERS FILENE

1923

The lights are burning far into the evening on the eighth floor of the Filene building this winter. For this floor houses the store's executive office and both its President and its General Manager, along with some of their staff members, are working late. As it so happens, they are at work on similar, if wholly separate, projects. Edward Filene and Lincoln Filene are both writing books.

***

Lincoln would entitle his book *Merchant's Horizon* and its contents reveal that this merchant's horizon extended quite far into the future. For many of Lincoln's ideas anticipate not only the spirit and broad principles but even some of the practical applications of what today we call modern management.

Lincoln stressed, for example, the importance of organizational goals. "The most perfect organization cannot travel very far toward success unless it is driven by a high purpose," he noted, and though such a statement may not strike the present-day reader as very original, it has become an underlying theme of many contemporary management authorities. Lincoln also writes that the modern worker "has much in him to give. More than the mere skill of his hands. Few of us realize how widely the creative instinct, and even a feeling for artistry, are diffused among those who work with their hands." Again, a statement which to contemporary ears may sound piously soporific but which another notable theorist of modern management, MIT's Douglas MacGregor, would promulgate and propound with great success during the 1950's and 60's.

Lincoln also favored and foresaw the coming alliance between business and academia. "Never has business had greater need of the educator and never could education better profit by the businessman's touch in its guidance," he writes. Why? "Because business has learned by now its dependence on the school for many of its most important advances. And the schools, on their part, have discovered the contribution that business can make to them, because business is life, it is daily bread, and so has its own lessons to teach."

Lincoln may have rushed things a bit on this issue for at the time he was writing this symbiotic relationship between the groves of academe and the workplace was far from glaringly apparent to either sector. It has since, however, been wholeheartedly embraced by most businessmen if not by many educators, large numbers of whom continue to view the world of commerce with distaste and disdain.

He also may have leaped too far into the future when he stressed the still greater importance of another crucial change. Business, he wrote, "has now taken to itself...*the service spirit.*" (Lincoln's emphasis). Although the concept was not entirely novel in the 1920's, it would not become a critical issue in business until the 1960's. It still remains an issue, and a contentious one at that, since some economists, such as Milton Freedman, claim that business can best serve society by making good profits through producing desirable goods cheaply, and allowing other organizations, including the government, to worry about broader ideals and goals.

Lincoln himself indicates that the "service spirit" had not spread as widely through business as he would like. In fact, most of the criticisms in his book are reserved for his fellow businessmen. He accuses them of overly indulging in cut-throat and ultimately wasteful competition instead of adopting more cooperative and actually more profitable approaches such as joint purchasing (One sees here the reasoning which led him to form the Retail Research Association and then the Associated Merchandising Corporation). He looks to the emergence of chain stores as one antidote to such a splintering and scattering of resources.

Lincoln also blames business for labor's heretheto poor record in cooperating with management to achieve greater production. "The enlightenment necessary to any further progress in bringing manager and employee in full working accord must start with the manager." Businessmen can hardly accuse their workers of apathy, he says when they themselves often remain apathetic when it comes to involving themselves in the welfare of their workers or their communities.

Predictably Lincoln lays great stress in his book on employee participation. He regards such participation as not just desirable but necessary. Employees must assume increasing power, responsibility and, eventually, at least some degree of ownership in the enterprises that employ them. To those who would claim that working people lacked the capabilities to play such an enlarged role, he points out how "two hundred years ago the same poor opinion was entertained of the average man's political capacity. What did he know of the enormously complicated process of government?" But, he points out, the country, under democracy, has not only survived but thrived.

The rights which a worker now exercises as a citizen he will eventually wish and demand to exercise as an employee, says Lincoln. The dichotomy between the political arena and the workplace can not and should not endure for "the two chief interests in the average human life, the maintenance of life itself and the maintenance of a country to live in, must be brought into something of likeness."

The growing trend towards big corporations, in his view, makes such a move more and more urgent. The big corporation must exert greater effort to make its employees feel less like cogs in a machine and more like designers of their own destiny. Otherwise, the employees will fail to furnish the information and cooperation the company needs to sustain itself.

He reviews some of Filene's efforts toward this end, scrupulously noting that not all of them had succeeded. The continued "timidity" of his employees to embrace and utilize the power offered them is "tragic in its nature and effects." Still, the results had been positive enough to reassure him that Filene's, and the Filenes, were on the right track.

Lincoln carefully points out, indeed he emphasizes, that what he is advocating is not only consistent with but conducive to improved profits. "The moves my brother Edward and I may have made toward sharing responsibility with our people were made primarily for good business reasons, and our work-associates so understood it. For it is safe to say that one must make a business a success if his contribution to the liberalizing of business in general is to count. Any broad advance that might come out of our efforts we preferred to regard as of secondary importance." But he goes on to say in words whose sincerity no one who knew him could ever doubt. "Call it honest interest or call it calculation, the fact remains that we wanted to deserve the friendship of our people. It was admittedly good business, but it was also something more. It was satisfying a sense of justice."

***

Edward's book, which he entitled *The Way Out*, parallels Lincoln's in many respects. He, too, takes as his basic theme the essential convergence and congruence between profit making and public service. "The real end of business is not to make money but to render a service to the public." But, he adds, "it happens to be a profession in which money can be made in great amounts. In fact, the merchant must make money in great amounts if he really renders a great service."

Edward noted how common it was "for social critics to bewail the fact that American civilization is predominantly a business civilization." And he goes on to say, "I hope to live to see the day when that regret will be changed to pride, a change that waits only upon business sense, business vision and business statesmanship...the social progress of the future lies not in the destruction of the modern business system but in its further and future development."

Yet this change will not come easily. Immediately ahead Edward sees surplus production leading to cut-throat competition which in turn will lead to wage-cutting, a development which could prove catastrophic as well as cruel. His prescription for avoiding this prognosis was long-term credits to the still war-shattered European nations so that they could buy American goods, plus increasing adoption of the techniques of mass production and mass distributions at home. We will be compelled, he says, "to Fordize American business and industry."

Edward's concocting of the term "Fordize" show how greatly impressed he had become by Henry Ford's mass production techniques which had brought car ownership within the reach of the average American family. He was struck not only by Ford's assembly line methods and standardized style but by his approach to setting prices. Ford priced his cars first and then set about reducing costs to meet that price rather than producing the car first and then pricing it to reflect its cost. In other words, he adjusted his costs to meet what he considered to be a marketable price rather than adjusting the price to meet his expenses.

At the same time, Ford was paying high wages, extraordinary high for factory work at that time. This also elicited Edward's enthusiasm, for high wages, so Edward felt, enabled producers to become consumers and this should avert the scourge of surplus production which he saw lurking just over the horizon.

188 ---- George E. Berkley

Edward thus wanted more standardization of production, a development which, in his view, would lead to less waste and duplication. Hundreds of brands of wallpaper were far too many, he said. Concentrating on fewer brands would bring down the costs considerably. Even such a small step as standardizing the thickness of walls could appreciably cut the cost of new houses. Mass production techniques generally, he averred, would lead to better work scheduling, less interrupted production, better stockpiling of materials and more prosperity for everyone. He wanted to see such methods become the rule not only in manufacturing but in distribution as well. There is an indication in his book, and also in his other writings, that he was hoping to become the Henry Ford of distribution.

Edward was well aware of the mounting chorus of criticism being leveled against mass production. These criticisms, which have hardly changed in over 70 years, include its presumed destruction of creativity in work, its similar destruction of variety in products, its impetus toward heavy-handed centralization, its rape of the environment, its ravaging of raw materials, its quickening of the materialistic impulse, etc. etc. After drawing up an extensive catalogue of such criticisms he then proceeds to rebut them.

On the whole, he does a fairly effective job at doing so. The key element in his case is the freedom which he sees flowing from the increased bounties of more efficient production. "...now the motives of the masses are mainly material," he says, "But free them from the bondage of bread and butter, and their desires will go out for better education, for instance, and better education will in turn give men a better sense of values."

Of course, machine work is monotonous but so is most work, says Edward, and in any event, machinery will make a shorter day possible. As for standardization, this will allow more people to buy more goods, thus actually extending, not curtailing, the variety available to the average American. And if it brings more simplicity to design, then this could increase rather than decrease beauty. In any case, Edward was confident that the increased leisure, wealth and education which mass production would produce would bring "a new competition for beauty and refinement."

Edward did not foresee any increased centralization resulting from such changes but rather the opposite. Growing specialization makes it more and more difficult to produce an entire commodity under one roof, he noted, and he pointed to Ford's success in decentralizing its operations.

But though Edward gives Henry Ford rave reviews for many of his industrial innovations, he carefully dissociates himself from many of Ford's other policies. He repudiates Ford's anti-Semitism though he does so only in passing and without mentioning that it touches him personally. He also throws cold water on the auto maker's rather crackpot currency theories and "sentimental" efforts to insure world peace. (Edward believed that international organization, to wit: the League of Nations, offered a more realistic solution to the peace problem.)

Edward goes far beyond Ford by calling for industrial democracy. His main argument rests on what he sees as its inevitability. In words that indicate how closely his views match those of his younger brother on such issues, Edward points out that a people accustomed to controlling their own political fortunes will eventually seek to control their economic and social conditions as well, since these latter factors affect them more directly. Should their employers seek to deny them such power then they will use their political power to obtain it. "It is important to remember," he writes, "that every time the masses have become conscious of their power, and have achieved a sense of solidarity, they have inaugurated a new epoch in history."

Edward urges his fellow businessmen not only to accept such a development but to accelerate its advent, and, like Lincoln, he targets most of his criticisms at his commercial colleagues. He expresses particular distaste for certain finance-oriented businessmen such as land and stock speculators, saying "We employers must become the sworn enemies of every avoidable and speculative increase in business costs." On the other hand, he deplores the tendency of so many businessmen to spend three-quarters of their lives making money and the last quarter giving it away. A businessman best serves society, he says, not through philanthropy but through operating his business efficiently, holding down costs, meeting the customer's needs, and, as a result of all these steps, making healthy profits.

In his last chapter Edward sheds some light on his own problems for in it he returns to the theme he had expounded after his ouster from the Board of the International Chamber of Commerce. This is the loneliness of the liberal businessman. Once again, he seems to put some of the blame for his removal on his own shoulders for he admits that the liberal businessman too readily becomes impatient, fails to do the necessary preparatory work, and forgets "the normal courtesies and amenities of human relations." At the age of 63 Edward Filene was finally starting to understand how his failure to get more people more interested in his ideas may have been caused not so much by their shortcomings as by his own.

Edward would write six more books during the remaining 14 years of his life, but none of them would be as revealing of the full range of his thought. For in this short work he incorporates the basic ideas which had begun to condition and color his approach to virtually every problem. A series of quotations from the book provides a further key to his thinking:

We must pay as much attention to our prophets as our forefathers paid to their profits...

The businessman of the future, whether manufacturer or merchant, will make more money by reducing prices than the businessman of the past ever made by raising them.

The businessman of the future must fill the pockets of the workers and consumers before he can fill his own pockets.

Who causes the most dangerous discontent, the reactionary businessman or the radical agitator?

...to see what is ignored by all is a sure way to be ignored by all.

...the first business of reform is to succeed.

***

The fact that the two brothers were working on their books at about the same time, leads to speculation that some sort of rivalry was going on. If this were the case, then knowing them as we now do, we must suppose that the rivalry was Edward's doing, not Lincoln's. One likely explanation is that Lincoln had first made the decision to do a book and this had stimulated his more competitive older brother to follow suit. In his introduction, Edward notes how he had been asked several times to write a book. Very likely he had never wanted to make time to do so until he learned that Lincoln had started to write one.

Both books came out in 1924 under the imprint of well-established publishers. But, though the thoughts expressed were remarkably similar, Edward's was the most far-ranging and would have by far the greater impact. *The Way Out* received generally favorable notices including one from *The New York Times Book Review*. Although the *Times* gave it only five paragraphs under its Books In Brief column, its reviewer called it "admirably ample and lucid in its statement and absorbing interesting from start to finish." The review concluded by noting "There has been within recent years no book on business methods, affairs and outlook quite so suggestive, so inspiring, so clear-minded and far-sighted as this. One may not agree with all that Mr. Filene says, but at least he makes the reader do a lot of thinking. It is a particularly good book for the young businessman to read, but, for that matter, it is also a good book for almost anyone to read who is intelligently interested in life."

Buoyed up by reviews such as this, as well as by enthusiastic endorsements from several business leaders such as the head of the American Bankers Association and the executive secretary of the American Association of Advertising Agencies, *The Way Out* went through six editions. It was also published extensively abroad. Lincoln's book, by contrast, received scant notice outside of mercantile circles and sold only a few thousand copies.

Of course, the two books, though markedly alike in their viewpoints, differed greatly in scope and tone. Lincoln confined his thoughts largely to labor relations, while Edward embraced the whole spectrum of social problems. Their tone also diverged. In their support of worker participation and possible ownership, for example, Lincoln issued a plea while Edward set forth a prophecy.

Both brothers drew extensively on the help of others in preparing their manuscripts. Lincoln was greatly aided by Dr. Benjamin Selekman, a professor at Harvard's new business school. Edward's primary ghost writer was Glenn Frank, a professional newspaperman. But both books reflect their respective authors. For example, Lincoln frequently uses the phrase "My brother and I," while Edward on the other hand simply says "I," making not a single mention of his younger brother in the entire book. To be sure, Lincoln's book continually refers to their experiences at the store while Edward's does not, thus affording its author far fewer occasions to refer to his fraternal business partner. Still, the contrast seems striking. Also, Lincoln dedicates his book, "To my wife" while Edward dedicates his to no one, though he does acknowledge Frank's "assistance in the organization of the material..."

The two books, then, vividly point up the personalities of their two authors, men who thought so much alike on so many important issues and yet who differed so widely in so many important ways.

***

While Edward and Lincoln were writing their books, the enterprise which incorporated so many of their ideas continued to prosper. In fact, sales rose every year during the 1920's, soaring well past the thirty million dollar mark by the decade's end. Frequently in business a growth in sales, while it produces an increase in total profit, fails to produce an increase in profit margin. Indeed, its profit margin may, and often does, go down. But this had not happened to the World's largest specialty store. While the store's profit margins fluctuated somewhat they tended to go up as well. Of the 30 million which it grossed in 1929, it earned over one and one-half million in net income. This gave the store a profit margin of about five percent as compared to the three-to-four percent which similar stores were earning. Business was indeed better than ever at Filene's.

Its continued growth had stimulated the store to seek out fresh fields for expansion. In 1922 it opened its first branch operation. It was a modest undertaking housed on the second floor over a five-and-ten cent store in Providence, Rhode Island. It was followed during the next six years by nine more branch stores throughout New England. Some were located in substantial cities, some in resort areas and some in towns having women's colleges. The sequence and sites of the new stores, after Providence, was as follows: Northampton, Hyannis, and York Harbor, Maine in 1923, Wellesley and Laconia, New Hampshire in 1924, Portland, Maine in 1925, Magnolia and South Hadley in 1926, Falmouth in 1927 and Worcester in 1928. In 1928 Filene's also enlarged its Hyannis, Wellesley, and Magnolia operations.

Back in Boston, meanwhile, the home store was also on the move. It acquired the two remaining buildings in its own block and in 1928 purchased the R.H White Company, a long-established and full-line department store on the other side of Washington Street. The firm took over the White Company with the intention of using its building to house some of its own non-clothing departments. For although Filene's still insisted that it was a specialty store and not a department store, the range of its specialties had spread far beyond its initial involvement in apparel.

This trend had already become apparent by 1912 when the new store opened its doors. It continued to grow during the ensuing years. In 1923, for example, Filene's opened its "Bobber Shop," the first hairdressing salon ever established in a store. The same year its men's barber shop began introducing such novelties as sun tan lamps and air hoses for drying hair quickly. Men arriving in Boston by overnight train could get buttons sewn, clothes pressed and hats blocked while they waited. Filene's had also set up a children's barber shop where youngsters could get their hair cut while perched atop gayly-colored, merry-go-round horses. By the mid 1920's the store had added a restaurant, a travel and theater-ticket bureau and a clothing information bureau to its spreading spectrum of customer services.

Its clothing information service was designed to help customers find out not only what the store had to offer, but what the customer could best use. It counseled customers on what styles best suited them in terms of their own physique, coloring, tastes etc. It inspired a great deal of interest and a good many imitators. In 1925 *The New York Times* noted how "the number of personal shopping bureaus in retail stores has increased rapidly during the past few years" and cited Filene's as the forerunner in this development.

The store was certainly not neglecting the more mundane aspects of merchandising. As mentioned earlier, it took out large display ads in early September, 1922 to celebrate the tenth anniversary of its new store building. The ads trumpeted the triumphant progress which the store had made. Filene's also sponsored, in conjunction with the advertisement, a three day parade of Fall Fashions in the ballroom of a local hotel, complete with an exhibition of ballroom dancing. Six years later when the Zeppelin dirigible made its first transatlantic commercial flight, Filene's buyers seized the opportunity to bring over the latest in French fashions, thus beating out all other American stores in displaying the most recent creations of the Paris courtiers.

The store's most aggressive promotions, however, were coming from its Automatic Bargain Basement which by the end of the decade was producing nearly a third of the store's net income. The basement's 36 buyers were fanning out all over the country and Europe seeking cheap but choice merchandise. And they were getting it. When they came to New York City in September 1929 for one of their regular buying missions, over 1,000 manufacturing representatives showed up to offer seconds, odd lots, samples and other surplus items. As a result the basement continually managed to have a good supply of desirable, and desirably priced, merchandise to sell.

And the basement was selling it, often as fast as its stock boys could get it on the counters. Nearly 3,000 aprons and over 3,000 pairs of women's stockings sold in a single day; 300 capes were sold in an hour and 115 women's coats were once snapped up in eight minutes. In 1929, Robert Ripley started his widely-syndicated "Believe it or Not" cartoon series with a story about the now famous Filene's Basement.

Behind much of the store's success was its continuing progress in improving its internal operations. The systems approach was constantly being expanded and enhanced. In 1921 it added to its already elaborate information-gathering apparatus a new procedure called an "inventory of demand."

Sales clerks now had to make a note of every customer who did not buy and why they didn't. It was intended to supplement the daily inventories which only showed what the customers did want. This latter operation, meanwhile, was constantly improved so that by 1928 the store's buyers were receiving fresh reports every day as to which goods were selling and which were not. Long before the age when computers would encourage other stores to start up such information systems, Filene's already had one in successful operation.

The store continued to be a pace-setter in labor relations. Its medical clinic added a podiatrist to its staff and its nurses began making home visits. In 1924, it became the first store in Boston and possibly the country, to offer winter vacations to its employees. With 3,000 on its payroll, it still managed to maintain some of its old informal and intimate spirit. Joining the work force in 1922, a young woman named Tracey Brown was pleasantly surprised to find that most any employee could speak to most any member of management quite easily. Many years later in retirement she would recall how, "Filene's was like a family."

Self-development programs for employees continued to grow and bear fruit. A check of Filene's nearly 100 buyers in 1928 found only five who had started in that position. All the rest had worked, and studied, their way up.

Many of those who were taking advantage of the store's advancement opportunities were women. By the end of the 1920's, when a woman's place was still widely regarded as the home, women in Filene's were managing the store's Training Department, the Expense Control Bureau, the Personal Service Bureau, the Bureau of Standards, the Beauty Shop, the Women's Alterations Department and various selling departments. Although many seem like typically women's positions, elsewhere they were still often held by men.

In 1930 the Russell Sage Foundation published *The Filene Store*. Nearly nine years in the making, the book was, and would remain, the most extensive study ever undertaken of a mercantile organization. It gains credibility not only from the wealth of investigation it represented but from the experience of its principal researcher, Mary La Dame, who had, earlier in her life, worked for some six years in retail sales including a year at Filene's. The store had welcomed her back as a researcher and had cooperated fully in the study.

The report centers largely on the store's efforts at promoting industrial democracy, and while it does not find perfection it does award high marks. Its only serious criticism was of the store's failure to work out a realistic and detailed plan for making its workers into co-owners. At the same time, the researchers ruefully noted that the employees themselves had to bear most of the blame for this failure since they had demonstrated little desire for such responsibility.

In general, La Dame and her associates found Filene's efforts at promoting the involvement and welfare of its workers to be sincere and, within limits, successful. "Personnel administration at Filene's has not been tacked on as a frill to management or as an afterthought suddenly created by the stress of war-time production," they say. "Nor was it devised for purposes of publicity, however much it may have served them. Furthermore, it was not stimulated by philanthropic feelings or sociological considerations. Rooted in a philosophy of cooperation, it has grown up as an organic part of management , cutting across its entire content, as a body of policies and methods designed to insure the permanency, profit and service of the business."

***

While the public at large tended to attribute the store's success almost entirely to its publicity-conscious president, the retailing world knew differently. It knew of the contribution which the store" conscientious and capable general manager had made to its growth. It also knew of his initiation of the Retail Research Association and the unique Associated Merchandising Corporation. Finally, it knew Lincoln Filene to be a likable man and a most competent conciliator.

As his fellow merchants became more aware of Lincoln's abilities, they began looking to him to provide leadership to the industry. In 1920 the National Distribution Conference asked him to chair an important committee on the sensitive issue of trade relations. The committee worked for five years, delving into all aspects of the topic and all areas of their industry before issuing a report. The report bore the obvious stamp of Lincoln's outlook for in summarizing it in a speech to the Conference he called for the establishment of a cooperative organization between producers and distributors to draw up standards, exchange information and settle disputes.

"Heretheto, attempts to improve business practices have proceeded on the assumption that the principal necessity is to make the businessman want to do right," noted Lincoln "The committee's findings indicated that unethical actions in business would be entered into less frequently if those who practice them were more aware of the harmful effect of doing wrong, both to themselves and others." He also stressed that "in developing means to organize better trade relations we must not lose sight of the need for constant emphasis of the viewpoint of the consumer whom we serve."

Lincoln's contributions to the industry had even begun to earn him some recognition abroad. In 1927 the French government made him a Knight of the Legion of Honor in appreciation for his help in making the Modern Furniture Exposition , held earlier that year in Paris, a singular success. Now both Filene brothers could wear the small, highly-prized red ribbon in their lapels.

Locally, Lincoln had become involved in a highly controversial issue. The Sacco-Vanzetti murder case had concluded with a finding of guilty against the two Italian anarchists. The case had aroused the passions of many throughout the world. Liberals, leftists of all kinds, plus more than a few moderates, had expressed outrage at the verdict and the seemingly questionable evidence on which it was based. Committees had been formed, demonstrations had been held and even poems had been written to denounce what so many viewed as a gross miscarriage of justice.

Lincoln wrote no poems and marched in no parades but he did join with 225 other prominent Bostonians in a letter to Massachusetts Governor Alvin Fuller calling for an extensive investigation of certain disturbing aspects of the case. Although several of the signers came from illustrious Brahmin families, Lincoln was one of the very few businessmen, and the only merchant, among them. Given the strong feelings which the case had aroused, especially in the Boston area, he risked alienating a sizable share of the store's clientele in lining up on one side, and, locally, the least popular side, of the controversial case. However, whatever fall-off in business his stand may have caused was apparently more than offset by the store's ability to attract customers on other grounds for, as we have seen, Filene's continued to flourish.

Lincoln had not abandoned his efforts to bring about Federal aid to education. In 1928 he published an article "The Need For a Department of Education As Seen By a Businessman" in *School and Society*. He argued for such an agency on the same basic grounds he used in advocating his advanced labor policies, namely that such a Federal role in education would help business meet its challenges and earn better profits.

The following year he published "The Fallacy of an Industrial Panacea" in *The Atlantic Monthly*. In this piece he expressed a view toward mass production which differed from the one being constantly advocated by Edward. While mass production was correcting many problems, said the younger brother, it was also creating new ones. He worried over the often costly competition it was generating and wondered whether its centralization and attendant lack of flexibility suited an age in which style and taste were changing rapidly.

Lincoln also warned American business to be on guard against "the effects of a superabundance of energy and over-confidence natural to youth and young nations." Careful and cautious planning might be required, he said, to cope with the challenges which lay ahead. His article probably stuck a discordant note with most of his fellow businessmen who, caught up in the swelling stock market boom, believed that prosperity would last indefinitely. But five months later the stock market crashed and the Great Depression began. So, Lincoln Filene, ill-educated and overshadowed by his older brother, had shown himself to be not only a pioneering business thinker, but something of an economic prophet as well.

***

Although he loved outdoor activity, Lincoln had never been especially robust and during the war years his health had begun to deteriorate. During the 1920's, though he managed to stay active, he complained frequently of flagging energy. While a soon-to-be-mentioned personal crisis that was building up within the executive offices of Filene's undoubtedly contributed to his condition, other factors were also at work. For example, a leg ailment, possibly complicated if not caused by a touch of diabetes, had begun to plague him but his doctor ruled out an operation, fearing that his patient, who was now in his sixties and not in good health, would not survive.

At this particular juncture of his life neither of his daughters were around to comfort him. Catherine, once she had separated from her husband, had returned to Washington where she soon established herself as a new female force in national affairs. Soon after her 26th birthday in 1925, she co-founded the Women's National Democratic Club. The next year she became chairperson of the Advisory Committee for the Federal Government's first prison for women. She soon instituted a job training and rehabilitation program for the inmates that ignited world-wide interest and imitation. Three years later she founded the Institute of Women's Professional Relations.

Her dynamism and drive continued to perplex her father who, despite having opened up many new opportunities for women at his store, had yet remained somewhat old fashioned in his thinking. He would never completely understand his oldest daughter though he would always admire her abilities and treasure her affection.

His youngest daughter had left for New York soon after her marriage. For her husband had decided to enter the retailing field, and Filene's rigid rule against nepotism meant that he would have to go elsewhere to do so. So George Ladd took a job with Abraham & Strauss of Brooklyn. The Ladds had three sons during their first six years of marriage and named one of them after Lincoln. However, the births, plus George Ladd's demanding duties at Abraham & Strauss, prevented them from visiting Lincoln as often as he, and they, would have liked. As a result of these developments, neither of his daughters would be around when the storm long gathering inside Filene's executive offices finally broke.

***

The 1920's brought a great expansion of Edward's role as a public figure. His work with Wilson, his peace prizes and his successful book, combined with his presidency of the nation's most innovative store, made him a man to be reckoned with in political, business and even religious circles. What he said was listened to and what he did was noticed. *The New York Times* regularly reported his statements and speeches, for Edward Filene was now news.

His adherence to the Democratic party at a time when most millionaire business men had become staunch Republicans only made him more newsworthy. When he toyed with the idea of trying to get his party to nominate Herbert Hoover for President in 1920, the press reported it. And when in 1928 he refused to support Hoover, now running for President as a Republican, and endorsed Al Smith instead, the press again reported it. (In his statement, Edward acknowledged Hoover's impressive qualifications but felt that Smith's election would produce more prosperity for the average worker.) And when, following Hoover's election, rumors began circulating that, despite Edward's endorsement of his opponent, Hoover was thinking of naming the Boston merchant Secretary of Labor, the press took proper notice. (The rumors were quickly denounced by the White House as "baseless," which apparently they were.)

Edward continued to speak out on a variety of issues. When Henry Ford called for a five-day week in 1926, he enthusiastically rallied to his side. Such a step, said Edward, would increase net production by forcing producers to improve their methods. It would also improve worker-management relations. All in all, he said, a shortened work week "will bring about a reduction of waste in industry."

Reducing waste, long an obsession of Edward's, became, if anything, even more central to his thought. He told a national real estate association that mass production of housing could lower housing costs and stimulate sales. And he urged a conference of business leaders to establish a "businessmen's institute" to work out ways for coordinating their activities to cut costs.

Although cost reduction had become and would remain a life-long passion with Edward, he at all times made clear that he did not equate it with wage reduction. On the contrary, he believed, along with Ford, in raising wages. Only in this way, argued Edward, could the menace of over-production be met. In fact, there was no such thing as over-production, he maintained, but rather a problem of under-consumption which required steadily rising wages to resolve.

His constant calls for cost saving also did not reflect any pronounced materialistic bent, but rather his belief that such efforts, if successful, would increasingly free people from materialistic concerns. As he put it in an address before a university audience, "In the final analysis, beauty is the greatest objective in the world. But we cannot teach spiritual truths effectively to starving people. One great way to make more beauty in the world is to make the obtaining of a living...so mechanical and so little time-consuming that we shall have time for avocations-have time to work for and search for better things--to search for beauty."

In a subsequent address, he went so far as to stress the essential compatibility between profit-making and religious values. He did so in a speech before the Laymen's Committee of the Federal Council of Churches. He was already a member of the committee but his new affiliation did not reflect any further repudiation of his Jewish background. In fact, he became more consciously identified with it.

His increased Jewish consciousness began as World War I drew to a close and he read of the plight of Polish and other East European Jews caught up in the increased anti-Semitism which the war and its aftermath had fostered or at least facilitated. This development prompted him to start contributing to various Jewish aid societies. However, he angrily refused an invitation by one of them to accept formal membership, saying "it is against my established custom of many years to become a member of any organized charity or sectarian charitable or educational movement."

But Europe was not the only place where anti-Semitism was on the march. In this country the Klu Klux Klan was spreading its wings and attracting thousands of new members in the North where it was making Jews its number one target. This, too, troubled Edward, so when he learned that the Federal Council of Churches was organizing a campaign to combat anti Semitism, he opened up his checkbook and began contributing to its support. It was then that he decided to join the Council's Laymen's Group.

Edward was not altogether happy with his new affiliation. He was dismayed that most of its funds for fighting anti-Semitism were coming from Jewish sources. He had hoped that its Protestant members would do more. He also felt it was not organizing its work properly for he wanted it to set up state and local committees. In 1928, he stopped sending money to the Council but he remained on fairly friendly terms with the organization until his death.

As part of his new awareness of his Jewishness, Edward in 1922 took out a subscription to *The American Hebrew*, a magazine designed for modern-thinking and highly Americanized Jews. However, he dropped his subscription in 1928. It would take the outbreak of Nazism in Germany five years later to make him fully conscious once again of his Jewish identity.

***

Edward had wanted to visit the Soviet Union ever since it was established. He had listened to Lincoln Steffens' rapturous reports of the Soviet experiment with interest tinged with skepticism. Furthermore, Lenin had, in a way, flattered him by issuing "An Open Letter to E. A. Filene and the progressive Capitalists" in which the Russian leader asked, "Mr. Filene, do you think the workers of the world are fools?" So when the Soviets in 1927 began lowering their barriers to foreign visitors, Edward quickly applied for, and received, a visa.

He was especially eager to study how the world's first socialist country was handling the problem of distribution. Unfortunately for him there was little to study along this line for the still impoverished nation had little to distribute. Nevertheless, Edward came away impressed with the vigor and boldness of those he met. He hoped to come back when the Russian experiment was farther advanced and there would be more to study and see.

On returning to the U.S., Edward called for formal American recognition of the Soviet government and chastised the press for not accurately and fully informing their readers as to what was taking place in Russia. He expressed the belief that the Soviet system, contrary to what many economists and most businessmen were saying, would last a long time. But, he felt that it would gradually shift more toward the center in the coming years.

***

Edward's lively interest in progress was not confined to international, national or even business problems. He also manifested and supported new ideas in more narrow areas of human endeavor. In May, 1925 he startled the members of the American Marine Association, whose dinner meeting he was addressing, by urging them to abolish the customary three class system on ocean liners and adopt a one class system instead. Passengers would still pay different rates according to the size, location and amenities of their cabins but there would be no segregation between groups. All would have the run of the ship.

Such a system, said Edward, would make ocean travel simpler and much cheaper for there would no longer be a need for separate dining rooms, recreation rooms, etc. It would make ocean travel more democratic as well.

The New York Times supported the notion and eventually two shipping lines announced intentions of implementing it. One said it would build eight ships for single-service, trans-Atlantic crossings. However, the advent of the Depression greatly depressed ocean travel, and Edward's idea fell by the wayside.

Edward had also acquired a good deal of familiarity with doctors and with the problems of medical care, both as a patient and as the operator of a medical clinic. Speaking to the American Hospital Association in 1929, he put forth the notion of "medical guilds" under which groups of doctors would agree to provide medical care for a set fee. His proposal anticipates the Health Maintenance Organization of several decades later and which now offers complete medical care for a pre-determined yearly or monthly amount.

The following year Edward took advantage of an invitation to address the National Boot and Shoe Manufacturer's Association to polish up and present still another idea. This was for a nationwide network of footpaths to make walking safe, enjoyable and attractive. It would also, he told them, promote footwear.

"Bravo, Mr. Filene...More power to his voice," wrote an enthusiastic reader to the Times after reading Edward's remarks. The paper itself liked the paths but not the purpose, at least not the one he emphasized, for, as it commented editorially, "pedestrians will endorse his generous proposal of safe by-paths but will not sell their souls or wear out their soles to promote an industry, honorable or essential as it is."

***

The 1920's saw Edward take on a new role, that of inventor. Not that he had any mechanical aptitude for, as noted earlier, he had never even learned to drive. But he did have an interest in inventions, probably acquired from his father, and had once tried to have a new footstool developed but the idea had fizzled.

It was the Versailles Peace Conference which triggered his new effort in this field. Edward had attended the conference as a bystander and what he saw and heard convinced him that communication problems bore the primary responsibility for the conclave's many problems. This feeling was further strengthened when he attended an International Chamber of Commerce the following year. In pondering the problem, he came up with the idea of a device for overcoming it.

The League of Nations was already being badly hampered by the problem and so he went to Geneva to discuss his idea with the head of its translation section. This official introduced him to a Captain Gordon Findlay, a British engineer who was then working part-time for the League's International Labor Organization. Findley was interested and immediately began experimenting.

What Edward had in mind was a device that would allow a speaker's words to be translated into various languages while he was speaking them. Findley soon came up with an experimental model and the labor organization agreed to try it out at one of its meetings. The new simultaneous translator worked quite well and so Edward offered to pay for its installation in the new League of Nations building that was then being planned. His offer was gratefully accepted and the device was patented. Edward invited Findlay to share the credit and the Filene-Findlay translator made its formal debut.

Edward was eager to have a commercial concern produce and market the system. He first approached AT & T but the stodgy giant said no. He then turned to a newer, smaller and more innovative firm called International Business Machines. He had met its President, Thomas Watson, while attending International Chamber of Commerce gatherings. Like Edward, Watson was a businessmen who was concerned in public problems, especially with the task of fostering international accord. Also, like Edward, Watson greatly hungered for and enjoyed the favorable publicity which the role of businessman-statesman could produce.

Watson was interested and called in his staff to examine the device. His engineers could find nothing wrong with the translator but his marketing people could see no real sales potential for it. But since Watson could see its potential for promoting international communication, as well as the image of Thomas Watson, he put it into production. He even agreed to pay its inventors a small royalty.

The League of Nations began to break up before the translator would ever become an established part of its proceedings. However, after the war the device was used in prosecuting Nazi leaders in the famed Nuremberg trials. Afterwards, Chief U.S. Prosecutor, and later Supreme Court Justice, Robert Jackson said, "It does work and without it the trial would not have been accomplished in this amount of time, if at all."

Today, Edward's creation, albeit in a more perfected form, has virtually become a fixed feature at international gatherings everywhere. And anyone who picks up an earphone at the United Nations and carefully inspects it, will find inconspicuously inscribed on it the words "Filene-Findlay." It is another reminder of the Boston storekeeper's far-reaching creativity and far-ranging concerns.

Despite his continual incursions into diverse areas, Edward had not abandoned or even greatly neglected his long-standing projects and interests. To be sure, he grumbled frequently over the Twentieth Century Fund, believing that it was dissipating its resources by getting involved in too many projects. (That this tendency was, in all likelihood merely the reflection of its founder and financier apparently did not occur to him). Yet he continued to support it generously.

He also continued to support the credit union movement, and one day in 1921 he summoned Bergengren to his office and told him that he wanted to take "one more chance." By this he meant that he wanted to try one more time to establish a nationwide network of "People's Banks."

What had sparked such an ambitious move was a crisis in his own state organization. Max Mitchell, the Boston businessman who had faithfully shared with Edward the cost of financing the Massachusetts Credit Union Association, had gone bankrupt. He would obviously be unable to continue his support. Confronted with this problem, Edward, rather characteristically, decided to meet it not by retreat but with a bold advance. If he was going to have to put more of his money and time into keeping the movement alive, why not do it on a grand scale?

One factor which encouraged him was the availability of someone competent enough to translate such a dream into reality. For in his first year with the MCUA Bergengren had almost single-handedly established 19 new credit unions in Massachusetts.

Knowing that Mitchell's business failure had placed his own future in jeopardy, Bergengren had begun winding up his affairs preparatory to accepting an attractive position in private industry which had been offered him. But when Edward outlined his desire to finance a nationwide campaign to spread the credit union concept or, as he put it, "to take one more chance" at creating a nationwide movement, the former Lynn Commissioner immediately became interested. And when Edward asked if he would like to head it up, he promptly said yes. "It looked fascinating", Bergengren later recalled. "We talked it over and we found a partnership without any papers. We decided that we must have, and so we created, The Credit Union National Extension Bureau. We agreed that no one else should have anything to do with the Bureau; that he would put up the money ...and that we would make the plans which I would execute. I was given extraordinary latitude."

The two set up CUNEB's headquarters in Boston's Park Square right next to the Offices of the Massachusetts Credit Union Association. Edward would finance its operations in part directly out of his own pocket and in part from the Twentieth Century Fund.

Bergengren saw from the first that the movement's future depended on his ability to get appropriate legislation enacted in the various states. He decided to make the South his primary target and toured the area extensively in late 1921 and early 1922. Having, so he felt, softened up the terrain, he persuaded Edward to go with him on a second tour of the region. Knowing by now of Edward's fondness for the limelight, Bergengren set up a series of meetings, luncheons and other events where his boss, could play the central role.

The trip was a great success. At a luncheon in Atlanta, Edward rubbed shoulders with the mayor and the state's governor, and, so the delighted Boston merchant wrote home to his mother "sitting by the governor I persuaded him of the merits of the unions so well that he came out for them in a speech and is so quoted in today's papers."

Edward then went on to Louisville, Kentucky where he spoke before a legislative committee that was considering a credit union bill and then addressed a luncheon meeting of the City's Board of Trade. Here, too, the publicity was extensive and generally favorable. The fact that Edward was already something of a national figure and prominent member of the political party which then dominated the South, aided his efforts considerably. Georgia, Kentucky and Virginia all subsequently passed credit union laws.

The following year Edward headed into the Midwest. Here the sledding was somewhat tougher but nevertheless he managed to drum up substantial publicity for himself and his cause. In Illinois the state bankers association came out against credit unions but the state's manufacturers association, together with the Illinois Federation of Labor, supported them, and eventually the necessary legislation was passed. In Indiana, an influenza epidemic came to his aid. The disease had struck the ranks of the "loan shark adherents" more heavily than it had the ranks of the credit union backers, and so when the Illinois legislative voted on the bill, the proponents managed to muster a bare majority.

Thanks to a bit of luck and lot of wise work, Bergengren and his busy boss had by 1926 succeeded in getting credit union laws on the books of 26 states. But enacting a law was only a first step, for by itself such a law would not create a single association. Follow up work was necessary to see that the law was utilized.

When it came to organizing actual credit unions, Bergengren again focused much of his attention on the South. He hired a woman field secretary who spent much of her time trying to set up such unions in impoverished Appalachia. This did not, however, please the bureau's benefactor. "Fine charity," he snorted and accused Bergengren of "thinking with your heart, not with your mind." Edward wanted to concentrate on the bigger industrial areas and so Bergengren shifted his field secretary to eastern industrial cities.

Edward also wanted more state laws enacted, but this time Bergengren came up with a new idea. Why not try to get a Federal Credit Union statute enacted that would solve the whole legislative problem in one fell swoop? They would then be spared the enormous effort and expense of trying to bring the other states into line. Edward, however, vetoed the suggestion. Although admitting that he could be wrong, Edward claimed that the country was too diverse for one all-embracing law. Furthermore, only the state-by-state approach would generate the necessary grass roots awareness of, and support for, credit unions that would result in their wide-scale growth. Bergengren argued his case with adroitness but Edward remained adamant. So the Bureau continued to press forward on the state level.

Other disputes also clouded the Bergengren-Filene relationship. Edward believed that his ideas would interest others as much as they did himself, and that they would work as hard to implement them as he did. He therefore wanted more emphasis placed on public relations and less on field work since he felt certain that once a state's leading citizens knew about the advantages of credit unions, they would be happy to join or even set up volunteer organizations to support them. Bergengren more often than not went along with Edward for, as he acknowledged in a letter to him, "the Bureau is just as much your property as your house in Otis Place and you have the right to do with it what you will..."

But Bergengren won his share of battles with his often bumptious boss. He managed to get a field secretary on the payroll, to get Edward to give up his idea for a speaker's bureau and even to get his own weekly salary raised from $75.00 at the start to $90.00 by 1925. He had come to learn the older man's weakness and so when he started a credit union publication called *The Bridge*, he mentioned the name of Edward Filene in almost every column. Edward was asked to write articles of his own for the publication and gladly did so.

Bergengren had also learned not to expect any praise from his boss. When in 1929 he wrote Edward triumphantly that two prominent Catholic organizations, one of them the National Catholic Welfare Conference, had set up credit unions, he was not surprised when his superior replied asking why he couldn't do the same among Protestants.

Edward, as noted earlier, was starting to become aware of some of his troubling personal mannerisms. Once he blurted out to Bergengren "You think I am dogmatic and I think I am too." It was too late for him to undergo any radical change but their relationship continued nonetheless, cemented by ties of mutual respect and of mutual devotion to the credit unions cause. By 1930 the lanky lawyer and his stubby, and stubborn, boss, had persuaded 32 states to sanction credit unions. Moreover, the number of such associations in existence had gone from 200 in 1920 to 1100 and several hundred more would soon join them. Edward had taken "one more chance" and won.

The credit union campaign brought Edward into contact with a vast and varied number of people. None of them, however, would play a more significant role in his remaining years than the newly elected governor of New York. Shortly after Franklin Roosevelt's inaugural, Edward sent him a long letter, vaunting the virtues of credit unions and asking that he support moves to strengthen credit unions in the Empire State. (New York already had a credit union law but in Edward's view it was weak and defective.) In closing, Edward wrote "Needless to say, I was happy indeed at the result of the New York election, and I want to extend to you every good wish for a happy and successful administration."

Edward's letter evoked a prompt and cordial reply. "Thank you for your extremely interesting letter which has taught me much," wrote Roosevelt. "I had no idea that the credit unions had had such widespread, effective and sound growth." The governor then went on to say how some railroad officials he had recently met with had praised the "vast amount if good" which their own railroad's credit union had done for their employees. "It is fine of you to do what you are doing to encourage the growth of the good work." And Roosevelt concluded by saying "I shall hope to have the pleasure of seeing you in Boston next month when I am there for my twenty-fifth [Harvard] reunion."

Although no record of their meeting in Boston exists, it apparently took place and forged a link between the two men. For Edward would become one of Roosevelt's enthusiastic supporters and the next American President would find the Boston shopkeeper to be an increasingly useful, if sometimes troublesome, ally.

***

A mother and her six year old daughter are passing the glove counter at Filene's when the youngster becomes attracted by a pair of rather expensive kid gloves. She asks her mother to buy them for her and when the mother says no, the girl starts to stage a mild but disturbing tantrum. Suddenly a dignified gentleman carrying a cane approaches the pair and asks the youngster her name and what is bothering her. When she tells him, he has her outfitted with a pair of the gloves she wanted, signs the sales slip and with a pat on the head for the child and nod to her mother, disappears down the aisle.

Nearing 70 years of age, Edward Filene had lost none of his love for children. He had, fortunately, lost some of his awkwardness. Although he would always bristle whenever he felt himself challenged, and although he would remain difficult to work with or for, he had learned to handle many major and minor social situations with a modicum of urbanity and grace. The ugly duckling's defensiveness, while by no means eradicated, had become coated over with a veneer, albeit a thin one, of courtliness and charm.

He had met and consorted with some of the world's leading figures and not just those in business and politics. He had, for example, become friendly with the popular philosopher--writer on philosophy would perhaps be more accurate--Will Durant and his wife. He had also gotten to know a well-known psychiatrist, Joseph Jastrow and a well-read French novelist and biographer, Andre Maurois.

Many of these celebrities would call on him at his office in Filene's when they came to Boston and some would even stay at his home. Maurois and Jastrow were among the house guests with the psychiatrist being remembered mostly for his endless expositions on the brilliance of his son. Another house guest was Colonel Julius Deutsch, the minister of War in Austria's first socialist government. Princess Kropotkin, widow of the famed Russian anarchist, and the eminent black scientist Dr. George Washington Carver called on him at the store. Edward Filene had become a man to be visited and seen.

He had remained close to Lincoln Steffens despite the fact that the former muckraker had moved politically far to the left. Steffens spent much of 1920's in Europe and Edward would spend time with him during his annual summer trips to the continent. In 1922 they attended the Carpentier-Siki boxing match in Paris and watched Siki, an untrained Senegalese, knock out Carpentier, the world's champion heavyweight, renown for his deftness and skill, in six rounds. Two years later they went together to Salzburg to hear Mozart being played.

They also kept up a lively and revealing correspondence. Edward's insecurities show themselves when, in a downcast mood in 1924 he writes Steffens seeking reassurances that he retains the journalist's affections and even asking whether his appearance has become more pleasing. Steffens replied, "Yes, I still love...it matters not at all even if no other person gives you his or her heart. Mine, you have. But why do you ask?"

As to the 63-year old man's hopes about his looks, Steffens answers, "I can't tell you at this distance whether you are more comely than of yore but why should you wish me to think you are? It doesn't matter what I call handsome, does it? Even if it is you; especially if it is you."

In 1926, after hearing that Edward had suffered a bout of illness, Steffens wrote asking him "to arrange somehow so that if you are ever ill again I may be told..if there is anybody in the world that has a right to know how you are and not to be ever surprised about you, it is this same me." And a few months later Steffens wrote again urging Edward to retire from active life in order to reflect and report on what he has seen, done and thought. "There is a long, helpful, happy chapter ahead of you if you can cease from over-doing."

But despite the warmth and intimacy of their correspondence there are indications that their love for one another had its limits. In fact, it may not have been without some taint of self-interest on both sides. Edward was a wealthy man, while Steffens, though famous, was not, and it may be assumed that when the two went somewhere together, the merchant usually picked up the bill. Edward also supported Steffens' writing even though he had come to disagree with most of what he said. When Steffens' book *Moses in Red* came out, Edward purchased 50 copies and sent them to various distinguished people he knew.

Steffens at one time tried to borrow money from Edward and received instead a reprimand for his extravagance. Edward probably thought his friend was trying to take advantage of him and so re-acted characteristically and predictably. Steffens, on his part, was understandably miffed on getting a lecture instead of a loan and it rankled him for quite a while thereafter. At the same time, however, he had indicated to others that he regarded Edward in a somewhat different light than he may have given Edward to understand. For example, in a letter to his sister in 1923, Steffens referred to his Boston friend as one of those "idiots that one can enjoy."

The success of *The Way Out* had whetted Edward's appetite for authorship and two years later he followed it up with another book. *More Profits in Merchandising* did not attain the widespread reader-ship of his first book; as its title indicates, it was not designed to do so. But it did get Edward's ideas about merchandising across to his fellow merchants in a more expanded and substantial form. It was respectably received if not widely followed.

But, it was another book that was weighing most heavily on the businessman-statesman-author at this time. This was a book that would be written not by him but about him. Edward wanted to have his biography done.

As with most of his endeavors, the motives behind it were mixed. Knowing Edward as we do, it is quite safe to assume that his ego had made him deeply desirous of seeing his life inscribed between hard covers. But Edward offered another reason for having his biography done and this reason also commands some credence.

Edward liked to tell people that he was essentially a failure. Why? Because he had not achieved his two great goals in life. These were, first, getting his workers to take over his store and, second, substantially cutting the cost of distribution.

Edward thought that an able biographer in going over his life would be able to discover and point out to him and others just where he had gone wrong. He was perfectly prepared for criticism, he maintained, for he thought that most biographers erred in being too flattering to their subjects. His biography should state the plain unvarnished truth. He also had a title for it: An Unsuccessful Millionaire.

As early as 1925 he had tried to interest Steffens in taking on the assignment but Steffens begged off, saying he was working on his own autobiography. There would be "a dandy chapter on you," Steffens wrote back, and so, he added, "I don't feel so much like writing your life." By 1928, Edward and his aides had sounded out a host of others but had so far come up with no well-established writer willing to take on the task. (Although Samuel Crowther, who had written Ford's biography, had offered to do Edward's for $25,000). Then, someone suggested the name of Charles W. Wood.

Wood was a former locomotive fireman who had started writing to fill in the time between stoking engines on long trips. His natural talent had eventually won him first prize in a national magazine contest and he had gone on to become a professional magazine writer. Originally a socialist, he had come to believe that capital and labor could and should collaborate and had recently written a book entitled, *Make Everybody Rich--Industry's New Goal* for Benjamin Javits, a believer in worker ownership and the elder brother of the future New York Senator, Jacob Javits.

Wood thus seemed an almost ideal person for the job and negotiations between him and Edward got underway. They agreed that it was to be Wood's own book and that Edward was to let him write it as he wished. The biographer would have carte blanche to say what he felt he should say.

Wood, by this time, had become aware of Edward's sensitive ego and was therefore skeptical that the arrangement would last. So instead of seeking a contract for the book itself he asked for a salary, payable every week. Should they reach an impasse, that is should Edward take objection to what he wrote, Edward could fire him immediately. The salary agreed upon was $74 a week, which was more than double that of a newspaper writer in those days. Wood and his wife then moved to Boston where they took an apartment in the Fenway, a 20 minute walk from Edward's home on Otis Place.

Edward quickly became so impressed with Wood's fluent writing style and his fund of information on world problems that he soon had him working on other projects, especially speeches. Wood protested that these new tasks were preventing him from carrying out the assignment for which Edward had engaged him, but Edward pointed out that since he was on salary, he need not worry. The loss was Edward's not Wood's.

Suddenly one day Edward told him that he was leaving for Europe in three weeks and would like to see a good part of his biography before he left. Wood packed up his portable and went off to a beach cottage leaving no address. There he quickly pounded out a half-dozen chapters of *The Life Story of an Unsuccessful Millionaire*.

Only one of these chapters, the first, survives, carefully tucked away in the well-maintained Filene Files of the Credit Union National Association in Madison, Wisconsin. Entitled, "A Strange Unhappy Man," this chapter portrays its subject as a complex web of contradictions. Edward, according to Wood, is "a merciless apostle of mercy—a despotic champion of democracy," and "a cross between the prophet Isaiah and a Jewish pack peddler." While "the welfare of the masses was his passion," this "aesthetic, artistic and enormously rich old bachelor...never knew the masses, had never shared in their pleasures or perplexities and was utterly unfitted by temperament to mingle with the common people."

While Wood's introductory pages point up many of Edward's virtues, they also single out many of his problems. Moreover, the remaining chapters may have even bore down still harder, for someone who read the entire manuscript described it as "an extraordinary piece of work—shrewdly aimed, brilliantly written and utterly ruthless."

Wood showed up at Otis Place with his manuscript under his arm. There, in the library, he sat up until midnight reading what he had written to his boss and his boss' secretary. When he finished he quietly took his hat and left. There was no "good night" from his host and Wood intended to start looking for another job the next day.

But the next day brought no phone call informing him of his dismissal. In fact, three days passed with no word from or about Edward at all. Finally, when his phone did ring, it was not Edward or his secretary on the line but Edward's physician, L.R.G. Crandon.

"What the hell did you do to E.A?" demanded the doctor, wrathfully.

The nonplused Wood replied that he hadn't even seen him for three days.

"I know you haven't, snapped the physician. "He's been in bed and you put him there. Now you go and see him at once and straighten this out or I won't answer for the consequences."

Wood promptly returned to Otis place. He explained to his still bedridden boss that he had certainly meant him no injury. If he had written without mercy, he had also written without malice, that he admired many of Edward's ideas (which was true) and that they could part with no ill will.

Edward said he would like to retain his services, though not as a biographer, and offered him a three-year contract with a yearly salary. Wood said he preferred the existing arrangement which permitted him to quit or Edward to fire him any Saturday when he drew his weekly wage.

Wood would remain with Edward until the latter's death. He is remembered as a grey, gaunt man who liked to get up at three or four in the morning to write his boss' prose. He is also remembered as a delightfully zany character—like someone out of John Steinbeck's *Sweet Thursday* was the way one associate recalls him—whose favorite hobbies were drinking, talking and joking. Since Edward was always using the term "inevitable" in making his prophecies, Wood once amused Edward's other aides by suggesting that they form the Society of the Evitable so that when something that was inevitable came along they could oppose it.

But despite these occasional sallies at his boss' expense, Wood shared most of Edward's ideas and showed great facility in putting them into words. Edward would later say of their relationship, "I furnished the meat and some seasonings. Charles Wood furnished the fats and spices and made them into the dishes that the public ate with gusto." He may have overstated the relish with which the public received the intellectual fodder that he sought to feed them but he correctly, so it seems, summed up the relationship between the sober merchant-statesman and his off-beat scribe.

***

When Wood went to work for Edward he became the part of a three-member team of principal aides. The other two were Robert Moore and Percy Brown. Moore had been introduced to Edward in an elevator at Filene's in 1924.

A World War I pilot, now in his late twenties, Moore was planning to leave in a few weeks for Europe with his friend and business partner Ernest Henderson, to buy surplus war material. When they learned that Edward was also going to Europe but on a different ship, Moore and Henderson revised their travel arrangements in order to voyage on the same vessel.

Edward and Moore saw a lot of each other on the ship as well as in Europe that summer, and in the fall, Edward offered him a staff position at the then princely sum of $6,600 a year. Moore, accepted the offer and became Edward's principal assistant for handling all his activities in connection with the store. He would stay with him until 1932, leaving only to join Henderson again in a series of ventures that would culminate in the creation of the Sheraton Hotel chain. (Moore would become the corporation's board chairman while Henderson would serve as its president.)

The other aide, Percy Brown, entered Edward's employ in 1927. A tall, large man with a warm, expansive demeanor, he gave many the impression of being a former social worker with a socialist orientation. Actually, he had worked in business in the Midwest and believed in a progressive capitalism along the lines suggested by Edward. He handled Edward's outside activities, frequently serving as a mediator between his boss and Bergengren in their many disputes over credit union matters.

The fourth and final, and by far the most important, member of Edward's team joined him in the Spring of 1930. Edward had advertised in *The New York Times* for a secretary and general assistant. It was an attractive-sounding position and he received over 400 replies. He and Moore pared down the list to a dozen or so of the most eligible and scheduled interviews with these top contenders at the suite Edward customarily engaged at the Commodore Hotel during his visits to New York. One of the candidates, when her turn was announced, entered the suite, spotted a disorderly pile of papers on the desk; without waiting to be interviewed, hung up her coat, sat down at the desk and went to work sorting out the mess all the while chastising the two men for having allowed it to accumulate. Lillian Schoedler had marched into the life of Edward Filene--for good.

Born on September 6, 1891 and therefore 38 years old when she swept into Edward's hotel suite that day, Schoedler was the eldest of five daughters of an educated, German-American family. On her graduation in 1911 from Columbia's Barnard College, where many considered her the brightest member of her class, she had gone on to hold a variety of challenging positions including that of executive secretary of the Women's Division of the National Amateur Athletic Association.

While she was greatly interested in women's athletics, she was even more interested in travel and had turned down an offer to become the secretary of Mrs. Herbert Hoover in 1926 in order to journey around the world. She had recently returned to New York and had just started to think of going to work again when she spotted Edward's advertisement.

Once she had sat down at the desk to work there was no further question as to who would get the position. The other applicants were sent home and Lillian Schoedler became Edward Filene's all-around assistant. A large woman--she stood nearly a head taller than her boss—she was quite pleasant looking though not what one could call attractive. And despite her dynamic and forceful personality, she possessed a cheerful disposition and a good sense of humor. When Steffens visited Edward, she would occasionally engage him in a wrestling match on the floor. Onlookers had no doubt as to who would have won if the match had been serious for she towered over the diminutive Steffens as well.

Edward took to her at once—most people did—and she quickly became an indispensable part of his life, running his home, typing some of his manuscripts, bringing information to his attention, making his travel arrangements and often traveling with him to see that all went well. Edward, on his part, treated her more like a daughter than an employee, and frequently took her with him when he went to dinners, receptions and other gatherings that she knew how to converse with and even charm the many distinguished people he would deal with in his remaining years only made her presence more helpful.

Edward Filene had long needed a Lillian Schoedler but she couldn't have come into his life at a more opportune time. For despite his many triumphs as author, credit union organizer, inventor, etc. during the 1920's, he had simultaneously been undergoing a strenuous ordeal. And this ordeal had just culminated in the most severe and stunning set back of his career.

Chapter 10
STRUGGLE, STRIFE, SCHISM

1927

The Filene store has closed for the day but its employee restaurant still resounds with the clatter of dishes and the sounds of laughter. The Filene Cooperative Association is holding a birthday party for one of its long-time benefactors. Clara Filene, who has contributed money and materials to the Filene Cooperative Association since its inception, has turned 92. Although she will die the following year, she is still spry enough to attend and enjoy the event, and, of course, the presence of Edward and Lincoln only adds to her pleasure. She does not realize that this is the last truly festive occasion her two sons will ever share together.

***

Since 1912 Edward's expanding activities had increasingly removed him for his store's daily operations. During many of these years he spent more time away from Boston than in the city. Even when he was in town, he was often engaged in matters that had little to do with Filene's. He had in many ways become an absentee president.

But he was president just the same, and he had not the slightest intention of relinquishing either the position or the powers that went with it. When he did show up at the store, he immediately immersed himself in what was going on.

The problem was that he often did not know what was going on. He would see something he didn't like and immediately start to correct it without realizing the reason that may have made it necessary. He would give orders without realizing that they clashed with orders that others had given. Once he went to great trouble preparing a proposal for a director's meeting only to learn that what he proposed was already being done. The man who had done so much to create the world's largest clothing store was now rapidly becoming the store's biggest nuisance.

And he was a rather nasty nuisance at that. For although he had become more diplomatic in dealing with the world outside the store, he had, if anything, become less tactful in handling people in his domain. For one thing, he was constantly becoming irritated in seeing so many things going on which he did not like or which in any case he would have done differently but which his proliferating outside activities made him helpless to control. For another, his enlarged stature in the world at large made him expect more deference from his own employees and associates. If some of the country's leading citizens were willing to listen to and even applaud what Edward Filene had to say, then certainly his own board of directors should do no less. And in fact, he viewed directors' meetings as an opportunity to lecture to the others on what they should do.

Another mannerism further aggravated the situation, one that had been part of his personality since youth but had become more pronounced as he had grown older and become more deeply involved in so many diverse activities. This was his habit of skipping from one idea to another without letting his listeners follow the sequence of his thought. For example, he could be explaining something, stop to answer the phone, talk for five minutes, then hang up and go on with the subject not at the point where he left off but at a new point for he had been thinking more about it while on the phone.

To some this minor quirk was a major factor in his failure to get along with those he worked with. "With all his genius," said Harold Hodphkinson after Edward's death, "he could never make himself understood. He tried, he wanted to be understood, to be liked. He was not a misanthrope, but he lacked the gift of getting in touch with other minds. I think in part it was because his own was so swift; he would explain half an idea, then his mind would leap ahead to the conclusion, and he couldn't believe that he hadn't explained it all."

But this idiosyncrasy was but one manifestation of Edward's overall problem. He was so walled in by his complexes that he could never fully see things from the another's point of view. He appreciated intellectual arguments but not personal reactions. "He seemed to have no idea of the impact he made on other people," says Edward Bernays. And as his achievements mounted this failing was gradually undermining the base from which these achievements had sprung.

If Edward's associates were finding him an ever greater cross to bear, there was now one associate who had never been prepared to bear such a burden at all. Lincoln, the younger brother, had grown up more or less in Edward's shadow. Frost, Cory and Simpson had built their careers in following Edward's lead. But Louis Kirstein was a different story altogether.

Kirstein, it will be recalled, had already made a name for himself before joining Filene's. He was independently wealthy, and when he cast his lot with the Filenes he brought not just his fame but his fortune to the job. He had made a great investment in the firm and he was not prepared to let Edward do what he wished with it.

There were many similarities between the most senior and the most junior member of the Filene's management team. Both were dynamic, hard-driving men who worked hard themselves and expected others to do the same. Both believed in approaching their tasks systematically. In one of the few articles he ever wrote, Kirstein began by saying "The basic trouble with merchandising is that we merchandise on opinion, not on facts." Indeed, so systematic was Louis Kirstein in his fact-gathering that he kept separate files on each of his three children.

Though nowhere near as original, or, as he would have said, radical, as Edward in his thinking, Kirstein was also becoming known for his observations on the merchandising field. These included such one-liners as:

Retailing needs less figuring and more fingering;

No industry can rise higher than the caliber of the men in it.

Advertising pays when it is believed;

Overnight we have all become accountants rather than merchants.

Like Edward, Kirstein was self-educated, and though he lacked Edward's breath of knowledge and command of languages, he nevertheless read extensively in those areas that interested him. (History, especially the Civil War, was one of these areas) He also involved himself extensively in public affairs, although his interests here took a more conventional turn. He contributed generously to schools, hospitals and, most of all, Jewish charities. For many years he served as the "Jewish Trustee" on the Board of Trustees of the Boston Public Library and would later establish one of that library's more unique branches.

His lifestyle was in most respects also quite conventional. He lived with his family in a rented house in the Back Bay, played golf avidly at a Jewish country club and attended Red Sox games. But he could go against the tide when he felt the need to do so. For example, he not only spoke out in behalf of Sacco & Vanzettti but for many years employed Sacco's son Dante as his chauffeur. And though he worshipped Harvard and would send his sons there, he spoke out forcibly when the University sought to promulgate a quota on Jewish faculty members.

At the store he would be remembered as a taciturn giant who spoke alternatively in grunts and growls. Yet he would also be remembered as scrupulously fair in his dealings with associates, subordinates and even competitors. If a dispute arose between, say, a manufacturer and the store over an order, Kirstein would readily side with the manufacturer if he felt the latter was in the right.

In his way then, Louis Kirstein was as strong-minded and as stubborn in his beliefs as was Edward Filene. And if their points of view occasionally coincided, they more often diverged, sometimes sharply so. They were probably embarked on a collision course from the moment Kirstein became a vice president of the Filene firm. But what made the collision both more rapid and rancorous was that Kirstein was the vice president of merchandising, Edward might listen to what the others might have to say regarding their own areas of authority and even, on occasion, modify his own opinion as a result. But merchandising was his particular specialty, one in which he had gained national, indeed international, renown. He was not about to yield many points in this field to a former baseball team manager from Rochester, New York. Given these sets of events and the personalities involved it was not long before the sparks had begun to fly between the company's president and its merchandising vice president.

In the growing tension between himself and the other associates, especially Kirstein, Edward looked to Lincoln as an ally. His younger brother had in the past generally gone along with him on most matters and, as we have seen, their thinking on major issues had more or less followed parallel lines. On a personal level, Edward, in his way, was quite attached to Lincoln. H had expressed a paternal uneasiness when Lincoln went off on his own to Europe, and even in their later days, Edward on his own travels, would sign his letters to him "your loving brother." He had always assumed that he could count on Lincoln's steadfast loyalty.

But while Edward was becoming, in store matters at least, increasingly testy and troublesome, Lincoln, now entering his fifties, was becoming increasingly independent. As he handled more and more matters on his own, and as the store grew, he became more and more confident of his abilities. And when Edward, returning from one of his absences would attempt to seize the reins and drive off in new directions, barking out orders for everyone to follow him, and even chastising them for not having done what he had wanted, Lincoln's devotion to his older brother began to diminish

Another factor in the situation was Lincoln's growing closeness to Kirstein. His health problems, plus the fact that Edward's absences left Kirstein the only merchandising specialist in the firm's director-ate, caused him to lean on Kirstein more and more. But more importantly the two men genuinely liked each other. They played golf together regularly and when Kirstein read a biography he enjoyed he passed it on to Lincoln. He even named his younger son after him.

This closeness between the two men was not shared by their families. Therese and her daughters regarded both Kirstein and his wife as "pushers" and Therese had heard that Rose Kirstein had tried to pose at the store as Therese Filene. However, Lincoln carefully kept his store life separate from his home life and his family knew little of what was going on in the increasingly acerbic board meetings on Washington Street.

Lincoln sought to maintain peace between his brother and Kirstein but his knack for conciliation proved no match for the situation that confronted him. In 1917 he wrote Edward pleading with him to adopt "a more generous attitude" toward their junior partners. But Edward probably could not have acted any differently even if he had wished. He still regarded himself as the store's leader and he expected the others to follow him. Lincoln meanwhile was drawing further away from him and closer to the others, especially Kirstein. When the latter, fed up with having to deal with Edward, began thinking of severing his connection with the store, Lincoln begged him not to do so. "If you were to withdraw from the business which I hope will never occur," Lincoln wrote him, "I would not stay in the business myself. This sounds rather drastic but the fact of it is my health would never permit of my working again in the business if EAF were to assume control of the details and I should have no choice in the matter."

* * *

The first major battle occurred in 1918. Simpson, who headed the advertising and publicity pyramid, had taken leave to serve in the army. He had distinguished himself, earning a medal and rising to the rank of Colonel. With the war ending, he decided to pursue a career in the oil business and so he tended his resignation.

He also, under the terms of the partnership agreement of 1912, tendered his stock. If the company declined to buy it back from him, he could sell it to whomever he chose. There was no question of allowing the stock to be sold to outsiders for all stockholders were to be company employees wholly committed to its welfare. The stock was repurchased but now a new problem appeared. Kirstein & Frost wanted to buy it.

It is easy to understand and even to sympathize with their desire to do so. Frost had worked for Filene's nearly all his adult life. Kirstein had only been with the store seven years, but had given up a good position, moved to Boston and invested a quarter-of-a-million dollars in the store at a time when its position was less secure than it was in 1918. Both men felt entitled to expand their holdings in the firm's common stock, the stock that gave its holders the right to vote on company policy.

Edward vigorously opposed the sale and Lincoln reluctantly went along with him. Simpson's twelve shares were held in escrow. But on another issue Edward was less successful. Kirstein wanted to take over Simpson's responsibilities and combine the advertising and merchandising pyramids under his control. Edward argued against such a move on the grounds of his long-held belief that it would enable and encourage a merchandising head to cover up his mistakes by spending too much of the advertising budget in trying to dispose of these mistakes. His opposition was buttressed by his growing animosity to Kirstein. Lincoln on this occasion sided with Kirstein and so Edward's enemy emerged from the fray with greater power.

Despite this defeat, Edward kept trying to impose his ideas on what he still regarded as his store. The fact that his favorite project, the bargain basement, turned its first profit the following year, and soon thereafter became the store's most profitable operation only strengthened his determination. He even began to fantasize about multiplying store sales by 100 and 200 percent while the others were racking their brains for ways to boost sales by 10 or 15 percent.

The breadth of his ideas were attuned to the amplitude of his ambitions. For example, he wanted to consolidate all the store's goods into three basic lines, a proposal he was advocating in his books and speeches. He also wanted completely separate accounts kept for all departments so that those which lost money could be identified and shut down. He even urged setting turnover targets for every item and discontinuing those items that failed to meet these goals. Under this plan, the store would decide how many calls per week or month would justify carrying, for example, 12½ size men's shoes, and if the calls were insufficient, then such a shoe size would be dropped from stock.

He also had less sweeping proposals to suggest. For example, he recommended setting up separate counters, each with a sign saying "any gift at this counter for $5, or $10 or $2.50" as the case might be. Now in his sixties, Edward Filene believed he was only hitting his stride as an innovative merchandiser.

Few of his ideas lacked merit. Many stores would adopt his concept of three basic price lines, though some would later abandon it. Completely separate accounts for departments would eventually become standard practice in large-scale retailing operations. Sears Roebuck, Woolworth and other retailers would also implement the plan for counters carrying diverse goods with a common price tag.

But the prophet was without honor in his own bailiwick. In part, because his proposals seemed unrealistic, in part because they threatened one or more of their own interests, in part because they were not carefully thought through and packaged, and in part because of personal antagonisms, most of Edward's proposals received a frigid reception.

One which was accepted was his plan for selling staple items at a reduced mark-up. It was tried out in an underwear department but resulted in substantial losses and so was discontinued in six months. Although the same idea would later be inaugurated successfully by many chain stores, its failure to prove itself in Filene's only made the other management members more wary than ever of their President's brainstorms.

Even the President's proven successes sometimes became sources of discord and dispute. This was especially true when it came to dealing with items purchased in large quantities for the Basement.

For example, if a buyer for the Basement managed to acquire, say, three thousand blue serge suits at an attractive price, the other board members would wish to put out only 500 of them for sale at a time. Putting all 3,000 on sale at once would temporarily saturate the market, forcing the store to mark down large numbers of them and possibly even give some away when the 30 day sales period expired. Furthermore, the 3,000 suits would take up so much rack space that other salable items would be crowded out.

Edward, however, refused to see it that way. To him, holding merchandise back out of such concerns was unethical and contrary to the Basement's principles. The customer was entitled to buy merchandise at marked down prices when it had not sold by the stipulated time and holding goods in the storeroom to prevent such markdowns boarded on deception.

The Basement and its operations deepened the division between Edward and the others in other ways. It was his pet project and he favored it in all its relationships with the main store. Consequently, it had developed a high degree of independence, too much so in the eyes of the other managers. It functioned almost as a separate entity with its own buyers, its own procedures, its own *esprit de corps*. At times, it seemed to be in competition with the main store.

Edward encouraged this and liked to use the Basement as an example of successful retailing which would teach the others a lesson. When, for example, he discovered that the main store was touting a perfume named Christmas Night for $25 a bottle while the Basement was offering it at $2.99, he gleefully informed his colleagues of this fact. They, however, were not amused.

Edward used the Basement's success especially to taunt Kirstein for Kirstein's particular project was the men's store and the men's store was struggling. Year after year it continued to operate at a substantial loss and by the mid 1920's it had cost the company almost two million dollars. Even when it finally at this time edged into the black, it failed to produce an appreciable return.[10]

Edward continually reminded the other board members of this fact. His doing so plus his moves to discover and discontinue unprofitable operations and slow-selling items, seemed especially directed at undermining Kirstein, the firm's merchandising vice president. Needless to say, his efforts only increased Kirstein's hostility.

But if Kirstein had emerged as Edward's greatest enemy, he certainly was not the only one. Edward Frost was also frequently at loggerheads with Edward Filene. The finance head challenged his president's persistent plea for large increases in sales in order to cut down the percentage of gross revenue eaten up by overhead costs. This, of course, was one of Edward's main goals in life, i.e. to reduce distribution costs. Frost, however, claimed that contrary to Edward's contention the store's expense rate had not increased and that stepping up the volume of sales would not lower it.[11]

Frost further nettled Edward by questioning the need for the store to continue its membership in the U.S.Chamber of Commerce. Every year when the bill for Chamber dues arrived he would urge that it not be paid. This infuriated Edward who, despite his ouster from the directorship of the International Chamber, continued to consider himself a leader of the U.S. Chamber of Commerce.

In their enmity toward Edward, Frost and Kirstein could count on near total support from the junior management members, some of whom had become members by virtue of FCA elections to the board of directors. As Stuart later wrote, both Frost and Kirstein were regarded as "considerate, understanding, and at least as liberal in rewarding good work as they were stern in condemning poor work." Each, he says, was "spoken of as a fine man to work for..." Edward, on the other hand, had become an increasing source of trouble for them since he refused to accept any decision by the board of directors of the broader-based junior management board, that ran contrary to his wishes. Consequently, when he saw an employee or executive carrying out a store policy which he had opposed, he would strongly and often loudly bawl him out, giving no heed to the fact that the hapless fellow was only following orders. Edward still viewed the store much as Louis XIV viewed the French State, i.e. as an extension and embodiment of himself. But the French King had had no partners to worry about; Edward Filene did.

***

Impossible as the situation was becoming, it might still have continued indefinitely as long as Lincoln's loyalty to his older brother remained intact. But this loyalty had already begun to weaken, and as matters progressed--perhaps regressed would be a better word to describe the situation--it dissolved still more.

Edward did much to bring this about. He had apparently never forgiven Lincoln for allowing Kirstein to take over the advertising function and he regarded with deepening resentment his brother's growing friendship with the new partner. But instead of trying to woo Lincoln, he rather typically only drove him further away by displaying his resentment in harsh and heedless ways.

The branch operations which the store started up in the post-war period were primarily Lincoln's projects. Edward attacked them mercilessly. We are "selling our heritage for a mess of potage," he once said, claiming that the store was "frittering away" energies which should go into establishing a chain of department stores, each in a major city. He was at least partly correct for many of these branches would never become profitable and in later years would be shut down. But Lincoln believed in them and fought off his brother's attempts to abolish them. When, at a board meeting in early 1924, Edward proposed keeping separate accounts for the Providence and Northhampton stores, Lincoln replied "if we keep separate accounts, we'll want to close these shops, and I don't want them closed up."

Even minor matters frequently placed the two brothers at odds. Lincoln, together with Frost and Kirstein, wanted Filene's to contribute to an endowed chair at the Harvard Law School that would be named after Brandeis. Since Brandeis had served the store well as its counsel during its formative years, and had written the constitution of the Filene Cooperative Association, such a donation seemed properly within the store's range of activities. But the decision incensed Edward who insisted that the money given would end up being extracted from the customers through higher prices. Such contributions, he maintained, should come out of their individual incomes instead. But once again he found himself outvoted. Such outcomes were becoming habitual and were posing a greater peril to his future than he seemed to realize.

***

In 1925 Thomas Dan Cory, an affable man who found himself caught up in all these troublesome tensions, suffered a sudden heart attack and died. His death was a great loss to Lincoln who had always prized Cory's friendship as well as his ability. It was also a turning point in Lincoln's relationship with Edward.

Once again, some voting stock became available and once again Kirstein & Frost wanted to buy it. Consequently, Lincoln found himself torn once again between his brother and his two junior partners. Finally, at a directors' meeting on November 15, 1926, Lincoln voted to allow the sale. Kirstein and Frost also took over Cory's duties as head of store administration. The original four pyramids had shrunk to two.

"As my brother more and more left the management of the business to the rest of us," said Lincoln in explaining the decision in later years, "we developed convictions of our own. And one of them is that the attempt to fix for two generations the control and organization of a business corporation is extremely unwise." He described the stock sale as "the only fair and logical procedure" for Kirstein and Frost had worked conscientiously and competently to make the store a success. Furthermore, he noted that they had indicated that they would offer some of this stock to their own assistants.

For Edward it was a major blow. Kirstein and Frost together now owned 36 shares or over one third of the company while Edward had only 26. He was somewhat protected by the partnership agreement which required Lincoln and him to vote their shares together as joint tenants of their mutual holdings. But that did not require them to vote together on the Board of Directors where the major battles were being fought. More ominously, the partnership agreement itself would not last forever. In fact, it would expire in a little over a year.

On April 27, 1927, Clara Filene, aged 93, died. Her death dealt Edward a double blow for he lost not only his single source of female affection but also a valuable link to his younger brother. While Clara lived, her sons had sought to shield her from their growing division and, had she lived on, Lincoln would probably have prevented his differences with Edward from becoming too pronounced. Her removal from the scene left him with a freer hand in shaping his own future conduct.

Edward apparently assessed the significance of the event and this, plus his awareness of his weakening position generally, made him start to seek a way out. He had long been preaching the need for department store chains as a way of lowering distribution costs and now he set about seeing if he could start one up. A month or so after Clara's funeral, he went to New York to confer with officials of

Manufacturer's Trust with an eye to securing financing for such a chain. The ambitious scheme would have required a very large loan and the New York bank declined to supply it.

Undaunted he continued to discuss with his aides the possibilities of developing such a chain through other means. He also began discussing with them the possibility of buying out the other partners. Both such enterprising endeavors struck them as hopeless.

In the midst of these discussions, Stuart suddenly resigned to accept another position. He had received an attractive offer from the Goodyear Company but its acceptance required him to limit his notice to Edward to two weeks, nowhere near the amount of time it would take his boss to find and train a suitable replacement. Stuart knew the problem his leaving on such short notice would cause Edward and he had consulted with some of the other management members as to what he should do. Frost had told him to go ahead for, said Frost, Edward would fire him on five minutes notice if it suited his convenience. Frost also reminded him that his boss had never given him a raise or a bonus and had done nothing to make his work easier or pleasanter.

Kirstein's response was predictably similar, "Stuart, you know there is no chance for advancement for you in this business. Mr. Edward would not let you have it." Stuart, realizing that both men were, for whatever reasons, telling him essentially the truth, thereupon decided to leave.

Edward was furious at Stuart but even more furious at Frost and Kirstein. He suspected that they had secured the position for his aide with the sole view of depriving him of his services. This charge was baseless for Stuart had merely answered a blind ad placed by an employment agency. But Edward remained convinced that Frost and Kirstein had figured prominently in Stuart's departure and the atmosphere at board meetings became more acrimonious still.

As the last year of the partnership agreement drew to a close, relations between the two principal partners, Edward and Lincoln, continued to deteriorate. An incident, minor in itself, which occurred during the Christmas shopping season illustrates just what was happening. On December 29, Lincoln sent Edward a memo saying how he had been passing through the luggage department when he noticed some valises grouped under a sign which said in bold letters "Mr. E. A. Filene's Bag".

Lincoln asked what the sign was doing there. The supervisor said Edward had ordered him to put up the sign because Edward used these valises himself and thought an announcement of the fact would facilitate their sale. Lincoln's memo then relates how he removed and destroyed the sign, telling the supervisor how he felt "very sure that this could not have been so and that probably in his zeal to carry out some suggestion from you, he accepted it as an order."

Edward replied the next day that he had merely told the supervisor how much he liked the bags and that all that was needed to sell them was a to call people's attention to them, "and that I would not object if it was thought to be a good way, to have them called the Edward A. Filene bag." Edward protested that he did not mean for the supervisor to put up a sign without consulting the publicity department. He ended his memo by saying, "Your note impressed me that you may have belittled me with the buyer."

Their partnership agreement had twelve more days to run.

***

Certain premises underlay the partnership agreement of 1912. These were that Edward and Lincoln would only be able to give, and would only want to give, 15 more years of active service to the business; that the four younger partners would stay with the store and take over its direction when the Filenes faded from the scene; and that the store's employees would become increasingly interested in, and increasingly prepared for, assuming a greater role in its operations along with a greater share of its ownership.

None of these premises had proven true. Most of the store's employees had manifested little desire to own or operate the enterprise, only two of the four junior partners were still with the store and the two Filenes, despite the touchy health of the younger one, still seemed addicted to shopkeeping.

However, the most important of the premises upon which the partnership agreement had been based was that Edward and Lincoln would continue as a team. It was this premise that now confronted the brothers with the greatest dilemma of their merchandising careers, and, indeed, their lives.

Isolated and alone, Edward was obviously in the weakest position. Yet he nevertheless possessed weapons with which to fight. He was still the joint owner with Lincoln of 52 percent of the company. He still was the company's president and most famous figure so that any public outcry he might make could prove costly. And he was still tied by bonds of blood and a lifetime of association to Lincoln Filene.

Lincoln did not welcome his pivotal role in determining his brother's future. He certainly did not wish to humiliate him in any way and yet he knew that things could not continue as they had been going. As if to underscore this point, Edward had chosen to ignore his now shaky position and to attack vigorously Lincoln's latest project, the new Filene store in Worcester. At a meeting of the board on January 9, 1928, Edward's bitter objections to the venture caused Lincoln to say. "It is because of these statements the president is now making and has been making right along that I think the directors are entitled to have him look into this so that he is not doing it in ignorance any longer." The two-member band of brothers which had built the world's largest specialty store had come apart—for good.

In casting about for a solution Lincoln consulted with all those who could help. He even invited out to Weston some of these closest to Edward such as John Fahey and Henry Dennison to see if they could suggest ways to resolve the problem with a minimum of pain to his brother. Edward meanwhile hired a battery of lawyers to help negotiate his future status with the store.

The best hope of a solution seemed to lie in letting Edward retain his position but not his powers. Needless to say, Edward was far from enchanted with the idea but there seemed little he could do to win anything better. Characteristically, he bothered his negotiators so much that they finally urged him to go off on a fishing vacation in Florida, saying that they could do better in his absence. Edward reluctantly agreed and from a hotel in Key West he wrote Lincoln Steffens a letter somewhat pathetically summarizing his plight.

"The store situation is distressing," said Edward. "Frost and Kirstein have completely won over Lincoln and we are practically estranged. It's unimportant and my own fault. I was too one-sided—not human enough to play more with my brother instead of working only, with him."

He goes on to bemoan the fact that the idea of instituting true industrial democracy through enabling the employees to become major stockholders also seemed lost. He then returns to his own sorry state. "I have lost all power to lead or advise and my lawyers have made me agree to negotiations for a compromise by which I give up the last possibility of gaining leadership again—which possibly can only come to me by the total incapacity or death of A.L and I don't want to live with that in mind."

Edward points out that "two different groups are after me to make a new chain of department stores" but he does not believe he can obtain the right conditions from either of them. And he ends his letter by saying, "I envy you your wife and son. I wish I had a family like yours." The unsuccessful millionaire was learning, and experiencing, just how unsuccessful he was.[12]

By early summer, the negotiations were finally completed. Edward emerged as still the company's president and its principal stockholder as well. But he also emerged as a virtual eunuch in his own store. For while he retained his title and all its trappings including his $100,000-a-year salary, his eighth-floor corner office and his assistants and secretaries, he could not give a single order to anyone outside his office. Even the lowliest store supervisor would now possess more direct power than the store's president.

His contract as president was to run until 1940 when he would be nearly 80. If it gave him no authority it also removed him from any responsibility. He objected to having duties spelled out for him for, he somewhat paranoically said, "they will harass and humiliate me as they do now if I am bound to definite duties." However, the others were only too happy to grant his wish. In a letter sent to him to confirm the new agreement, the store's management acknowledged the fact "that your duties will be such as to make the manner of their performance and the time to be devoted thereto a matter largely within your personal discretion." Edward also was given the right to terminate the contract at any time. It was in all likelihood the most unusual employment contract in the history of American retailing. In his own ironic way, Edward had achieved another Filene first.

The other partners were also only too glad to grant another of Edward's demands. He had wanted the company to go public, that is to list its stock on the New York Stock Exchange. This would enable him more easily to sell his shares, should he wish to start a new enterprise, or to purchase additional shares should he wish to strengthen his position in Filene's. Kirstein & Frost had long wanted to go public so that they could also dispose of their shares should Lincoln die and Edward assume control of the company.

It was thus agreed that the 100 shares of voting stock would be replaced with 500,000 shares of new common stock. Of this, Edward would hold 150,000 giving him 30 percent of the company. But Lincoln, Kirstein and Frost would hold, collectively, 250,100 shares giving them a majority control. Each of the five members of the operating committee was to receive 4,000 shares or 20,000 in all, while 4,900 shares were earmarked for 150 employees to be selected by management. The remaining 75,000 shares would be offered to the public.[13]

Although the new financial arrangement would give the store a more broadly-based ownership and allow five percent of its employees to own voting stock, it failed by far to carry out the provisions of the 1912 partnership agreement which called for the employees to acquire nearly half of the store's voting stock. The dream of full-fledged industrial democracy had died. Why?

To some extent its death resulted from insufficient desire on the part of management to bring it about. Kirstein and Frost had always considered such a scheme unsound as well as threatening to their own interests. Lincoln had probably become more conservative as he had grown older and his growing closeness to the two remaining junior partners would no doubt have strengthened this trend. But even Edward himself, while continuing to call for fulfillment of the 1912 agreement, was most likely having second thoughts for he had rarely received much support from the employee representatives on the Board of Directors.

Another reason for the firm's failure to implement the agreement was that it had never created any arrangement for doing so. When the time for the transfer of the stock came due, there was no mechanism in place for effecting it. Just who was to get how much and on what terms were questions that had never been considered, let alone answered.

Yet the biggest factor was simply the employees own lack of interest in owning or operating Filene's. All through the 1920's Lincoln had sought to strengthen the Filene Cooperative Association. He had, as we have seen, given its Board of Arbitration the right to initiate inquiries on its own and in 1922 he arranged for it to have final jurisdiction in all cases it considered. Yet the Board's work load actually declined. In one subsequent year it heard only four cases.

In 1925 Lincoln wrote in *The Echo*, "I want to call your attention to the very little use to which the Arbitration Board is being put of late. While I should like to think the inherent justice in our organization makes the Arbitration Board non-essential, I am afraid we cannot answer the question in that way." But despite his inquiry the board's activities continued to stagnate. By the time the partnership agreement had expired, the Board had yet to initiate a single inquiry on its own.

Elsewhere the employees were displaying a similar disinterest in developing or utilizing the powers they possessed. The store's credit union, for example, was having great difficulty in obtaining quorums for its meetings. Even membership in employee hobby and social clubs had begun to dip as the growth of car ownership, movie houses, and dance halls made outside distractions more easily available.

Several, more fundamental, factors underlay this failure in employee involvement. One was the lack of education. Less than 20 percent of the store's work force had finished high school while over a quarter had never completed grammar school. Less than two percent had a college education and some of these had attended low-level teacher's colleges or "normal schools" as these institutions were called at the time. Then there was the store's high turnover rate. Some 20 percent of its employees left its employ every year, most of them women who were getting married. An unstable and insufficiently educated workforce would not normally be eager for, let alone prepared for, widening its responsibilities, especially in those much more conservative days.

The Russell Sage study then underway in the store would fully acknowledge the problem. While it took management to task for not trying harder to effect their dreams of industrial democracy, it would also note that "the employees themselves are more than a little responsible. Their lack of initiative in using their powers for participation in management has been conspicuous." The greatest killers of the dream, then, were those for whom it had been designed.

***

Once the agreement had been signed, Edward hastily departed on his annual summer trip to Europe. The others, however, journeyed to New York where they sought to interest Lehman Brothers, the leading stock underwriters at the time, in marketing the 75,000 shares of common stock plus the 35,000 share of preferred stock that Filene's was offering to the public. Knowing that the stock of the well-known store would be quickly snapped up by the buoyant, indeed boiling, stock market, the underwriting firm quickly said yes. But the offering came with an important string attached. The Filene management group had never forgotten how the First National Bank of Boston had rescued their store from the brink of bankruptcy in 1913, and although the financial obligation had long since been paid, the moral debt remained. The Boston bank, they said, would have to share fully and equally in the underwriting.

Lehman Brothers protested such a stipulation. As Wall Street's pre-eminent underwriter, it did not wish to co-underwrite a stock offering with a provincial bank. But Lincoln, Kirstein and Frost were adamant, and Lehman Brothers, not wishing to lose such a choice bit of business, capitulated.

In late September the stock of William Filene's Sons, Inc. came on the market at $38 a share. Edward wrote his assistant, Robert Moore, authorizing him to borrow money on Edward's existing Filene stock and buy up to a quarter-of-a-million dollars worth as long as he could get it at no more than $50 a share. But thanks to the store's reputation and the speculation spree then engulfing Wall Street, the stock immediately took off, soon soaring to a high of $97. Moore managed to acquire only a few hundred shares within the ceiling Edward set.

The avidity with which Wall Street took to the Filene stock made Edward a much wealthier man. At $97 a share, his common stock alone was worth nearly $15 million. (Of course, the stock would tumble along with other stocks in next year's crash, eventually dipping to half its offering price.) Of greater importance to him at the time was that its rise prevented him from appreciably strengthening his position at the store.

But there were further disappointments in the offing, disappointments that would make Edward's life at this time increasingly difficult. Even while the new contract was being negotiated, his role as store spokesman was being curtailed. For example, Moore had once given out copies of Edward's recent speeches and other materials to some German visitors who were inspecting the store. The aftermath was described by Moore in a memo to his absent boss. "This morning Mr. A. L. came into the office and warned me that I should not tell visitors that Mr. Edward Filene's ideas were being exemplified in store operations." Later, said Moore, Lincoln had called him into his office and told him that all letters relating to store business should be delivered to him when Edward was absent. Under no circumstances was such mail to be answered by Edward's staff.

In early October, Edward tried to obtain a raise for Moore whose $6,600 a year salary had not been increased in the four years he had worked for his boss. The memo recommending such an increase drew a frosty, though polite, reply from Lincoln who pointed out that no one in a similar position was being paid more than what Moore was already getting, and increasing his pay to $10,000 a year as Edward wished would raise him well above what all the other assistants were earning. Later that month when Edward was preparing to leave for the annual meeting of the Associated Merchandising Corporation, he received a memo from Lincoln saying "I understand that you contemplate attending the meeting of the Associated Merchandising Corporation in Columbus next week. I assume that in doing so you will not undertake to speak for our company at the meeting."

The form of this communication was perhaps even more revealing of their present relationship than its contents. They were now referring to each other as "President" and "Chairman of the Board" the last title having been officially assumed by Lincoln under the new set-up. And they were communicating almost exclusively by memos although their offices still adjoined. (Edward and Kirstein had even stopped saying hello. When they passed in the corridor, according to an aide, they just glowered at one another.)

The 1928 presidential campaign was also underway and Edward was actively supporting Al Smith. His activities included giving speeches to audiences where he would be introduced as the president of Filene's. This predictably perturbed the other board members and at a meeting on Oct. 31 they voted the following resolution, "that officers of the corporation be asked to refrain from making public expression of individual opinion on controversial questions unless prior sanction is given by the Board of Directors in each case." Edward, secure in his 12-year contract, simply ignored the resolution and went right on speaking his mind.

The following year, however, brought some fresh humiliations. He had finally found in Percy Brown an aide to take the place vacated by Stuart. Edward wanted Brown shown through the store but when Brown called the Personnel Office to make the arrangements, he was told that such a tour could not be arranged for under the circum-stances it could lead to misunderstandings. It might, so he was told, prove embarrassing to Brown himself. But perhaps nothing more forcefully brought home to Edward the fragility of his position than a minor incident which occurred in March, 1929.

Edward wanted to look at the balance sheets and operating statements of all the other stores in the Retail Research Association and sent Frost a memo requesting these documents. His contract did guarantee him the right to scrutinize all of Filene's records but said nothing about the stores with which it was now linked through the Retail Research Association. Frost, mindful that Edward was still hoping to start a chain of stores of his own, was reluctant to give such figures to the store's figurehead president. He replied to Edward's memo the next day saying that these records could not leave his office. If Edward wanted to look at them, he would have to come to Frost's office to do so. This meant that Edward, the company president, would have to troop to Frost's suite and sit in his outer office among the secretaries and wait for Frost to parcel out the records for him to examine. Edward was painfully learning the limitations of his paper presidency.

***

When Frost refused to let Edward see the records of the other RRA stores, except under circumstances which made it almost certain that Edward would refuse, he was not seeking to humiliate him. Far more critical considerations prompted his action. Filene's was then preparing to take the most significant single step in its history and it was a step that Edward was vigorously, vehemently, contesting. Filene's was preparing for a merger.

According to one account, the initial move took place aboard a yacht in Long Island Sound. The yacht belonged to Walter Rothschild; President of Abraham and Strauss of Brooklyn, NY. On board, in addition to Rothschild, were Fred Lazarus of F and R Lazarus of Columbus, Ohio, Samuel Bloomingdale of the well-known New York Store which bore his family name, Louis Kirstein of Filene's and Paul Mazur of Lehman Brothers. On the cruise, Mazur proposed that the four stores carry the cooperative arrangements they already enjoyed through the Retail Research Association and the AMC one step further and consolidate into a single company.

The consolidation which Mazur suggested would take the form of a holding company. This would place all the stores under common ownership while allowing each of them to retain its own identity and methods of operation. Although the stores would form a chain it would not be a chain like Sears Roebuck or Woolworth for there would be no central headquarters and no central direction and control. The benefits would come in the form of increased cooperation and, most importantly, a spreading of risk. Should any one store ever falter or fail, the effects would be partially offset by income from, and equity in, the others.

Rothschild, Lazarus and Kirstein quickly agreed and each returned home to sell the proposal to their associates. Kirstein had little trouble convincing Lincoln and Frost. Lincoln had always favored cooperative approaches and he saw in the proposed holding company a continuation and further development of his work in developing the Retail Research Association and the AMC. Frost, along with Kirstein, had an additional reason for favoring the merger. It would remove them still further from danger should anything happen to Lincoln. Edward's ownership of over 30 percent of the Filene voting stock still made them uneasy but in the new holding company his ownership and voice would be substantially diminished.

Edward, of course, saw the same thing. He also saw his positions as president publicly weakened. Up to now few had learned of his actual impotence in the operation of Filene's, but with the merger, all would know that he was president of merely one of a group of collectively-owned stores.

The news broke on March 6, 1929 with a report in *The New York Times*. It said that "negotiations involving a merger of Abraham & Strauss, Incorporated of Brooklyn and William Filene's Sons Co. of Boston are underway." Rothschild of the Brooklyn store was quoted as admitting it, and reached in Boston, Kirstein was quoted as confirming it, saying "negotiations are pending looking to such a merger, but details have not been completed and nothing has been signed."

The details were soon completed and it was later learned that F & R Lazarus was also included in the proposed new holding company. On March 27, the three stores sent out letters to their stockholders asking them to deposit their stock preparatory to exchanging such stock for shares in a new company to be called Federated Department Stores.

***

The 1920's had witnessed a great growth in department store chains and by 1924 they were handling one-fifth of the nation's retail business. Edward had long hailed this trend. Just a year previously he had written an article for *The New York Times* lamenting the nation's over-supply of retailers and middlemen and looking to chain stores for a remedy. "The growth of the chains is largely due to the low prices at which they can sell because of the successful fight they have waged against all kinds of waste in distribution," he said. He seemed quite oblivious to the irony that when it came to his own store he was now fighting the trend he had so long and so fervently favored.

He first sought to convince his fellow board members to abandon the idea, but, predictably, his efforts did not avail. In desperation, he then turned to the courts. Hiring Sherman A. Whipple, Massachusetts' leading trial lawyer, to represent him, he filed a suit on June 18 to block the merger.

In his petition, Edward accused Lincoln, Kirstein and Frost of bypassing him in the conduct of the business, and claimed that they now "have contrived and are attempting to carry out by wrongful means a scheme to deprive the plaintiff of the rights, benefits and advantages secured to him by the settlement agreement." His financial interest in the store would of necessity be reduced through the merger. So would his influence for, so his petition alleges, "the defendants propose and intend to cause themselves to be elected as directors, officers and managers of said merger company but not to elect the plaintiff either as a director or as an officer..."

His complaints were to a great extent true. But did they violate the terms of this contract? Lincoln, Kirstein and Frost insisted that they did not and in his answering argument their counsel dismissed most of Edward contentions as "impertinent and inelegant", maintaining that the proposed merger abrogated none of the rights accorded to the plaintiff in his agreement with the firm.

"For many years," their lawyer said, "the plaintiff has arbitrarily and unreasonably opposed many of the well-chosen plans for the administration of the business which were approved unanimously by the other directors and said directors repeatedly indulged the plaintiff in many ways because of his past relationship to the business and to one of the defendants."

The defendants put forth a further notice regarding Edward's effort to block the merger through litigation. As their attorney put it, Edward was tying "to obtain from the defendants rights and advantages to which he is not entitled and with the knowledge of the danger that publication of the fact that the president of William Filene's Sons Company had created internal discord and strife might injure the business of the corporation and the value of the defendants' stock therein..."

Their assertion that Edward had acted deliberately with this end in mind seems dubious. But that his suit had accomplished at least the aim of revealing publicly the split between him and the others can not be denied. Wile the Boston newspapers soft-pedaled this story out of consideration for a major advertiser, *The New York Times* put it at the top of its business page. Under the headline "E.A. Filene Seeks To Stop Store Merger" the newspaper devoted nearly half a column to the story on June 20 and gave it some additional space the following day. This, plus the expense and effort that Edward's suit was costing the store, only further embittered the atmosphere and enlarged the estrangement between Edward and Lincoln.

The presiding judge granted Edward's request for a temporary injunction restraining the other three from tending their stock to the new holding company pending a full hearing and weighing of the arguments. But on July 8, he dissolved the injunction and dismissed Edward's suit, finding it to be without merit.

Action aimed at effecting the merger promptly resumed and soon virtually all stock but Edward's was deposited. Then a new and, at least to all those concerned except Edward, welcome development occurred. On September 17, *The New York Times* in a front page headline declared "Bloomingdale's Joins Huge Store Merger." There were now four members of the new chain and further ones were anticipated. However, Filene's was still the largest of the four for its annual sales of $46 million doubled that of Bloomingdale's.[14]

In November, the new holding company was officially incorporated. Its president was Walter Rothschild but Lincoln was given the highest post, that of Chairman of the Board of Directors, while both Kirstein and Frost were made board members. Frost was the only non-Jew among the holding company's directors and one can't help wondering how this austere Yankee felt in taking his place among a group of men, none of whom could pass through the door of the country club where he spent so much of his leisure time.

Lincoln Steffens sent a sympathetic letter to Edward. "You are facing your problem, and I would like to have a voice in the solution of it. I have no advice for you," he wrote from his new retreat in

California. "But E.A., if you do get sick of the fighting in Boston...remember that there is a quiet spot in Carmel, California where you can always be loved and insulted, laughed at and admired."

Edward, however, had no intention of conceding defeat and then retiring to California to lick his wounds. He brought attorney John W. Davis, the Democratic Party's 1924 presidential candidate to Boston to appeal the court's decision to the Massachusetts Supreme Court. On December 5th Davis appeared before the court to ask it to restrain Lincoln, Kirstein and Frost from going forward with the consolidation. The three, said Davis, "conceived the idea of this merger" with the aim of securing "peculiar advantages to themselves, they to be officers and directors of the new corporation, voting trustees and to have employment with it to the exclusion of the plaintiff." These charges were resolutely resisted by the defendants' attorney Edward McLennen who insisted that "there is nothing of which the plaintiff is deprived in any way."

Within two weeks the judges rendered their decision. "The benefits accruing to the defendants in which the plaintiff does not share do not amount to a deprivation of the property rights of the plaintiff; these benefits are not inconsistent with the plaintiff's right as a stockholder or with his rights under the settlement agreement," said the presiding justice as he upheld the lower court's finding. Edward was finally, and decisively, beaten.

The same week brought still another victory for Lincoln, Kirstein and Frost. Federated applied for listing on the New York Stock Exchange and in so doing it revealed the terms under which its stock had been exchanged for the stock of its constituent companies. Because of the high value which the securities market had accorded Filene's stock, the store had succeeded in swapping its stock for Federated stock on a one-for-one basis, that is one share of Filene stock for one share in the new holding company. The remaining three firms had felt constrained to accept less, putting up more than one share of their stocks for each Federated share they received in return. (Years later Fred Lazarus would wonder if they hadn't been foolish in allowing Filene's such generous exchange terms.)

The year 1929 thus ended on a note of triumph for Lincoln Filene. He had emerged as the leader of a four-member chain of prestigious stores. His store would serve as something of a flagship for the new chain and the chain itself seemed likely to grow for other members of the Retail Research Association and AMC were already indicating an interest in joining it. Finally, he had reduced still further the role of the man who had done so much during the past decade to hamper his efforts and bedevil his whole existence.

Nevertheless it was not a triumph he could fully savor. For Lincoln Filene, who had lived 65 years without acquiring a single significant enemy, now had one: his own brother.

As for Edward, he found himself not only defeated but exposed. By taking his fight to court he had spread before the public the fictional nature of his position as President of the store which bore his name, and his resulting defeat had only emphasized how weak that position really was. The ugly duckling--and he had never seemed more like one as he vigorously protested through his court briefs his exclusion from what the others were doing--had also showed himself to be an emperor without clothes.

After the battle had finally ended, his ghostwriter Charles Wood, in a zany effort to console his embittered boss, produced what he said should be Edward's epitaph. It ran as follows.

> Here lies the body of Edward A.,
> Who died defending his right-of-way;
> He was always right as he sped along,
> But he's just as dead as if he'd been wrong.

According to another aide who was present at the time, Edward managed to respond with a slight, sad smile.

Chapter 11
EDWARD: STORMING THE HEIGHTS

1936

T he most spectacular, and one of the hardest-fought, presidential campaigns in American history is drawing to a close. Franklin Roosevelt, considered at the outset the underdog despite his incumbency, has been steadily gaining ground. To wind up his campaign on election eve, he has lined up three of his more notable supporters to speak on radio in his behalf. He will then wind up the round-robin program with a 15-minute address from his Hyde Park home.

Senator Robert Wagner of New York speaks first, followed by James Farley. Then, for the final address before Roosevelt's own talk, the program switches to Boston and the program's announcer introduces Edward A. Filene.

***

Public relations pioneer Edward Bernays was sitting in his New York office in November, 1929 when he received a phone call from Boston. On the line was "an Edward Filene" who wanted him to come to Boston to discuss a possible assignment.

Bernays arrived at 12 Otis Place to find a "small and wizened," but also immaculately dressed and mentally alert man sitting in a rocking chair surrounded by five aides whom he occasionally needled but continually referred to as "my team", Edward told Bernays "I want you to get my observations into the newspapers of the country." He had big plans in the making including the establishment of a chain of department stores and therefore needed a good reputation, he said, "to raise the necessary financing. I am unappreciated as a businessman by other businessmen. I want to be known throughout the world as a business leader."

When Bernays named the outlandish, indeed almost outrageous, fee of $15,000 a year to handle Edward's publicity, Edward, though complaining of being financially hard pressed by the stock market crash--Filene's stock had plummeted from a high of $96 to $18--

agreed. Edward never regretted the expenditure since, under Bernays' guidance, his career as a public figure entered its most spectacular, and significant, phase.

One of Bernays' more enterprising efforts came when Lincoln Steffens published his autobiography in the Spring of 1931. Edward said he would like to do something to help promote both the book and also, if possible, himself. Bernays then suggested that he give a dinner for Steffens and invite all those mentioned in the book as honored guests. Edward did so and it was a great success. Among those who came were financier Bernard Baruch, Woodrow Wilson's secretary of State Bainbridge, Colly and Anne Morgan, sister of J. Pierpont Morgan. While Steffens was perforce the star of the occasion--it was, after all, his book that was being celebrated--Edward as the dinner host garnered his share of the spotlight.

Then there were Edward's annual trips to Europe which had become more important to him than ever, for in Europe his fall from power was less known. Indeed, in Europe he was still hailed even by fellow merchants as the great American retailer, although he was now retailing nothing but himself. When he left for his 1931 trip, Bernays got the editor of *Harper's*, Ordway Tead, to host a luncheon for Edward and invite to the American correspondents of the leading European newspapers. Bernays wrote a glowing introduction of Edward, which Tead delivered at the luncheon and the correspondents cabled accounts of it back to their papers. As a result, when Edward arrived in Europe ten days later, he was showered with requests for speaking engagements and interviews. It would be his most triumphant tour of the continent.

***

Edward's hunger for publicity continually amazed Bernays. His client would call up every newspaper editor in Boston to inform them, whenever he was going to be at a head table. Bernays told him he would become much more newsworthy if he spoke less, and he counseled him to take as his model the actress Greta Garbo whose reclusivity had become a Hollywood legend. For a while Edward went along with the suggestion and his news value increased. But while he stopped trying to solicit speaking engagements he found it hard to resist those that came his way. Bernays recalls only one speaking bid that Edward ever turned down. It was from the Homemakers

Institute on CBS radio and Edward felt he would be talking to a "bunch of women who will be listening while they are washing dishes."

The deepening depression certainly provided Edward with much to talk about. He viewed it as confirming his warnings of the excessive costs of distribution. If these costs could be drivers down, he claimed, then people could buy more and, therefore, business would improve.

But Edward did not stop there. He also called for increased wages to combat the slump. Employers should pay their employees not just a "living wage" but a "buying wage" so that the American people, through increased purchases, could revive the moribund economy. When he became deluged with letters from irate business men saying that they were already paying their employees as much as they could afford, and that any further hike would bankrupt their enterprises, Edward issued a clarifying statement. What was needed, he said, was legislation making higher wages compulsory for all. This would remove the competitive threat while allowing the economy to prosper as fatter pay envelopes led to increased consumption of goods and services. He brushed off complaints about the loss of freedom entailed in such a compulsory measure by asking what is better, compulsory prosperity or compulsory poverty?

Edward continued to press for consumer cooperatives even arguing their case before business groups by claiming they would help business in the same way that credit unions were helping the banks by training the masses in the sound administration of money and credit. He also anticipated Ralph Nader and the "Public Interest" lobbies of later years by saying "I want to create an organization called the Association for the Protection of the Consumer Dollar..."

Edward also articulated his ideas in two books published during these years. *The Model Stock Plan* in 1930 claimed that the secret of successful retailing lay in buying, not selling. "The primary function of the retailer is buying for the customer, not selling to the customer. Probably goods that are well bought are already more than half sold", he said. Though largely aimed at merchants, the book was eventually translated into five languages.[15]

The following years came *Successful Living in This Machine Age*, a much more wide-ranging book that attracted a much wider range of readership. "Heretofore", writes Edward, "whenever we have longed to create a better world we have thought it necessary first to change human nature; but no matter how many movements we started...the world we longed for never happened."

But the "second industrial revolution" has changed all that. For it has initiated and necessitated "intelligently selfish, actual, factual cooperation, not in accordance with some theory of what management should be, but in accordance with what management really is." Injustice, says Edward, has become, or soon will become, inefficient. The current crisis is making universal concordance not just desirable but mandatory.

Successful Living in The Machine Age would be published in British, French, Italian, German and even Dutch and Czech editions, adding not only to Edward's fame but to his fortune as well. It also, of course, added to his attractiveness as a speaker and he was now criss-crossing the country addressing various groups including radio audiences.

Though now in his seventies, Edward yet remained vigorous and alert. He had removed his birth date from his biography in *Who's Who* and would react angrily when anyone treated him with too much consideration. This did not often happen, however, for with his bouncing step and his quickness in climbing stairs he did not seem old to most who met him.

He frequently addressed college students as "My Fellow Students" to stress the point that in this new age his own experience counted for almost nothing. He emphasized that "We cannot conserve the values of the past by trying to conserve the formulas of the past." Lehigh University, Rollins College and Tulane University awarded him honorary doctorates. As his power at the store disappeared, his prominence as a public figure increased.

Though much of his speechmaking dealt with the "second industrial revolution" and its requirements, he did not abandon his more specific interests of the past. He continued to call for more systematic fact-finding, more footpaths, cheaper ocean travel and pre-paid medical care. Long an opponents of tariffs, he now blamed them for much of the depression and urged their repeal. Long a supporter of sanctions against aggressor nations, he spoke out stridently against the Japanese invasion of Manchuria in 1931 and worked with Bernays to stir up public disapproval.

To produce this vast outpouring of books, articles and speeches he kept his staff working overtime. He also called on outsiders for occasional help. One of them was Glen Frank who later became president of the University of Wisconsin.

Much of Edward's appeal lay in the fact that he seemed to be a spectacularly successful businessman with some spectacularly bold and unconventional ideas. And a nation, struggling desperately to overcome its worst depression, was definitely interested in bold ideas. As one anonymous commentator--it may have been his protégé Harold Hodgkinson--later put it, Edward was "not a polished speaker nor even a good speaker as the term was used." Yet, "he would eventually be able to interest and inspire audiences by the bold unconventionality of his thought and his direct and forceful language for expressing it."

Edward was not just interested in talking; he was also interested in doing. And since there was little for him to do at the store, he became increasingly immersed in other activities. He continued, despite the cost involved, to support the 20th Century Fund and even transferred its offices to New York. He assisted the World Peace Foundation in stirring up public disapproval of Japan's Manchurian invasion. He even became involved in a new invention. It was a cigar shaped like a pipe, which a Swiss inventor had created and which Edward sought, with little success, to introduce into this country.

Three developments in particular engaged his energies during the early 1930's: Hitler's persecution of the Jews, the Credit Union movement and the New Deal.

From the very first Edward, unlike so many both within and without Germany, took Hitler seriously. In the Spring of 1933 he protested the use of a German ship and a German port of debarkation for the American delegation to the International Chamber of Commerce of which he was a member. When the head of the delegation replied that the members wanted to minimize land travel, he grudgingly went along.

When the convention ended its meetings in Vienna he went on to Berlin where he found the situation as ominous as he had feared. After conferring with many informed observers, including Germany's former chancellor Heinrich Bruening, he sent back a telegram to his staff telling them to "subscribe a thousand dollars [to Jewish relief organizations] which my visit confirms desperately needed."

Edward also sought to help a Jewish journalist emigrate, and meeting Hjalmar Schacht, the head of the National Bank and Hitler's

Chief Economic Advisor at a dinner gathering, he pressed him on the emigration issue. Schacht admitted that no Jew could take out more than 10,000 marks ($2,500) but said all of them could emigrate. If Edward knew of any who were forbidden to leave, then Schacht urged him to let him know.

From Berlin Edward flew to London where, among other activities, he had tea with H.G. Wells. He sought to interest the British writer, then at the height of his popularity, in the anti-Nazi cause. Wells admitted that Nazism "is a crime against civilization" but noted "Like it or not, there is a certain number of Jews whose habitual manners offend the taste of many otherwise neutral people." The fight against Nazism, he said, should not therefore center on the Jewish problem.

Edward agreed and urged him to go to Germany and write articles on what he saw. Edward would seek to have these articles syndicated in the U.S. Wells hesitated but finally agreed to undertake the assignment when a definite offer was made. Buoyed up, Edward on his return contacted a literary agency which, equally enthusiastic, soon sparked the interest of Liberty, then one of the country's most popular magazines. But when Wells heard about it he suddenly had a change of heart, saying Edward was "peddling" his material and he did not want his wares "hawked about." When Edward, seeking to make amends, offered him $1,000 for expenses simply to visit Germany, the writer's secretary replied "Mr. H.G. Wells asks me to say that he could not think of accepting money from you, and that he will be obliged if you will abandon your claim to have any plan or project in association with him. Mr. Wells has been considerably inconvenienced by your attempts to participate in his arrangements for newspaper articles in America."

Another of Edward's efforts to aid German Jews also came to naught. A German Jewish physician told him that China would admit hundreds of German Jewish physicians if a "responsible organization" would handle the arrangements for their selection and resettlement. Edward passed on the letter to Brandeis who said he would pass it on to others, but the project died.

These developments did not deter Edward from his efforts. He now even kept a special file for his Jewish activities. But he continued to suffer setbacks. Once, when he sent a $100 check to a Jewish relief organization, the official who solicited it, sent it back, saying it represented too small a sum for a man of his means. This naturally incensed Edward who retorted "I am not in the charity end of it, and there are enough Jewish people not doing the big preventive work I am doing, who should spend their money for that sort of thing."

The depression had, in a way, proven a boon to the credit union movement for it showed just how durable such lending institutions were. While some 7,000 banks collapsed in 1932, and only government loans prevented another 5,000 from joining them, no credit union failed and only five required government aid.

The number of credit unions had also grown but neither Bergengren or his boss was satisfied. Bergengren urged Edward to make a our of the Midwest and in January, 1933, Edward, accompanied by Bergengren and Schoedler, set out. During the next 20 days the 72-year old merchant visited 20 cities, delivering, in all, 36 speeches.

The tour, at least from Edward's standpoint, was a stunning success. Thanks in part to Bergengren's careful advance arrangements, Edward's words, indeed his very appearance, evoked an enthusiastic response. The highlight of the tour came in Chicago when an overflow crowd leaped to its feet as he was introduced and then, as the band began to play, paraded in front of him cheering lustily. As one reporter described it, "I have seen a good many demonstrations but nothing quite equaled that given the founder of the credit union movement... It was the spontaneous love of disciples for a master." Edward, his eyes filled with tears, said to Bergengren, "You didn't tell me it was like this."

Notwithstanding Edward's appreciation of Bergengren's efforts on this and other occasions, the two continued constantly to bicker. After the tour Edward wanted to ask the newly-established Reconstruction Finance Corporation for a $100 million loan to set up 6,000 more credit unions but Bergengren opposed the idea, feeling it would disrupt and, in a way, corrupt the whole credit union concept. When Edward went West in 1934 to see if he could generate support for his idea among credit union leaders, he met with little success. Bergengren, who was in continual contact with these leaders, had primed them in advance to give Edward a warm welcome but no support for his proposed loan.

Though he disdained federal funding for his cause, Bergengren did want federal authorization. Specifically he wanted the Federal government to charter credit unions. This would not only extend the concept to the 12 states which had not passed credit union laws but would validate and facilitate the whole movement. Pursuant to this aim he had three bills introduced into the Senate in 1934. The Federal Reserve and the Post Office opposed two of the measures and managed to kill them in committee. The main measure encountered no substantial opposition but Congress went home without acting on it.

The next year Bergengren tried again. Differences between Edward and Bergengren over other matters, plus Edward's expanding schedule of other activities, prevented him from playing a major role in advancing the legislation but he did write some key senators as well as Roosevelt himself. He also talked with the President's son James who promised to put in a word with his father. Roosevelt subsequently asked his Treasury Secretary to "take it up with the congressional committee concerned to see if we can get it passed without opposition in the closing days." Bergengren, meanwhile, haunted the corridors of Congress to push the measure along.

On June 16, 1936, with Congress about to adjourn, the House passed a much amended but basically intact credit union bill and the Senate hastily and unanimously followed suit. It would allow any seven persons to apply for a Federal Charter to form a Credit Union. Roosevelt sent Edward the pen with which he signed the bill but Edward forwarded it to Bergengren saying "the pen clearly should have gone to you. You did the work without which the bill could not have passed..."

The new legislation brought about the formation of the Credit Union Nation Association which held its first annual meeting in Kansas City, Missouri in January, 1935. Bergengren nominated Edward as its president and the 37 delegates promptly elected him by acclamation. It represented the culminating step in the greatest achievement of his public career.

***

Edward naturally took to the New Deal. It's efforts to revive the economy through bold, ambitious programs aimed at helping the little man paralleled to a great extent his own thinking. He also genuinely like Roosevelt who as governor of New York had shown himself receptive to his ideas.

For his part, Roosevelt naturally took to Edward. For one thing he and his New Deal desperately needed support from leaders of big business, especially from leaders as articulate and as well-known as Edward Filene. But he also genuinely appreciated Edward's ideas and abilities. And, of course, he welcomed his financial support as well. Edward had contributed $3,000 to the Democratic Party's campaign chests in 1932 and had campaigned tirelessly for Roosevelt's election. He had been subsequently invited to the President's inaugural luncheon where he chatted with the President's wife and his vice president, John Garner.

Edward had already begun sending the President advance copies of 20th Century Fund reports and other materials, and Roosevelt had showed interest in receiving them. He also asked for Edward's ideas on ending unemployment, although when Edward proposed that the government finance the hiring of new workers by private industry, Roosevelt rejected it in favor of setting up government agencies such as the WPA, the PWA and CCC to put the unemployed to work on public projects. (In retrospect, Edward's proposal may have been best for it would have directly impacted on private industry, which remained depressed all through the New Deal. It would also have aroused much less opposition from businessmen.)

On June 11, 1933 Congress passed the President's sweeping National Industrial Recovery Act. The NRA set up codes for 700 industries, encouraged collective bargaining and established minimum wages and even minimum prices. (Under the bill, a pants presser was once fined for charging too little to press a pair of pants.) In a speech to the Advertising Club of Boston, Edward hailed the bill as a "sacred covenant between American government and the American public," and Roosevelt subsequently appointed Edward to head up the NRA in Massachusetts. When the Supreme Court a few months later declared the NRA unconstitutional, Roosevelt asked Edward to study business conditions in 14 major cities and report back to him.

Edward's relationship with Roosevelt, like most of his relationships, was not always smooth. In 1935 he became alarmed over business hostility to FDR and over the growing popularity of such demagogues as Huey Long and Father Coughlin. He prepared a speech warning that the Republicans might win the next election and then, through their reactionary policies, produce such chaos that extremists such as Long or Coughlin might take over. Fortunately, he sent the speech to the White House first and Roosevelt's aides, alarmed at the prospect of one of their most prominent supporters predicting a Republican victory, persuaded him to drop it.

Edward's deep involvement with Roosevelt only weakened his ties with large sectors of the business community, and when he sought to make a proposal at the annual meeting of the U.S. Chamber of Commerce in 1934, the meeting's chairman persistently refused to recognize his raised hand. Edward, who more than anyone had fathered the organization, now found himself spurned and rebuffed by his own offspring. Two years later Edward formally withdrew from the organization charging, in a publicly released letter, that it now "functions as a successful club of business men when times are good but as a potent center of reaction when changing times make some new great forward step necessary..."

Edward's break with the Chamber did not greatly hamper his effectiveness as a spokesman for the New Deal, for the public still regarded him as a successful business man. Consequently, Roosevelt's 1936 re-elective campaign saw the 76-year old Edward addressing rallies and radio audiences in dizzying progression. The high point came on election eve when Edward, as noted, was chosen to speak after such major figures as Postmaster General James Farley and New York Senator Robert Wagner. Writing ten years after his death, Gerald Johnson observed, "It was the apex of his public career and perhaps the happiest moment of his life."

Chapter 12
THE END OF EDWARD

Edward had never abandoned his effort to have his biography written. He persistently pestered Steffens to undertake the task, but Steffens persistently begged off. The journalist finally agreed to find someone else to do it and to then supervise his work, an arrangement to which Edward reluctantly agreed.

Steffens first attempted to persuade Whittaker Chambers, who many years later would achieve fame, or notoriety, for his accusations against Alger Hiss, to undertake the project but Chambers declined. Steffens then turned to Robert Cantwell, a staff writer with *The New Republic* who had authored two well-received novels, *Laugh and Lie Down*, published when he was 23, and *The Land of Plenty*. Steffens urged him to take on the assignment, saying of Edward "the man is a bore but not his life."

Although *The New Republic*'s editor, Malcom Crowley, offered him more advantageous arrangements to enable him to write his novels if he would stay with the magazine, Cantwell opted to go to Boston. A militant leftist, he saw in the assignment an opportunity to expose the faults and failings of capitalists and to show "how they justified to themselves the exploitation on which their wealth was based."

Cantwell arrived in Boston on New Year's Eve, 1933 to find the city shivering in below zero temperatures. But he encountered what seemed to him an even frostier reception at 12 Otis Place for there he learned that Steffens had suffered a severe stroke. Edward, in informing him of this turn of events, said that with Steffens unable to supervise the project he might not wish to go on with it.

This naturally shocked Cantwell who had not only quit his job but had made arrangements to move his wife and baby daughter to Boston. Still, Edward did take him into his library and, pointing to the bound copies of his speeches which came to thirty volumes, told him to go through them during the next day or so to get an idea of his thinking.

Just what arrangements finally developed remains unclear but Cantwell did stay on with Edward for at least six months and possibly a year. Described as slight, slick and humorless by Robert Moore and his wife, he never became comfortable with Edward or his aides. It apparently never occurred to him that his antipathy to Edward, formed before he even met him, might have made Edward less cordial in turn. Nor, apparently, did he ever think that he was doing anything underhanded in accepting the assignment with the intent of doing a hatchet job on the man who was paying him.[16]

***

Cantwell eventually produced a 240-page manuscript on Edward Filene. Fragmentary and discursive, it is a mixture of biography, commentary and personal reminiscence, held together only by its author's deep antipathy for his subject. But it contains a good deal of information about its subject as well.

The manuscript gives us a glimpse of Edwards life as Filene's figurehead president. For when in Boston, Edward would regularly show up at his office to preside over his lost domain.

Leaving his home at about 10:00 A.M. Cantwell describes him as walking across the Common and down to Washington Street, exchanging greetings and occasional small talk with policemen and doormen, all of whom treat him with cordial respect. Entering the store he is met with a cheery chorus of "Good morning, Mr. Filene," from smiling sales women. He responds with smiles, salutations and an occasional clumsy joke as he makes his way past the sales counters. A deferential elevator starter, seeing him approach, holds an elevator to whisk him to his eighth floor executive suite. To the working people of Boston, including those at Filene's, he is still the head of the city's best known and biggest specialty store.

But his office, while still the store's grandest, has become, as Bernays would later describe it, "an enclave in enemy territory like a small West Berlin." Once inside it he spends little time on store business but works with his aides on his outside affairs. When lunch time comes he heads not to the executive dining room, where he would probably end up eating alone, but, if he is not eating out, to the employees restaurant. There he sits with the young saleswomen or clerks and inquires solicitously about their concerns.

In awkwardly seeking to play the role of the paternal boss, Edward often embarrasses them or makes them frightened and nervous. But sometimes they do the same to him. When they present him with work problems and ask for help, the now powerless president squirms and says "I haven't anything to do with details."

He is, to be sure, the store president and the single biggest stockholder in the corporation that controls it. As such he still attends the Board meetings which Lincoln chairs. But these meetings only underscore his impotence. He continually makes motions that no one ever seconds. On one occasion his fellow directors take a step which causes him great public embarrassment. In line with what other businesses are doing they decide to cut all employee salaries including their own. This does not in itself cause any undue hardship to those affected for the Depression has lowered the cost of living considerably. But Edward has been calling for increased salaries to combat the depression and now he must put out a statement trying to explain why his own firm has gone in the opposite direction. His statement points out that control over the store has passed to the Federated Department Stores, that the wage reduction, while passed over his objections, only duplicates what other business firms are doing, and that "I question no one's motives."

Edward believes, or believes he believes, in this last point for, he tells Cantwell, "they are not bad men" but simply misguided. Yet his bitter feud with Kirstein has, if anything, become more bitter still. In a 1934 memo prepared for his lawyers with a view to possible legal action, he accuses Kirstein of attacking him on a personal basis at Board Meetings and claims that Kirstein is "very definitely interested in becoming President of the company."[17]

Edward could derive some consolation from the fact that only his bargain basement was keeping the store from losing money during these difficult years, and that Filene's own credit union had become one of the largest in the state. Otherwise, his solace was coming increasingly from his ever-increasing outside activities.

While Edward's hostility to Kirstein and Frost continued to grow during the 1930's, his feelings toward Lincoln remained more favorable. And knowing Lincoln as we do, it seems safe to say that he must have found the breech between himself and his older brother not just uncomfortable but at times unbearable. In any event, the brothers made an attempt to reconcile in 1935. Evidence of the effort remains somewhat illusive but according to one report Edward came to dinner at Lincoln's home in Weston. Unfortunately, their new accord would soon disintegrate.

What killed it was a trip Edward made to Russia. He had always intended to return to the Soviet Union and in the Summer of 1935 he decided to do so. After an exhausting tour of Poland, he arrived in Moscow on the first day of August and immediately began a round of interviews. But when his interpreter called for him on August 5, he found his client seriously ill. Edward refused to have a doctor or even a nurse but the interpreter sounded the alarm and several physicians soon showed up at Edward's hotel bedroom, one sent by the American Embassy and another by the Kremlin. The confusion only increased Edward's irritation who kept insisting that he wasn't all that ill and kept getting out of bed to prove it.

Eventually, however, he collapsed into unconsciousness for he was suffering from a virulent form of pneumonia. It was said that only a Doctor Meyer from Berlin could save him. So Lillian Schoedler, who had parted from Edward in London but who had hastily come to Moscow at the first report of his illness, got Ambassador William C. Bullitt to persuade the Kremlin to grant Dr. Meyer a visa--the Soviet Government was then at great odds with Nazi Germany--and the physician flew to Moscow.

After spending ten days at Edward's bedside and managing to pull him through, Meyer returned to Berlin, leaving an assistant behind to supervise his patient's continued recovery. He also left a bill for $10,000.

Once back on his feet, Edward became incensed at Meyer's bill. Calling it outrageous and saying that the doctor had profited already from the publicity he had obtained from treating such a prominent patient, Edward left Moscow without paying it. Ambassador Bullitt, embarrassed over Edward's behavior, since he had summoned Meyer to Moscow, paid the bill himself. He then sent it to Lincoln, who, shaking his head over his brother's behavior, reimbursed the envoy. The incident soured relations between the brothers and so their reconciliation effort fizzled.

***

Though now a 75-year old man who had suffered a near-fatal illness, Edward Filene had no intention of retiring or even slowing down. On his return to the United States he not only resumed his speaking schedule and New Deal activities but also began taking steps to establish a chain of co-operative business enterprises.

He had set up the Consumer Distribution Corporation in 1935 but it was as yet only a paper entity. He now set about trying to gain backing for its aims and activities. Although he declined to run for re-election as president of the Credit Union National Association in 1936, he sought to involve the Association in establishing cooperative stores such as those being set up in Sweden. The Association's directors, however, reacted coolly to the idea. (They responded more favorably to another of Edward's suggestions, which called for setting up cooperative pre-paid medical care, and with Edward's financial support, they appointed a committee to develop a proposal. But nothing came of it.)

To help finance his cooperatives, Edward set up the Good Will Fund in 1936. He took care to include in its articles of incorporation a clause that would prevent it from engaging in propaganda, lobbying for legislation or contributing to strictly charitable endeavors. Working out of an office on West 42nd Street in New York, the Fund contributed to a pioneering co-op housing project in New York called Hillman House after the CIO Leader Sidney Hillman. But the Fund remained essentially a one-man enterprise with Edward as president and his aide Percy Brown as secretary-treasurer.

Edward had never lost his near obsession, born out of his school experience in Germany, with the role which reason should play in human affairs. In 1936 he invited a host of notables, including psychiatrist Alfred Adler and Wellesley College President Helen McAfee, to a dinner meeting in Boston. He told them that he wanted to put up $10,000 to help make American s think. What ideas did they have? But each attendee only offered suggestions along the lines of his or her own interest and the gathering ended with no clear cut course of action adopted or even indicated.

Undeterred, he convened another meeting, this one at Columbia University, a few months later. But again the talks bogged down. Finally, in near desperation, Edward turned to a Columbia professor named Clyde Miller and said, "You there—here is $10 thousand dollars for the first year. I don't care how you spend the money. I suggest you and two others form a committee. The American people must be taught to think."

Despite such an impromptu, and seemingly impulsive gesture, the money turned out to be well spent. Miller used it to establish the Institute for Propaganda Analysis which greatly helped the government and the media understand and deal with the masterly propaganda which Nazi Germany had begun to turn out.

While seeking to remain as active as ever, Edward was also mellowing. His letters to Lillian Schoedler when they were apart, as well as those to Steffens, show this. So do theirs to him. Steffens in a letter to Schoedler speaks appreciatively of "this sense of his that I should have or share all that he enjoys..."

Following his efforts in behalf of Roosevelt's re-election, Edward sent a warm message to Brandeis on the latter's 80th birthday. Brandeis replied saying, "I think often of the years we worked together in public causes and of the much I learned from you..." A few weeks later Edward entertained 32 children, including a group of underprivileged youngsters at his annual Christmas party.

But Edward was aging; at the first meeting on teaching Americans to think he had begun to doze off before it broke up. At the second he had rambled on somewhat incoherently about credit unions and consumer cooperatives before pressing his $10,000 check on Miller. The years and the bout with pneumonia were taking their toll.

As the Summer of 1937 approached he initially decided to forego his annual European trip, but then feeling somewhat tired and nervous, and being urged by his doctor to take a rest, he set sail on the Normandie on July 14. He met with the Finance Minister of France and the President of Czechoslovakia before settling down in a Czech spa for a "cure". Lillian Schoedler joined him there and together they proceeded to Switzerland. Although not fully rested, Edward insisted on scrambling up the Alps to bag a chamois and then had a picture taken of himself and his Alpine guide with the dead animal lying at their feet. The shooting of the chamois was to be his last achievement.

Refusing once again to rest completely, he set out with Schoedler in an open car for the embarkation port of Le Havre. The September weather was chilly and he arrived in Le Havre seriously ill. An alarmed Schoedler whisked the now semi-conscious Edward to the American hospital in Paris. But her 77-year old boss was too far gone. He never regained consciousness and in the early hours of the following morning, September 26, Edward A. Filene quietly died.

***

In accordance with his previously expressed wishes, Schoedler had Edward's body cremated and the ashes sent back to Boston. There, in further accordance with his wishes, a small group of friends took the ashes out in a small boat and scattered them on the Charles River. This was done at night to avoid attention and just who these friends were remains unknown.

In the meantime his death had produced an outpouring of condolences, both public and private. President Roosevelt hailed Edward Filene as a "unique personality" and "a prophet who perceived the true meaning of these changing times." In a lengthy statement Roosevelt went on to say "His democracy was more than a tradition. His liberalism was more than a mere assent to principles which have proved to be tried and true."

Socialist party leader, Norman Thomas and United Mine Workers President John L. Lewis, among others, also issued statements praising the departed merchant-statesman. Newspapers throughout the United States treated Edward's death as a major event, and even the *Times* of London devoted nearly an entire column to his obituary. As Gerald Johnson later observed, "Filene at seventy-seven, when he died, was a bigger man than he was at seventy-five, and at seventy-five he was afar bigger than he had been at fifty. He passed from sight still rising."

Filene's closed for a day and its management issued a statement lauding his abilities and contributions. But the statement was careful to point out that "as years went by, outside affairs gradually took up more and more of his time," forcing him "to withdraw himself from active management of the business." Consequently, "there should be no change in the policies of the store."

The Credit Union National Association scheduled 38 memorial meetings in cities throughout the country, beginning in Boston on October 13. This provoked an acerbic letter from Schoedler to Bergengren accusing the movement of capitalizing on Edward's death to promote itself. But the meetings took place with the last being held at Madison, Wisconsin, the Association's new home, on December 20. The mourning of Edward Filene thus lasted three months.

Much interest centered on Edward's will which became public nine days after his death. *The Boston Globe* gave it a banner headline saying FILENE'S $2,000,000 ESTATE LEFT MOSTLY FOR

CHARITY. Although Edward would have cringed, or more likely, flared up, at the word "Charity", the story was essentially correct. He left approximately one million each to the 20th Century Fund and the Good Will Foundation. Other bequests from the estate, which actually amounted to $2.2 million, included five thousand dollar legacies to his nieces and nephews and similar amounts to Brown, Wood and Schoedler to be used for any further publication of his writings. They would also draw their salaries for three months. He had previously made it clear to his aides that they could not count on him for any largesse on his death. As the *Globe* commented, "Among those who knew Mr. Filene, there was no element of surprise in the will. He was outspoken in his opposition to the handing down of great fortunes, either to relatives or personal friends."

Lillian Schoedler did receive the house along with most of the furnishings and she stayed on until Spring tidying up his affairs with her near legendary thoroughness. During this period Eleanor Roosevelt came to Boston twice and each time invited her out to lunch or tea. The First Lady had mentioned Edward three times in her popular newspaper column "My Day" and had once stayed in his house when her son Franklin Jr. was in a Boston hospital.

Percy Brown eventually left for Laconia, New Hampshire and was never heard from, or of, again. Charles Wood ended up steering barges down the Mississippi. Lillian Schoedler eventually became executive secretary of the Committee on Atomic Energy of the Carnegie Endowment for International Peace. She soon retired from that position to devote herself to travel and died in a car accident while touring the West Coast in 1963.

In the fall of 1938 some of Edward's "friends and former associates" as they called themselves published a collection of his speeches and writings made during his last years. (Edward had actually begun work on the project before taking off on his ill-fated trip to Europe in 1937.) During World War II the Federal Government named a Liberty ship the Edward A. Filene and Lincoln's daughter Catherine christened it.

In 1950 the Credit Union National Association established a new headquarters building in Madison. They named the building Filene House and invited President Harry Truman to dedicate it. In his remarks, Truman mentioned how often Edward had called on him when he was in the Senate "and always had some constructive idea to offer that was in the public interest and never a selfish one." In 1959 the association put up a plaque commemorating Edward on Boston Common and the following year passed a resolution declaring September as Filene Centennial Month.

But the posthumous honor which Edward might have most appreciated came in 1954 when he became one of six merchants to be elected to the Merchants Hall of Fame at the Chicago Merchandise Mart. (The others were John Wanamaker, Huntington Hartford, Marshall Field, F.W. Woolworth and Julian Rosenwald of Sears Roebuck who was honored at the same time as Edward.) Edward had always considered himself most of all a merchant, and despite the defeats which Kirstein, Frost and his own brother had dealt him, he had in a way triumphed after all.

Chapter 13
LINCOLN ALONE

1938

Heretherto, Cape Cod Yankees have tended to discourage Jewish visitors. Even Brandeis, who has become one of the U.S. Supreme Court's most distinguished justices, can find no one to rent to him in Harwich and so must settle for the then less desirable community of Chatham. And even in Chatham, opines Harwich native Tracey Brown, he might have found no vacation home had he not selected a site somewhat isolated from the rest of the community.[18]

But Lincoln Filene has decided to spend the summer on the Cape, and his graciousness and good humor, coupled with his prestige as head of the store where many Cape Codders shop when they go to Boston, easily enables him to secure their acceptance. "Call me Link," says the 73-year old Lincoln and soon most are doing so. When he starts to go swimming without removing his wrist watch, many shout to warn him of this fact. But Lincoln merely waves back and dives into the water, chuckling at the surprise and puzzlement of his well-wishers who do not know that waterproof wrist watches have just come on the market and he is wearing one.

On the Cape he meets Charles Saxe, a 46-year old outdoorsman who is recovering from a heart attack. Lincoln hires him as his paid companion and soon the two are swimming, boating and, most of all, fishing together. Before too long, the elderly businessman becomes a fairly proficient fly-rod fisherman.

Since Therese does not share these interests, and since the Cape seems to aggravate her neuralgia, she usually stays home. But she does come down on occasion, most often to act as a hostess when her husband entertains important guests. For not just business associates but Harvard and MIT professors, along with public figures such as Averill Harriman visit the clothing merchant at his new summer residence.

Eventually, Lincoln buys a home on the Cape. It is a substantial estate in the Marston Mills section of Sandwich. The property contains a small pond and when Lincoln comes down in the winter, he sometimes skates on it. In the summer he enjoys, among other things, the numerous birds which haunt the grounds.

His good nature has become almost legendary. Whenever he hears of an employee in trouble at the store he asks for their name. But his sympathetic streak is not confined to his business. When Charles Saxe and his wife respond to an announcement from the Fresh Air Fund and take a nine year old boy from New York City into their home for a few weeks one summer, Lincoln invites them all over to dinner. Amused at the youngster's amazement at such delicacies as cantaloupe topped with ice cream, Lincoln sees to it that the youth returns to New York totally outfitted for the winter from Filene's.

Underlying this upsurge in his leisure activities is an apparent improvement in his physical condition. When he was in his sixties, his partners feared continually for his health. Now, in his seventies, he seems in many respects more vigorous than ever. What has produced this apparent burst of vitality?

Lincoln attributes it to the honey which he has begun to eat at every meal. He even keeps a pot of honey on his desk. One of his assistants, Samuel Seegal believes it's the snifters of brandy which his doctor has prescribed for him and which Lincoln now downs faithfully every afternoon. Others ascribe it to the supposedly relaxing yet invigorating climate of Cape Cod where he is now spending so much of his time. But a major factor may have been Edward's demise. All his life Lincoln lived under the shadow of, and continually had to cope with, an increasingly troublesome older brother. Now that older brother has passed from the scene and Lincoln Filene is, in a sense, free at last.

***

When Lincoln assumed the presidency following Edward's death, he took over his brother's larger and more luxurious offices which, in addition to giving him more prestige, provided needed additional space for his staff. But his new title conferred little added power for as Chairman of the Board and Treasurer, he had been the store's *de facto* chief executive ever since the 1928 partnership agreement came to an end.

Sales had reached a high of 47½ million dollars in 1929, but then the depression hit. As Kirstein put it, "the honeymoon is over. Now the labor pains begin." Fortunately, Filene's had a not-so-secret weapon to counter the depression's impact: the Basement.

Thanks to Edward's increasingly famous brainchild, the store's sales would never fall below $30 million all thorough the depression and the store itself would never fail to make a profit of less than a million dollars. In 1930 it earned $2.85 a share compared to $3.38 a share the previous year, a remarkably small drop considering the drastic change in business conditions. When Roosevelt temporarily closed the banks in 1933, the store met its entire payroll from the Basement's cash sales.

The Basement actually benefited from the depression since it not only made people more eager for low priced goods but also made greater quantities of such goods available from bankrupt or over-stocked suppliers. Yet credit for its success during these years must also go to Harold Hodgkinson who became the Basement's manager in 1931. He and his buyers fanned out across the country, and to some degree across the globe, zealously looking for bargains.

And they found them too. Customers lined up for four blocks along Washington Street to buy a famous brand of irregular nylon stockings, purchasing 200,000 pairs the first day. And when a Paris buyer sent a large lot of hip-length silk stockings made for the chorus of the Folies Bergere, they sold quickly at 59 cents a pair. A lot of 20,000 discontinued furs from Saks Fifth Avenue were offered at half price, and 90 percent were snapped up before the day ended.

One of the prima ballerinas of Britain's Royal Ballet was seen buying formal evening wear in the basement while the popular American movie comedian Joe E. Brown boasted of his Basement-bought shirts. On their return from England, the Joseph Kennedy family also became basement shoppers. And each year the descendants of the Bounty mutineers would send one of their number to buy shoes. (He would take along pencil outlines of the feet of each resident on Pitcairn Island.)

In 1938 the Basement generated several stories in *The New York Times,* as well as pictures in *Life Magazine,* when it hired President Roosevelt's son, John. Fresh out of Harvard, the good looking young man went through the Filene training course with 60 other new employees and then started work as a Basement sales clerk. But when news of his employment broke, celebrity seekers mobbed the floor trying to get his handkerchief, a suspender button or some other memento. One portly matron showed up with a scroll to give him on which she had written an ode starting with the line "Oh, thou youth of sterling character." Because of the turmoil his presence aroused he was taken off the floor and made a stock clerk. He became an efficient employee, got along well with his fellow-workers and superiors and eventually became a branch manager.

A little over a year later, Hodgkinson and the Basement scored their biggest coup yet. The war in Europe had begun and Hodgkinson had read in the newspapers that the famed British liner *Queen Mary* was to be converted into a troop ship. At the time he gave it scarcely a moment's thought. But a few days later he was negotiating with a hosiery maker high up in the latter's New York skyscraper office when he glanced out the window and saw the famous liner steaming into port on its last crossing as a passenger vessel. Suddenly he remembered that the ship housed a host of shops filled with English bone china, heirloom silver, Bond Street luggage and other prized items which it now would have to get rid of.

Hodgkinson hurriedly broke off negotiations with the bewildered hosiery manufacturer and dashed to the liner's dock. In 24 hours he had bought out the whole ship. Brought to Boston and offered at a carefully-planned sale, the entire lot of merchandise sold out in two and one-half hours.

Thanks to its on-going profitability, the store, despite deflation-caused wage reductions, retained its employee benefits programs. The FCA continued to sponsor its numerous activities including its now thriving credit union. Management even offered the employees a retirement plan which included stock in the store's parent company. But since the plan required some contribution from the employees, they turned it down. Most would later regret doing so for the stock, then selling at depressed levels, would eventually rise and many would have made small fortunes.

In 1935, however, Congress passed the Wagner Labor Relations Act, a piece of legislation which, while providing a big boost for organized labor, dealt a death blow to the Filene Cooperative Association. For the Act prohibited employers from contributing to their employees' labor organizations, and without such contributions the FCA could not function. (When told of its effect on the store's unique employee association, Wagner replied with a shrug, "Yes, but it is the only one of its kind.")

With the FCA gone the store's employees had to choose between a CIO or a company union. To Lincoln's great satisfaction and surprise, some 92 per cent voted for the company union. They were apparently hoping to continue the FCA in a somewhat modified form.

The depression failed to deter the company from new initiatives. In 1930 it installed charge plates and two years later it became the first business firm to take out full color newspaper ads. It also became the first store to operate a cruise and travel shop, a separate play clothes section for women, a special ski clothes shop for women and to offer individual coat cleaning. It also opened some new branches, one of which, in suburban Winchester, it had to expand only five months after its opening in March, 1940.

Joining the Filene staff that year, Stacy Holmes was struck by the change in atmosphere from the proper Bostonian bond house where he had previously worked. There, he said, his fellow WASPS spent most of their time bemoaning the state of the economy and cursing Roosevelt. At Filene's he found Jews, Anglo-Saxons and everyone else thinking about the future. At Filene's, he said, they were not just planning what to do; they were doing it.

***

In 1932 Catherine Filene Dodd married Jouette Shouse, a former Congressman and one-time member of Woodrow Wilson's kitchen Cabinet, who was now Chairman of the Democratic Executive Committee. Lincoln, remembering his older daughter's first marriage, had misgiving about the second. "If you had trembled as much the second time as you had the first, I would have stopped the ceremony," he later told her, ignoring the fact that she was already a woman of 33 who was well used to making her own decisions. Fortunately, the marriage turned out well.[19]

A year later Lincoln used the couple's Washington apartment to outline a plan for unemployment insurance to an influential group which included Senator Robert Wagner and Secretary of Labor Frances Perkins. Although Lincoln had done much work on this issue--he was already serving on a committee set up by the Governor of Massachusetts to study it--most of his ideas apparently came from Brandeis who, as a Supreme Court Justice, could not participate directly in governmental affairs. Brandeis' daughter, Elizabeth

Raushenbush was present and while Lincoln convened the meeting, she actually presented the plan. In any event, the proposal greatly resembled, and therefore apparently laid the groundwork for, the scheme later adopted by the Roosevelt Administration.

In Massachusetts Lincoln was continuing to push for expansion of Brandeis' Savings Bank Life Insurance scheme for the Justice was upset that only 16 banks in the state were offering it. Lincoln was also continually in contact with Felix Frankfurther, the Harvard Law professor who had become Brandeis' ally and Lincoln's as well. As the New Deal's first economic chief Raymond Moley later observed, "the only two important business men whom he [Frankfurter] constantly quoted were oddities and non-conformists, Lincoln Filene of Boston and Samuel Zemurray of the United Fruit Company."

But Lincoln was doing more in the public arena than merely assisting Brandeis and Frankfurter. Many of the guests he invited to Cape Cod came not just to cavort but to confer for the times were serious and there was work to be done. Although Lincoln would never, and would never try to, match his brother's place in public affairs, he nevertheless felt it his duty to devote some of his resources to pressing public issues. He remained especially active in education. He served on a committee set up originally under Hoover to survey secondary education, as well as on a variety of Massachusetts and Boston educational committees. In August, 1935, Roosevelt appointed him to his new Federal Board for Vocational Education.

Although he officially dropped the name Abraham in 1933, he became more openly identified with his Jewish origins. It happened when Kirstein marched into his office one day and said "Lincoln, you are now a Jew. Hitler has made you one." Lincoln, who was also reading the newspapers concerning Hitler's new racial laws, did not protest. Instead, he began contributing to various Jewish relief agencies. He also sought to contact some cousins in Germany whom he had never seen with the aim of helping them get out. He failed to reach them, although after the war he managed to locate one surviving cousin and brought her over for a visit.

As might be expected, his biggest efforts at advancing the public interest centered on business, and more especially retailing. Addressing a manufacturer's organization in 1933, he called for a national council on trade relations saying, "The era of laissez faire, free competition and untrammeled private initiative is gone, and perhaps gone forever." Less than two months later, the American Arbitration Association announced the formation of just such an organization with Lincoln selected as its chairman. The council was designed to act impartially to rectify unfair trade practices. In 1936 the U.S. Department of Commerce named him to chair a committee it had created to study this problem. Back in Boston, meanwhile, Lincoln was helping to organize the Boston Better Business.

Unfair trade practices were also the subject and title of a book he published in 1935. The practices he inveighs against were generally those which the Federal Trade Commission was already seeking to suppress, such as intimidation, obstruction, molestation of a competitor or his customers, misrepresentation of goods, etc. Lincoln's viewpoint, rather unique in the business world at that time, was that private enterprise could and should work hand-in-hand with the Federal government to eliminate such unsavory tactics.

He also called for stepped up coordination between manufacturers and distributors, believing that they and the consumer would all benefit. He pointed out how his store had contracted with a manufacturer to obtain goods of excellent quality which could be sold at exceptionally low prices by simply allowing the manufacturer to choose the time of year best suited for him to produce and ship them. This enabled the manufacturer to utilize his dull season.

Although Lincoln refrained from explicitly endorsing the New Deal, he endorsed many of its programs such as unemployment insurance, minimum wages and the outlawing of sweatshops and child labor. Characteristically, he claimed such steps would benefit business. In any event there is no turning back, he said, "to the days when business was a law unto itself..."

Lincoln's book is short, the main text being only 97 pages. It is also quite choppy, lacking continuity and stuffed with quotes from reports, his own speeches, etc. Yet it does convey quite forcefully his basic belief in cooperation and convergence between business and business, business and government and business and consumers.

In 1938 Lincoln cooperated with three other business men, Henry Dennison, Ralph E. Flanders and Morris Leeds, on another book, *Toward Full Employment.* Although his own contribution remains unclear for each of the book's three sections is credited to one of the other three authors, still his name appears with theirs on the cover and the text itself certainly reflects his point of view. It not only favors social security and unemployment compensation but seeks to allay the fears of many business men and others over the New Deal's great increase in public expenditure.

While calling for increased business cooperation, Lincoln continued to guide his own initial, and successful, effort in this area, the Retail Research Association. Re-elected unanimously every year as its chairman, he presided over its meetings with unfailing courtesy and consideration. Mrs. Kirstein's former dressmaker, the now successful but still semi-literate Ben Forman, often hesitated to speak out in front of the better-educated members from the larger stores. So during a discussion Lincoln would often turn to him with the words "Let's now hear what Mr. Forman has to say."

In 1941 the Retail Research Association observed its 25th anniversary by presenting its chairman with a silver gavel accompanied by a silver sounding board on which the signatures of all its members had been etched. It symbolized not just their appreciation, but their great personal regard for the president of Filene's.

As Europe plunged into war and America began to re-arm, Filene's revenues shot up, allowing the store in 1941 to pay its first bonuses in 10 years. The war also brought new opportunities. Arriving in Paris shortly before the Germans troops in the Spring of 1940, the store's buyers snapped up hundreds of fashionable gowns from panicky French courtiers and shipped them back to Boston. Later that summer the store could boast in its ads of having "the largest collection of exclusive Paris models in existence."

When America entered the war, the store held dances for servicemen, sponsored a Navy cruiser, the USS Massachusetts, outfitted the first batch of women sailors, and in 1944 staged a birthday celebration for the Women's Army Corps. Following the precedent it set in World War I, it paid its 400 employees in military service the difference between their service pay and their store pay.

Filene's made its most significant contribution to the war effort through selling war bonds. It brought to Boston band leader Eddie Duchin, the then famed chanteuse Hildegaard, the comely Powers models and even a circus to help sell over $50 million of war bonds. Over 97 percent of the store's own employees signed up for the bonds and one of them, a supervisor named Ackley Stee, personally sold nearly 5 million dollars worth, the highest amount sold by any individual in World War II. Filene's biggest competitor, Jordan

Marsh, took out advertisements to congratulate its rival on its achievements in helping the war effort.

With the war grinding to an end in 1944, Filene's inaugurated helicopter flights from its Cambridge warehouse to its suburban Belmont shop, another retailing first. Its buyers followed the allied armies into Paris to pick up 400 of the latest model dresses from famous modistes and ship them out through Spain. When the Basement put them on sale for $11 to $49, some 15,000 women, some of whom had come from New York and even Chicago, thronged Washington Street waiting for the store to open. Fifteen minutes after they had surged through the doors, every dress was gone. Meanwhile, American GI's attending the Folies Bergere in liberated Paris were seeing a conspicuous advertisement for Filene's basement on the theater's asbestos curtain.

But the event that may have elated the Basement's staff the most occurred when a German army sergeant who had once lived in Boston was taken prisoner during the invasion of Italy. His first words to his captors were "How's everything in Filene's Basement?"

For Lincoln Filene personally, the war years brought both gains and losses. While his store, despite shortages of goods and personnel, managed to increase its revenues and, as we have seen, distinguish itself in the war effort, the two major members of his management team departed from the scene.

The first to go was Kirstein who was struck with terminal cancer. The gruff and often fearsome executive now endeared himself to many by individually inviting nearly everyone who had ever worked with him to come to his home for a personal good-bye. He died on December 10, 1942 at the age of 75.

Harold Hodgkinson now became merchandising vice president while Samuel Seegal, a bright young MIT graduate and Kirstein protégé, became his second in command. Edward Frost, meanwhile, had become the store's president.

Just why Lincoln, while remaining Board Chairman, relinquished the presidency to Frost remains somewhat unclear. Apparently, Frost had asked for the position and Lincoln wanted to appease him, not just out of good nature but to get Frost to go along with him in other matters. In any event, the change of title did not last long for Frost died on June 6, 1944. Lincoln after a decent interval resumed the position.

The end of the war thus found Lincoln, for whose health the others had always feared, the sole surviving member of the management team, which he and Edward had put together thirty-five years earlier. Although now 80, he remained reasonably active and alert. As such, he felt ready to meet whatever challenges the post-war era might bring.

***

As the war was ending, Fred Lazarus, the head of Federated's Cincinnati store went to Houston to visit his son who was stationed there at an Army Air Force base. Lazarus came away impressed with Houston's possibilities and persuaded his fellow board members to set up a department store in the city. With this step Federated changed from a holding company to an operating company. Within ten years, Federated would become collectively the nation's biggest retailer with a network of 38 stores doing a total of over half a billion dollars in sales a year.

Filene's remained, to some degree, the hub of this network. It also retained its essential independence, and, under Lincoln's overall guidance and Hodgkinson's active direction, it retained its enterprising ethos as well. When President Truman announced the end of price controls at 10 P.M. one Saturday evening, many Boston stores took out advertisements in the Monday newspapers to announce they were holding the line. But Filene's managed to prepare and insert its ad in the later editions of the more widely-read Sunday papers. When airline service from Boston to France started up, Filene's Fashion Director, Harriet Wilensky, boarded the first flight to Paris to stage a fashion show for French war brides and to answer their questions. (The most frequent question was "How do I get along with my American mother-in-law?)

In 1946 Filene's sales passed the $60 million mark, exceeding by far that of any apparel and soft goods store in the world.

As might be expected, its bargain basement continued to contribute heavily to the store's success. The production of nylon stockings had been discontinued during the war for the material was needed for parachutes. So when the basement offered its first post-war sale of nylons, some 15,000 women lined up on Washington Street waiting for its doors to open. Nearly 37,000 pairs were sold in the first three hours. In other post-war sales, the Basement sold 500 radios in five minutes flat, 14,000 umbrellas in a single hour when it wasn't even raining and 1500 bathing suits during a snow storm!

The Basement's biggest coup by far came when the Nieman-Marcus store suffered a fire during the 1946 Christmas season. Since the highly-regarded Texas store felt it would be beneath its dignity to hold a fire sale, it sold nearly 1½ million dollars worth of merchandise, most of it only slightly damaged from smoke or water, to the Basement. It was the biggest single purchase in retailing history.

Hodgkinson, who negotiated the deal, brought the goods to Boston in a caravan of 12 trucks, each carrying huge signs on its sides saying "From Nieman Marcus to Filene's Basement." Offered to the public in six separate sales before Easter, the sales produced near pandemonium since the savings averaged about 60 cents on the dollar. Some articles represented even bigger bargains. A black imported lace bra, which Nieman-Marcus had priced at $190, went for $8.95, and a picture taken at the same sale shows six women struggling over a French lace girdle that had been marked down from 175 to 27 dollars. On one sale day a frantic out-of-town customer dashed into the store, and grabbing the first salesgirl she met, asked "Where is Nieman Marcus?" The salesgirl, a temporary, looked at her blankly and muttered, "I think he's out to lunch."

By 1950 the Basement was selling over a half million dresses plus millions of other articles of clothing a year. Over 90 percent of its wares were purchased during the first 12 days before the first scheduled markdown and only one-tenth of one percent had to be given to charity.[20] Once the Basement put a $10,000 bill in a window of the main store to dramatize the savings it claimed to have made available to shoppers, and in 1957 it identified 25 basic items which were selling, so it said, at the same price as in 1909, the year it opened.

Celebrities continued to spread its name and fame. The British playwright-composer Noel Coward, noting how he had once written a song entitled, "The Customer Is Always Right," added "You know, I never really believed it until I saw Filene's Basement." The highly-regarded political commentator Dorothy Thompson devoted a column on the Basement, hailing it as an example of the superior effectiveness of the American economy. (The column resulted from a visit which Thomson had made to the Basement on a hot August day in which she found bargains galore and purchased several of them, including a Bergdorf Goodman housecoat for $4.) Several stores, including Selfridge's of London, had sought to imitate its unique operation but none had truly succeeded.

The main store also continued to move ahead as Hodgkinson brought to it the same flare for bold initiatives or, as detractors might say, public relations stunts with which he had governed and guided the basement. He persuaded the French government to send the Ile de France on a special visit to Boston, with such famed courtiers as Christain Dior and Jacques Fath, to participate in a Filene fashion show. He also held a fashion show at Boston's Museum of Fine Arts, staged the city's first fashion show for men—this one at the store—and set up a board of high school students to advise the store on teenage fashions. In 1949 the store sent the Board's chairman, a 15-year old girl from Quincy, on a buying trip to Europe. *Look*, then the country's second most popular picture magazine, devoted eight pages to her trip.

Not all the store's initiatives succeeded. In 1950 it opened up a mercantile machine operation at Boston's Greyhound Bus terminal. Called "U-Ser-U" and modeled after Horn and Hardett's restaurant "Automats" in New York, it sold 21 items such as hosiery, toys, stationery, etc. Although *The New York Times* called it "one of the most revolutionary experiments in recent retailing history," in a year or so it folded. Many of the store's branches also closed down including one established at Boston's Logan Airport. In 1954 Filene,s installed on its roof a zoo, complete with a lion, a tiger, some monkeys and even a baby elephant from Bangkok. But a major hurricane that year destroyed the facility, and although the animals were saved, the zoo was never re-built.

But despite such setbacks Filene's continued to flourish. Such early TV shows as Candid Camera and the Camel News Caravan did pieces on the store and *The New York Times* in one of its Sunday Crossword puzzles asked for a "Famous name in Boston" in six letters. By the mid 1950's, not just the basement but the store as a whole, was doing more business per square foot of selling space than any store of any kind in the world.

***

As Filene's sailed comfortably through the initial post-war years, so, in a sense did its president. While Hodgkinson was now running the store on an every day basis, and while Fred Lazarus had become the chief executive officer of the Federated chain, Lincoln remained the presiding head of Federated's flagship. Except during the summer, he was in the store nearly every day, overseeing its operations and handling personally some of its more specific problems and projects.

He continued to make the store's employees, now 4,000 in number, one of his main concerns. They now had such facilities as a card room and sun deck, while the store's clinic, long a special project of Lincoln's, was staffed by five nurses and a part-time physician. In 1946 Filene's became the first of Boston's major stores to institute the five-day week.

The store had begun hiring 50 promising college graduates a year and giving them an extensive two-year educational program consisting of both classroom instruction and on-the-job training. It had also expanded its training opportunities for its regular employees. By the early 1950's it was operating a virtual retailing school featuring 82 different courses of instruction. It was actually producing more trained people than it needed but the growing Federated chain absorbed much of its surplus. The first president of Federated's first new store in Houston was a Filene "graduate" named Max Levine.

With Hodgkinson handling the daily operations. Lincoln spent much of his time walking the aisles, asking his "work associates" how they were faring. As noted earlier, when he heard of a case of genuine distress, he tried to remedy or at least alleviate it. Many employees took to calling him "Father", a practice which prompted him to beam with pleasure.

He had become especially vigilant over dismissals for the Wagner Act, plus some labor legislation enacted by Massachusetts, had ended the FCA's Board of Arbitration which had previously kept watch on such matters. Once Samuel Seegal came to him saying that he had to fire four of the store's buyers. "Have you talked to them, counseled them?" asked Lincoln. When Seegal assured him that he had done everything he could, Lincoln, still loath to act, asked "Have you looked into their health?"

Seegal promptly did so and found a health problem underlying each case. The problems were corrected and the employees were retained.[21]

One day Lincoln asked Seegal "Has Judge Kaplan talked to you?" (Kaplan, a part-time justice, was Lincoln's attorney.) Told, no, he said, "Well, he will." A week or two later, Kaplan told him that

Lincoln was leaving both Seegal and Hodgkinson $100,000 worth of Federated stock each in his will. The bequest, which represents well over a half million in 1998 dollars, astounded Seegal but when he went to thank Lincoln, the latter waived him away saying "I just wanted you to have an interest in the business." He did, however, ask him to look after Catherine after his death although his elder daughter was already a grandmother. (She was, however, a widow, for Shouse had died in 1941.)

An indicator of how Lincoln's attitudes and policies had paid off came in the mid 1950's when a survey showed that one-fifth of the employees had been with the store for 15 years and nearly one-seventh had been with the store for 25 years or more. Since retail establishments, especially those specializing in women's apparel and therefore employing large numbers of young women, were known to have high turnover rates, such a large block of long-term employees was considered unusual if not unique.

Lincoln remained fairly active in public affairs and established the Lincoln and Therese Filene Foundation to sponsor or support activities which he or Therese especially favored. Among other things, the Foundation contributed substantially to building Boston's first public television station WGBH-TV.

In 1949, the National Retail Dry Foods Association awarded him a gold medal as "America's Outstanding Merchant", and the following year Bates College made him an honorary Doctor of Laws. But the honor he appreciated most occurred in th Fall of 1949 when Harvard University announced the establishment at its business school of the Lincoln Filene Professorship of Retailing. It was the nation's first endowed professorship of retailing, and though its $300,000 endowment came from Federated Stores and his own Foundation, still it elated the education-conscious, high school drop-out. On his 85th birthday the following Fall, Harvard tended him a dinner to thank him for the gift and to introduce the man named to the professorship, Malcolm McNair.

The Harvard dinner was, and would remain, a high point for Lincoln for he had begun, to slow down. To be sure, he still showed up on most days at the store, he still made train trips to New York every other week to attend to Retail Research Association matters and in 1953, at the age of 88, he flew to the West Coast to attend a meeting of the Amalgamated Merchandising Corporation. He did not change much in appearance, while in demeanor he remained, in Stacy Holmes' words, "twinkly and sweet." But neither his honey pot nor his brandy ration, which his doctor now increased to two snifters a day, and which was brought to him at his desk punctually at 4:00 P.M., could hold off the inroads of advancing age. As a result, Hodgkinson became Filene's effective president.

The situation because quite galling to Hodgkinson, for he often found it difficult to act effectively as Filene's president while lacking the position's formal powers and prerequisites. Yet Lincoln showed no inclination to step down and so Hodgkinson tried to adjust. He managed to improve his situation somewhat by exchanging his title of General Manager for the more authoritative-sounding British title of Managing Director.

When debilitating illness did finally strike the Lincoln Filene household, it struck first at Therese. An artery to her brain had begun to harden, producing often bizarre behavior. For example, she kept re-modeling the house, complaining that its acoustics did not allow the organ she had installed to give the proper sound. Lincoln indulged her as much as he could but as her condition deteriorated, he moved her into an apartment at Boston's Somerset Hotel and installed round-the-clock nurses to look after her.

He took the apartment next to hers for himself but arteriosclerosis was starting to affect him as well and eventually he suffered a series of small shocks. One weekend when his daughter Helen came up from Providence, where her husband had become President of that city's leading department store, she found her mother and father both invalids in their adjoining apartments.

Lincoln made a partial recovery and Helen took him down to his home at Marston Mills. (Much of this estate had earlier been destroyed in a fire but had been substantially rebuilt.) She also installed benches every few feet so that despite his inability now to walk very far, he could still make his way around the grounds he had come to love so well.

Every weekend Helen and her husband would visit him. Lincoln would almost invariably greet his son-in-law with the words, "Have you got a joke for me, George?" for he continued to enjoy jokes and was always eager to hear a new one. Catherine, who lived in Washington, could not come so frequently but she tried to spend all of August with him.

Lincoln avoided mentioning Therese, whom he knew was dying, but on each of Helen's visits he would look at her meaningfully and ask, "Have you anything to tell me?" But as her mother was still alive, she merely shook her head.

Therese died in December 3, 1955 but Lincoln was now too frail, and often too fuzzy, to be told. Some months before he had finally resigned from the Presidency at Filene's, and although he remained Chairman of its Board, he no longer went to, or even thought of going to, its meetings. But though his mind was becoming increasingly unclear, he always recognized people. To Tracy Brown, this indicated the importance which people had always had for him.

As he weakened both physically and mentally, Helen installed round-the-clock nursing care. In the early summer of 1957, Lincoln, now 92, resigned as chairman of the board, and a month later, on August 27, he quietly and painlessly slipped away.

Lincoln's death evoked encomiums of praise in the national as well as the local press. *Time* devoted a full page to his obituary, hailing him as "The last of the 19th Century Merchant Princes." Nearly all accounts of his death paid tribute to his serene and kindly manner and to his many efforts at fostering improved human relations.

His will showed that he left an estate of four and one-quarter million dollars. In current dollars, this was just about double what Edward had left twenty years earlier, but adjusted for changes in prices it was actually a bit less. The estate was left principally in trust to his descendants, which now included 10 great grand children. As he pointed out in his testament, he had made substantial bequests to employees as well as to public causes during his life and he was confident that his heirs would continue to do the same. The will did include the $100,000 bequests to Hodgkinson and Seegal, and Hodgkinson, apparently fearing that some might think he had taken advantage of the elderly man, sought to keep his legacy out of the newspapers.

The burial itself was a small, private affair but it was followed on September 29 by a memorial service at Harvard University's non-denominational chapel. The Dean of the University's Divinity School offered up a simple prayer and a former Dean of its Business School, Donald K. David, delivered the eulogy.

"It is fitting that we remember him in this church of no denomination for he was one who recognized no differences in men except of character," said Dean David. He then went on to enumerate Lincoln's many endearing qualities and to speak of the good fortune which he and countless others had enjoyed in having worked for and with him. In conclusion, he said:

> As we go from this meeting we shall think of him, then, as a wise and kindly man. We shall carry with us pictures of him in his family circle--the good father--or gathered around the fireplace with friends... He lived a full life himself, to be sure, but in doing so he enriched the lives of those around him in ways which shall keep his spirit with us. For friendship, and charity, and good example, never die.

Chapter 14
THE BROTHERS' BEQUEST

The Filene brothers left many legacies not only in their wills at death but, one might say, in their wills during their lifetimes. What has happened with all these bequests? What have they achieved?

Edward, it will be recalled, left one million dollars to his Good Will Fund to establish cooperative stores. After the war, the Fund spent over half the amount to set up such a store in Arlington, Virginia outside Washington. Five years later it had to be liquidated. A similar experiment undertaken subsequently in Providence, Rhode Island suffered a similar fate.

Eventually, with its assets sharply reduced, the Fund confined itself to sponsoring scholarships for Black and Native American students at the business schools of Columbia and Roosevelt Universities. Finally, in 1987 its directors voted to dissolve the fund and hand over its remaining assets of $158,000 directly to these business schools with the stipulation that they use the money to aid such students.

The Twentieth Century Fund has fared much better with the $1 million it received. It has even attracted other funding and by 1998 its endowment had grown to $50 million. Under current president Richard Leone, its staff of over 30 continues to churn out informative and useful reports from its New York City offices. Faithful to the cooperative approach so often favored by its founder, it frequently teams up with other foundations on joint projects. The Fund was scheduled to change its name to the Century Fund in July 1998.

The Lincoln and Therese Filene Foundation also grew, and by 1990 its assets were nearing the $10 million mark. In the 33 years since its founder's death it had financed, in whole or in part, the Lincoln Filene Center for citizenship and Public Affairs at Tufts University, the Wolf Trap Arts Festival in Virginia, the Filene Auditorium at Dartmouth College and a host of lesser projects. It had also given money to several philanthropic organizations including Combined Jewish Philanthropies.

But it is the other category of bequests, the ones made during their lifetimes, which loom largest when one attempts to assess the legacy of Edward and Lincoln Filene. For it is through what they achieved, and in some instances failed to achieve, that has left their greatest imprint on our times.

There is little question regarding Edward's most notable, and noticeable, accomplishment: credit unions. Growing steadily since his death, they numbered over 21,000 by 1990 with combined assets of close to $100 billion. They have become the country's most conspicuous, and most conspicuously successful, self-help institution.

The movement's success can not, of course, be credited to Edward alone. As Bergengren once pointed out, Edward never organized a single credit union or, for that matter, authored a single credit union law. But, as Bergengren went on to say, "He equipped and financed the Crusade. Without the war chest, our battle could not have been won. Much more than that, he rode at the head of the Crusade, on a snow-white charger, cheering us on to follow his lead to the great glory which he could see quite beyond the sight of ordinary mortals."

Edward could see many things beyond the sight of ordinary mortals. They include the systematic analysis of systematically gathered data; they include worker ownership of or at least worker participation in, business operations; and they include discount merchandising. The Filene store experimented with, and to some degree incorporated, all these principles, and since then whole sectors of the American economy have followed suit. Discount stores of one kind or another, including supermarkets which earn good profits on one percent profit margins, have proliferated; all kinds of businesses including football teams, are using management information systems and other forms of systematic analysis; and worker participation, including substantial, and in a few cases total, ownership has become more and more common. As Gerald Johnson observed ten years after Edward's death, "Any adequate history of our economy must take account of what he said and did, for it has already had great influence upon our ways of thinking and acting and may have more."

On the international scene Edward has also had a lasting impact, most tangibly and specifically through his simultaneous translator. While such a device would likely have been developed sooner or later, most probably it would not have been available during the early years of the United Nations. And while it may seem an exaggeration to attribute much of the United Nations' success--and it has certainly been more successful than its predecessor, the League of Nations--to a simple mechanical device, still the translator facilitated the flow of communication in that multi-national body, and few today would downplay the importance of communication in international affairs.

Edward's belief in free trade has also borne the test of time for since his death the concept has become widely preached and increasingly practiced. Had it been widely adopted and acted upon during the Great Depression, then that great calamity would have been less calamitous and, just possibly, World War II might have been averted.

The use of economic sanctions against aggressor nations, which Edward also fervently espoused, has also come into practice, although with decidedly mixed results. When the League attempted to impose such sanctions against Fascist Italy for invading Ethiopia in the mid 1930's, it only helped drive Mussolini into the arms of Hitler, who, alone among major world leaders, supported him. Also, the use of such sanctions against Iraq following the Gulf War have been disappointing.

Edward's belief in high wages and government spending to maintain prosperity are more debatable still. Under the New Deal government spending rose and so did real wages since prices during those years declined more than did wage rates. Yet unemployment, except for public employment programs, remained high and the depression largely continued. After the war some European nations adopted similar policies, only to produce a situation called "stagflation." As Britain's Labor Party Minister James Callaghan said in 1977, "We used to think that you could just spend your way out of a recession... [But] it only worked by injecting a bigger dose of inflation into the economy followed by a higher level of unemployment..." Shortly thereafter Germany's Social Democratic Chancellor Helmut Schmidt said much the same thing.

On the mercantile scene, Edward's advocacy of chains within chains, that is chains of entirely separate departments located within one or more chains of department stores, has only to a limited extent materialized. (As we will see, his Bargain Basement has become such an operation.) As for his call for cooperative stores, the experience of his Good Will Fund in two such endeavors has cast doubt on the concept's viability, at least in the United States. Today, in fact, the country has only two well-established such cooperatives, one in Cambridge, Massachusetts and the other in Berkeley, California, both academic cities.

But if Edward erred in some things, his farsightedness remains remarkable. "He understood mass distribution before Ford understood mass production," said Harold Hodgkinson in unveiling the bust of his former boss at the Merchants Hall of Fame, while another of Edward's protégées, University of Wisconsin President Glenn Frank, made this assessment after Edward's death. "He came as near to being the philosopher of our machine age as we have yet produced."

In seeking to assess Lincoln's legacy, we run into a formidable problem. During most of his life he was the junior member of the Filene team and it is often difficult to distinguish his own particular contributions from those of his more articulate and intellectually more gifted older brother. Yet in reading his 1924 book, *Merchant's Horizon*, one easily sees that if his views paralleled Edward's in most important aspects, they nevertheless sprang from his own deeply-held convictions. Moreover, there are differences in emphasis and tone for Lincoln stresses in his book, as he did in his life, the priority of cooperation. Believing that cooperative approaches business usually yielded the best results, he lived to see his views vindicated.

In his public activities Lincoln Filene also displayed some farsightedness of his own. He espoused social security, employment insurance and, half a century before it came to pass, federal aid to education. Moreover, in 1929, when Edward was predicting the continuance of prosperity, Lincoln was counseling caution.

But in these broader areas of public concern, he again often marched to the same beat as his brother. This was particularly true when it came to viewing the relationship of business, and business men, to society. "One of the most noteworthy developments of our business age" wrote Edward in 1928, "is the fact that 'love your neighbor' which has been preached through the ages as a necessary religious, moral and ethical principle, has in the development of capitalism become the only sure basis of prosperity." Lincoln had made the same point four years earlier in *Merchants' Horizon* and never stopped making it until his death. It was a deeply help article of faith with both brothers that the private good could be consistent with the public good and that adherence to basic Judeo-Christian principles in business ultimately paid off in increased profits.

So they believed and, allowing for Edward's personal limitations, so they behaved. A biographer will find it difficult if not impossible to discover one truly dishonorable deed in the business activities of Edward and Lincoln Filene. They genuinely sought to do the right thing and became millionaires not in spite of, but rather because of, their doing so.

Their example in this regard may be their greatest legacy of all.

Epilogue
FILENE'S WITHOUT THE FILENES

Filene's continued to grow in the years following Lincoln's death. While it did have to close some of its stores, the suburban boom enabled it to open up others and by the 1980's it was operating 14 successful satellite stores throughout the Northeast. Its main store had also expanded in terms of both added space and added sales.

In 1988 the entire Filene network became a division of May Department Stores, a company that includes Lord and Taylor and several other well-known chains. Under its new affiliation Filene's continued to grow and by 1996 it was operating 40 stores with total sales of $1.4 billion.

These developments have necessarily cost the main store some of its centrality and singularity. It is now only the principal store of a division, and by no means the biggest division, of another company. Moreover, in the late 1970's it moved closer to becoming a regular department store by adding a home furnishing department. At the same time its Basement became an independent unit with branches of its own with over 20 stores.

Nevertheless, the store which the Filenes founded over a century ago yet retains some of its original flavor. It still does not carry the full range of merchandise that most other department stores carry. Its Bargain Basement is still the only one in the world that marks down prices automatically at specified intervals since its branch units have not adopted the unique feature. The main store still enjoys a reputation locally as a good place to work and it can still boast of many life-long employees. Finally, it still does business in the still distinctive building which Daniel Burnham designed in the early 1900's.

So, despite all the financial and administrative changes it has undergone, shades of its past still linger. In wandering among its busy counters, a visitor aware of this past can yet visualize the stubby figures of Edward and Lincoln trooping down the aisles, the former barking out orders to nervous employees, the latter reassuring one and all with his twinkly demeanor and his warm and winning smile.

NOTES

1. William's attitude was certainly not unusual for a German Jewish emigrant of 1848. As a group they tended to consider themselves more as Jewish Germans than German Jews. Many of them felt little kinship with the religion of their forefathers, and the arrival of the deeply orthodox Eastern European Jews late in the century only increased their estrangement. When the first Slavic Jews became noticeable in New York, the City's *Jewish Messinger*, published by earlier arrivals from Germany, spoke out sharply on the new emigrants' loud voices, vulgar manners and slovenly dress, and it expressed a rather fervent wish that they would become Americanized as rapidly as possible.

2. Although the time clock had been invented and was already in wide use throughout American business, Filene's never adopted it.

3. Edward wrote seven books and never dedicated any of them to anyone, though he acknowledged and thanked those who helped him in writing them.

4. Edward's apparently quite sincere affection for and attachment to his father is one of the reasons why an Oedipus complex is probably not the primary reason he never married or developed a satisfactory romantic relationship with a woman. It seems more likely that his inability to relate romantically to women was merely a part of his inability to relate to people generally. In other words, an inferiority complex rather than an Oedipus complex strikes this writer as a more likely, if somewhat simplistic, explanation for the barrenness of his romantic and sexual life. However, he obtained from his mother some of the warm, female affection which he would never arouse in any woman until he reached his seventieth year.

5. In all fairness it should be pointed out that New Hampshire was actually the birthplace of the movement in the United States, for some of the French-Canadian parishes in that state had made contact with Desjardins before Jay did so and had already started to organize such societies.

6. After the election, Storrow wrote to Edward, "You and your brother are among the few men in Boston who realize the necessity of twelve months' work the year round if we are to secure the result which we must have in Boston."

7. The North End where Therese began her work is now almost exclusively Italian. In her day, however, it was a much more ethnically diverse neighborhood containing, among others, many recent Jewish immigrants. The music settlement house eventually moved to the city's South End.

8. One thing which enabled the store to win most of its dismissal cases was its own elaborate system for preventing arbitrary action on such matters. Only the vice-president in charge of store operations could fire someone and he could do so only after the employee in question had received a warning and been given a chance to redeem himself.

9. Hodgkinson would later marry Laura Cabot, the flippant salesgirl who once provoked Edward's ire by saying, jokingly, that she was earning only half what she was worth. (See Chapter 4.)

10. According to figures compiled by Edward's aide Robert Moore, the Men's Store in 1927 earned $3.06 per square foot of store space. This contrasted with a figure of $8.77 for the main store and $15.55 for the basement.

11. Frederick Stuart, one of Edward's aides, felt that such an increase had occurred but that it was caused by increased outlays for such things as the Cambridge service building, the men's store, the New York City office and increased salaries and benefits to both employees and management.

12. A few years later, when he had mellowed a bit, Edward blamed his defeat on his social ineptness. "Basically, "he said, "my failure was that I never learned how to mix with people. I was alone a good deal--I was sickly, wasn't well, and I couldn't run with the other boys, so I never learned how to mix with people. Then they got after my brother, played golf with him, and did all that—all those men. They're not bad men...It's just wrong thinking, wrong education. They get them, you know, into those clubs and things."

13. The 24,900 shares reserved for the operating committee and other employees would cost them $18.00 a share. However, this was less than half the price the public would have to pay. Moreover, the store would lend them the money at low rates of interest to purchase their shares.

14. Actually, Bloomingdale's sales of 23 million were even less than Abraham & Strauss' 27 million. F and R. Lazares had sales of 12 million making the total of all four stores 106 million. Filene's thus accounted for nearly half of the new company's annual sales.

15. The heart of the book consisted of his plan for consolidating all goods into three price lines: the cheapest full-line price or the lowest price at which any class of worthwhile goods can be sold; the best-selling full-line price which captures the middle and largest range of buyers; and the highest full-line price made up of the highest priced goods that the great majority of customers can afford.

16. After leaving Edward's employ, Cantwell went to work for *Time* magazine. Like many radicals of this era he later became a staunch conservative. His last writings consisted mostly of articles for *Sports Illustrated*.

17. Adding to Edward's ire, in all likelihood, was Kirstein's own emergence as a public figure. In 1930 Kirstein gave $200,000 to establish a new and highly distinctive Boston branch library devoted to business and business-oriented publications and named after his father. In 1933 Harvard University gave Kirstein an honorary degree, something it had never given Edward, and, "For years thereafter," writes Leon Harris, "store executives who walked into Kirstein's office unexpected would occasionally find him sitting at his desk with tears in his eyes, starring at the framed degree he had taken down from the wall and was holding firmly in both hands." Kirstein's son Lincoln, however, told Harris that he felt his father's acceptance of the degree represented "a cowardly sellout" for Harvard was still imposing its quota on Jewish faculty members.

18. Today, Chatham is considered the more desirable community and no discernible prejudice against renting or selling to Jews exists.

19. Shouse, a horse-loving Kentuckian, frequently took his father-in-law to the races. Lincoln always dutifully reported his winnings on his income tax but for some unexplained reason, and despite exhortations from his family, refused to deduct his losses.

20. "Seconds" of new fashions comprised 65 percent of its dresses which sometimes went on sale before the "firsts" appeared on the racks of other stores. Discontinued merchandise made up 25 percent and samples the remaining 10 percent.

21. The most ticklish case for Seegal involved a woman buyer who was constantly forgetting things. The store's doctor attributed the problem to menopause and said he could give her some medicine to alleviate it. However, the woman was a Christian Scientist and refused the remedy. Seegal, a Jew, hated to have to persuade a Christian to depart from a sacred tenet of her faith but felt he had no choice but to tell her that if she did not take the medicine he would have to fire her. She decided to take it and her problems quickly cleared up.

SOURCES

Archives:

1. Credit Union National Association Library, Madison: Filene files.
2. Filene's: files
3. Radcliffe College Library, Cambridge: The Letters of Lillian Schoedler.
4. University of Oregon Library, Eugene: Robert Cantwell's unfinished manuscript biography of Edward Filene.

Bibliography:

1. Bernays, Edward L., *The Biography of an Idea*, New York, 1965.
2. Cowley, Malcolm, *The Dream of the Golden Mountains* New York, 1980.
3. Filene, Edward A., *The Way Out*, New York, 1926.
4. Filene, Edward A., *Successful Living in This Machine Age*, New York, 1931.
5. Filene, Edward A., and others, *Next Step Forward in Retailing*, Boston, 1937.
6. Filene, Edward A., *Speaking of Change*, New York, 1939.
7. Filene, A. Lincoln, *Merchant's Horizon*, New York, 1924.
8. Filene, Lincoln, *Unfair Trade Practices: How to Remove Them*, New York, 1934.
9. Gal, Allon, *Brandeis of Boston*, Cambridge, 1980.
10. Harris, Leon, *Merchant Princes*, New York, 1979.
11. Johnson, Gerald W., *Liberal's Progress*, New York, 1948.
12. Kaplan, Justin, *Lincoln Steffens*, New York, 1974.
13. La Dame, Mary, *The Filene Store*, New York, 1930.
14. Mason, Alpheus Thomas, *Brandeis: A Free Man's Life*, New York, The Viking Press, 1946.
15. Moody, J. Carroll and Fite, Gilbert C., *The Credit Union Movement*, Lincoln, 1971.

16. Pearson, Henry Greenleaf, *Son of New England: James Jackson Storrow*, Boston, 1932.
17. Steffens, Lincoln, *The Autobiography of Lincoln Steffens*, New York, 1931.
18. Urofsky, Melvin and Levy, David, editors, *The Letters of Louis D. Brandeis*, New York, 1971.

Interviews:

1. Austin Benton
2. Edward L. Bernays
3. Tracy Brown
4. Harold Hodgkinson
5. Stacy Holmes
6. George Ladd
7. Helen Filene Ladd
8. Robert Moore
9. Christine Saxe
10. Samuel Seegal
11. Catherine Filene Shouse
12. Benjamin Trustman

INDEX

THE FILENES ---- 291